At Seventy

At Seventy
A Journal

By *May Sarton*

W·W· NORTON & COMPANY · *New York* · *London*

Grateful acknowledgment is made to the following: Holt, Rinehart and
Winston, Publishers, for some lines from "I Could Give All to Time" from
The Poetry of Robert Frost edited by Edward Connery Lathem. Copyright
1942 by Robert Frost. Copyright © 1969 by Holt, Rinehart and Winston.
Copyright © 1970 by Lesley Frost Ballantine. Reprinted by permission of
Holt, Rinehart and Winston, Publishers; Alfred A. Knopf, Inc., for
permission to reprint "All Souls" from *Collected Poems of Elinor Wylie*.
Copyright 1932 by Alfred A. Knopf, Inc. and renewed 1960 by Edwina C.
Rubenstein. Reprinted by permission of the publisher.

The text of this book is composed in Caledonia, with display type set in
Garamont Italic. Composition and manufacturing by The Haddon
Craftsmen, Inc.

Library of Congress Cataloging in Publication Data

Sarton, May, 1912–
    At seventy.

    1. Sarton, May, 1912–   —Diaries. 2. Authors,
American—20th century—Biography. I. Title.
II. Title: At 70.
PS3537.A832Z463 1984   818'.5203 [B]   83–19369

ISBN 0-393-31030-2

W. W. Norton & Company, Inc.
500 Fifth Avenue, New York, N.Y. 10110
W. W. Norton & Company Ltd
10 Coptic Street, London WC1A 1PU

Printed in the United States of America

2 3 4 5 6 7 8 9 0

At Seventy

Monday, May 3rd, 1982

SUCH A PEACEFUL, windless morning here for my seventieth birthday—the sea is pale blue, and although the field is still brown, it is dotted with daffodils at last. It has seemed an endless winter. But now at night the peepers are in full fettle, peeping away. And I was awakened by the cardinal, who is back again with his two wives, and the raucous cries of the male pheasant. I lay there, breathing in spring, listening to the faint susurration of the waves and awfully glad to be alive.

The table is set downstairs, all blue and white, with a tiny bunch of miniature daffodils, blue starflowers, and, glory be, two fritillaries. They always seem unreal with their purple-and-white-checkered bells, and I have never succeeded with a real show of them.

Then at each corner of the square table I have put a miniature rose, two white and two pale yellow, part of a bounty of miniature roses that have come for my birthday and will go along the terrace wall when the nights are not quite so cold. They are from Edythe Haddaway, one of the blessings of the last five years, for she comes when I am away to take care of Tamas and Bramble, feels at peace in this house, she tells me, and makes it peaceful for me to know that she is in residence and all is well at home when I am off on poetry-reading trips.

What is it like to be seventy? If someone else had lived so long and could remember things sixty years ago with great clarity, she would seem very old to me. But I do not

feel old at all, not as much a survivor as a person still on
her way. I suppose real old age begins when one looks
backward rather than forward, but I look forward with joy
to the years ahead and especially to the surprises that any
day may bring.

In the middle of the night things well up from the past
that are not always cause for rejoicing—the unsolved, the
painful encounters, the mistakes, the reasons for shame or
woe. But all, good or bad, painful or delightful, weave
themselves into a rich tapestry, and all give me food for
thought, food to grow on.

I am just back from a month of poetry readings, in and
out through all of April. At Hartford College in Connecticut I had been asked to talk about old age—"The View
From Here," I called the reading—in a series on "The
Seasons of Womanhood." In the course of it I said, "This
is the best time of my life. I love being old." At that point
a voice from the audience asked loudly, "Why is it good
to be old?" I answered spontaneously and a little on the
defensive, for I sensed incredulity in the questioner, "Because I am more myself than I have ever been. There is
less conflict. I am happier, more balanced, and" (I heard
myself say rather aggressively) "more powerful." I felt it
was rather an odd word, "powerful," but I think it is true.
It might have been more accurate to say "I am better able
to use my powers." I am surer of what my life is all about,
have less self-doubt to conquer, although it has to be admitted that I wrote my new novel *Anger* in an agony of
self-doubt most of the year, the hardest subject I have
attempted to deal with in a novel since *Mrs. Stevens Hears
the Mermaids Singing.* There I was breaking new ground,
giving myself away. I was fifty-three and I deliberately
made Mrs. Stevens seventy, and now here I am at what
then seemed eons away, safely "old."

I have always longed to be old, and that is because all my life I have had such great exemplars of old age, such marvelous models to contemplate. First of all, of course, was Marie Closset (her pen name, Jean Dominique), whom I celebrated in my first novel and with whom I exchanged lives through letters and meetings from my twenty-fifth year until her death. I turn to her bound volumes of poetry this minute and open to the line

Au silence léger des nuits près de la mer

but I am bound to look for and find the long lyric addressed to Poetry, and as I write it here, I hear very clearly her light, grave voice, and we are sitting in her study, side by side:

Poésie! Je t'ai portée à mes lèvres
Comme un caillou frais pour ma soif,
Je t'ai gardée dans ma bouche obscure et sèche
Comme une petite pierre qu'on remasse
Et que l'on mâche avec du sang sur les lèvres!

Poésie, ah! je t'ai donné l'Amour,
L'Amour avec sa face comme une aube d'argent
Sur la mer,—et mon âme, avec la mer dedans,
Et la tempête avec le ciel du petit jour
Livide et frais comme un coquillage luisant.

How happy Jean-Do would be to know that at seventy I live by the sea, and all those images are newly minted for me today "like a cool pebble for my thirst," "and my soul with the sea in it, and the tempest at dawn, pale and fresh as a shining shell." (But where is the music in English?)

Then Lugné-Poë, my father in the theater, was a constant challenger and giver of courage during the theater years. I see his immense devouring smile and remember my pet name for him, "mon éléphant." So he always

signed his letters with an elephant head and a long trunk
waving triumphantly at the end of a page.

Basil de Selincourt, my father in poetry, fierce as a
hawk (and he looked rather like a hawk), wrote the first
really good review I ever had (in the London *Observer* on
Encounter in April, my first book of poems) and that was
before we became friends. He taught me many things, not
least how to garden into very old age by working at an
extremely slow tempo—but I never did really learn it.
That is still to come when, like Basil, I hope to put in a
vegetable garden in my late eighties.

Then there is Eva Le Gallienne, who was only thirty
when I first knew her as the star and creator of the Civic
Repertory Theatre, and who has again triumphed in her
eighties and shown a whole new generation what great
acting is. She is proof that one can be eighty-three and still
young. She too is a great gardener, so perhaps a good old
age has to do with being still a friend of the earth.

I think also of Camille Mayran, who has written a magnificent book in her nineties, *Portrait de Ma Mère en Son
Grand Âge.* She tells me that now, well over ninety, she
sees no change in herself except for a "slight slowing
down." She is all soul and mind, not a gardener at all! So
one cannot generalize. But Eleanor Blair has just tele-
phoned to wish me a happy birthday, as I write, and she
says her garden is flourishing. Her voice sounded so young
on the phone!

Perhaps the answer is not detachment as I used to
believe but rather to be deeply involved in something,
is to be attached. I am attached in a thousand ways—
and one of them compels me now to leave this airy room
high up in the house to go down and get ready for my
guests.

Tuesday, May 4th

FOR BREAKFAST at five I had a fresh egg from Anne and Barbara's chickens, a piece of homemade bread Donna brought last night with strawberry jam she had made, and I felt extraordinarily blessed by all that happened yesterday as I started to read a big manuscript on fathers and daughters that I promised to say something about. The price of being attached "in a thousand ways" is that there is never even twenty-four hours free of pressure, but this year I am clear in my mind that just this is what my life is all about, and what I have to learn (so late!) is to accept the multiple demands and understand that a rich life is bought at a high price in energy. If I can be wiser about not feeling so compulsive about everything, all will be well. Today, whatever happens, I am going out into the garden in the afternoon to plant the white impatiens Anne has been growing for me under lights, and the felicia, a charming blue flower I dearly love, and clean up the flower beds behind the house. Janice was hit in one eye by a bug when we walked down to the ocean yesterday—she, Anne, Barbara, Tamas and Bramble, and I—so I am going to take her some lunch. What a miserable bug that was!

The house is full of amazing flowers, among them huge pink rhododendrons flown from California, marvelous dark-red roses, yellow lilies in the blue and white Belgian jar, and a vase of pink African daisies and white chrysanthemums that Bob, the florist, brought as his birthday present. He read *Recovering* some weeks past and was so moved he has been bringing me flowers. Happy the writer who has a florist for a fan!

It is hard to accept that almost all the tulips I planted in October, imagining how rich the spring would be this year, have been eaten by mice and chipmunks. So there are bare spaces everywhere except in the big border below the terrace where the parrot tulips have emerged intact. I feel outraged. Must they have tulips, these creatures? "Let nature take its course," my father used to say when the pipes burst or the cat caught a bird. Thank goodness the mice do not like daffodil bulbs.

As I think over yesterday, I want to remember three special moments of amazement and delight. The first was at eleven, when Mary-Leigh Smart and Beverly Hallam arrived from their house across the field, trundling, in a bright red carrier, a case of Moët & Chandon champagne! That is a present I never thought to see. "Vintage 1912" was Beverly's splendid joke on the Moët & Chandon card shaped as a big bottle of champagne. Oh, to be seventy and be given a case of champagne! The second was greeting with peals of laughter a large stuffed blue parrot from Serena Sue Hilsinger and Lois Brynes. Its brilliant color and whiskers, short on one side, long on the other, give it a special nonsensical charm. An Edward Lear parrot, in fact. The third was opening an elegant black leather case that contained a necklace of pale-green aventurine beads from Charles Feldstein, one of my two adopted brothers. The card read, "The stone is aventurine (from the French *aventure*, so-called because of its accidental discovery).

Adventure is proper for this special birthday because of the adventures which lie ahead for you. And also because you taught those who love you that despite chronology, adventure is there for those who remain open to love."

And on all the cards and presents this birthday gathers to itself, I felt that, even though there is no longer one beloved person to center it all for me, I have a huge extended family and am (does the image work?) myself a centipede heart, so full of love it beats very fast and can race around.

Wednesday, May 5th

IT'S HARD to get going this morning because it is such a serene, quieting landscape—oh, what a tranquil ocean lies there, its deep breathing under the birdsong! The tree swallows are back, and I can hear them twittering as they fly. When I went down at six after my breakfast, the pheasant was on the lawn, lordly and magnificent. He is not afraid even of Tamas because he is so large and brilliant that he dominates the scene. Every now and then I hear his raucous cry that makes it quite clear. Now there is a moment of total silence except for the soft swish of the waves as they break, and that only accentuates the peace of the May morning.

I did get out into the garden yesterday afternoon at last and planted the white impatiens and the felicia near

"the pheasant was on the lawn"

TIMEtoSPA

Personal Program for: _____

Cruise Line: _____ NCC _____ Vessel: _____ Sun _____ Date: 20ᵗʰ / June 2011

Treatment	Recommendation
facial	- Pro-Collagen marine cream 124

Therapist Notes: Rosemary

CONTINUE YOUR EXPERIENCE AT HOME

Elemis, La Therapie and Ionithermie skin care products are available for purchase through

www.timetospa.com

You can also speak to a professional spa consultant by calling 1-800-423-5293.

970439

the house. Then I went down to the annual and vegetable plot and put in the twelve delphiniums that Raymond, the gardener, gave me. Last autumn friends brought a load of sheep manure, pure gold, so, with that spread, I am hoping the annuals will do better this year. I am really not a good gardener at all, full of hopeful plans but often in too much of a hurry to prepare the ground. Soon I must plant the seeds. What a shock when I was bitten by a blackfly yesterday! I had not expected them this early after such cold days. This is the first day without the sharp east wind and the first unclouded one in some time—in fact, it is our first day of spring. We have waited a long while.

But now everything will happen at once, too fast! Yesterday, as I came through the little wild garden with Tamas on the way back from our walk, I saw that the bloodroot Eleanor Blair gave me last year from her garden has survived. One group was in flower, the buds standing straight up on firm stalks, and this morning perhaps I shall come on them, wide-open white stars, the whitest white of any flower ever seen. It is the hour of the small early spring flowers—the scillas, brilliant blue in two thick patches along the wall, the small baroque clusters of puschkinia, the wonderful blue starflowers, all tiny along the borders, no great show yet. But the daffodils are beginning to shine in rich garlands, and above, against the sky, the red maples show their flowers.

I feel happy to be keeping a journal again. I have missed it, missed "naming things" as they appear, missed the half hour when I push all duties aside and savor the experience of being alive in this beautiful place.

One thing is certain, and I have always known it—the joys of my life have nothing to do with age. They do not change. Flowers, the morning and evening light, music, poetry, silence, the goldfinches darting about . . .

Thursday, May 6th

I HAVE BEEN putting together the poems for a reading at Westbrook College in Portland tonight. I love arranging poems around a theme, discovering old ones I had forgotten. Such as today "The Second Spring," which brings back vivid memories of Céline's garden in Belgium, for today is surely a day to celebrate spring again.

Yesterday afternoon Bill Heyen came with Bill Ewert and a friend. We have corresponded now and then since I quoted his poem "The Field" in *Recovering,* but we had not met. What a charming opener it was that, standing on the terrace, six-foot-tall Heyen exclaimed, "Look, a hummingbird, the first one I have seen this year!" To our amazement the usually vibrating wings were still, and we saw the hummingbird sitting on a branch of the cherry tree, a few feet away. He stayed quite still for several seconds.

So I felt at home with Bill at once, as I knew I would. It is odd that I have only a very few poet friends, now that Muriel Rukeyser and Louise Bogan have died, no one any longer with whom to exchange poems and lives. It was comforting to talk. I had put some of my birthday champagne in the refrigerator, and we drank a toast to Archie MacLeish. Bill was on his way to what would have been a celebration of Archie's ninetieth birthday, now a memorial service. We talked about that wonderfully fulfilled, generous life, and Bill said that in his last letter Archie had said that he hoped to live to his ninetieth birthday but then would be ready to go, and maybe it was a blessing not to have to respond to all the goings-on after all, to make his quiet exit just before. Two years ago I had a little word from him, saying, "Come soon. Time is running out." Why didn't I go then?

Among Archie's multiple graces was the ability to make real conversation, to draw out and appreciate those he chose to meet and to bring together. A wonderfully light touch, laughter, and keen intelligence all went into this. I feel that he deliberately chose to lead a life as balanced as possible, cutting away the extraneous, insisting that it be lived close to the marrow always. An arduous life, of course. These atmospheres do not just "happen" but are conscious creations.

In the wild jumble of these last days—public appearances, birthday presents to thank for, deaths of dear old poets and of small Sheltie puppies, days of everything-to-do in the garden, days of war in the world, of increasing poverty and desperation at home—I had a half hour of revelatory reading, an interview with Robert Coles in *Sojourner* on "The Faith of Children." It will do me good this morning to set down some of what he has to say and especially perhaps this story. It's the story, Coles tells us,

of a child who grew up in a very rich Florida family, whose experiences in the Presbyterian church somehow got to him when he was nine, ten or eleven, and prompted him to be very scrupulously concerned with the teachings of Christ. It got to the point that he was talking about them in school, upsetting teachers and fellow students by repeating certain statements that Christ made—namely, that it would be awfully hard for rich people to get into heaven (even though the child himself was very rich), that the poor

would indeed inherit the moral and spiritual kingdom, and so forth.

The more he talked like this, the more of a "problem" he became for his teachers, his parents, and
eventually for a local pediatrician. Ultimately this
boy ended up in psychotherapy because it was felt
that he had what was called, of course, a "problem,"
and needed help. His parents were told to stop taking him to church. He was accused of being too liter-
al-minded, at a very minimum.

ROBERT ELLSBURG, the interviewer: "And did they 'help'
him?"

COLES: "Well, they did 'help' him, and he lost a lot of these
Christian preoccupations and became another American entre-
preneur."

ELLSBURG: "Perhaps it's a good thing they didn't have psychotherapy in St. Francis' time."

COLES: "That's right! Psychiatry for St. Francis, psychiatry
for St. Paul, psychiatry for Jesus himself! But that is the Christian
dilemma. If you take Christianity seriously, it is a radical and,
indeed, a scandalous religion. And how close one feels to the
radical, scandalous nature of Christianity, how much we are
willing to be 'fools for Christ' is the problem for those of us who
become professional people and end up in institutions like, for
example, Harvard, where I teach."

Saturday, May 8th

I AM IN A WHIRLPOOL, so driven by what has to be done
immediately that a better image might be of a machine
that breaks down because all its circuits are overloaded.
And this is just when what I most want is time to notice

and savor the spring happenings. The mockingbird is back. I saw the first wood anemone open on my walk with Tamas yesterday, and the tiny plum tree I planted two years ago in the wild woods below the house at the back has grown into a beautiful tree and is just flowering, ravishing white flowers and bronzy leaves on its delicate branches. I picked a branch to set by my bed with a few small, pale-yellow and white daffodils. It reminds me of Japan when I was there just twenty years ago in March, and the plum blossom scented the air near a Zen monastery. It was very cold still and plum, the only flowering tree, unforgettable. Thinking of these things I center myself.

Outside in the world terrible things are happening— a British destroyer has been blown up by a single deadly missile in the war with Argentina. Perhaps this will stop the relentless clock; perhaps both sides will draw back, now each has struck hard, for the British sank a cruiser last week. But the QE2, filled with three thousand soldiers, steams toward the Falklands—a miniature war that could explode into such disaster and horror that one holds one's breath. I feel we have been irresponsible from the start. The Fascist macho junta imagined the British lion was toothless and because we had so buttered them up in our stupid wish to stop revolution in South America, they thought we would not interfere in their aggression.

There is never any depth in Reagan's perceptions of the world. He behaves like an animated cartoon, wound up to perform futile gestures and careless witticisms. It made me feel sick when his reaction to the despair of blacks about this administration was to engineer the other day a visit to a middle-class black family who had been threatened five years ago by a burning cross. So the TV cameras were marshaled, and Reagan and Nancy were shown kissing the family one by one. He made a few remarks about "this sort of thing" not tolerable in a democracy. But what is not tolerable is such a cheap ploy. Meanwhile, forty-eight percent of young blacks are jobless, and the administration offers no help. The black family behaved with perfect dignity, but the whole false "scene" was shown up clearly for what it was, a public-relations media event, an insult to the black community, neglected and shoved under the rug.

Other things are on my mind. The circuits *are* jammed. Proofs of *Anger* came yesterday just when I saw a small gap in the wall of tension because I gave my last spring poetry reading on Thursday at Westbrook College in Portland. Georgia called last night to tell me the awful news that Lisa, their Sheltie puppy, who has been such a comfort in the hard days they are going through, had died while being spayed. This happens so rarely I felt outraged that it had happened to my beleaguered, valiant adopted family.

Sunday, May 9th

LAST NIGHT the moon rose, a round, red disk, and this morning, just after five, I glimpsed the sun, red also, just before it disappeared in a bank of clouds, and now, as these signs foretold, it is raining a gentle rain, soothing for me and much needed in the garden. I did get in some seeds, two rows of cosmos, nasturtiums, and white radishes. It is always getting started that is the big hurdle into this spiral of work, remembering to lay down boards

© BEVERLY HALLAM

with Beverly Hallam—"a thousand dragonfly nymphs to put out"

on the newly raked big annuals bed, where I can stand to
sow the seeds, then move along as I proceed. It would be
nice if we had a few days without the chilling east wind,
although I expect it keeps the blackflies down and makes
the daffodils last a little longer.

But the real event yesterday was a new experience for
me, which can now become one of "les très riches heures
de York." Beverly, Mary-Leigh, and I set out at three
o'clock with a thousand dragonfly nymphs to put out in all
the marshy places and ponds around the place, Tamas and
Bramble tagging along. The air was cool. We had fun
finding the right place, near cattails, in water but not too
deep, so they could swim down into the mud and grow
into dragons. They came in twelve plastic containers,
lively looking beetley things that pricked one's hands with
their pointed tails. When the mosquitoes arrive, the hope
is that they will be decimated by the good dragons! It was
a wholly delightful expedition, scrambling around among
the moss and detritus on the borders of the salt marsh and
later the two fresh-water ponds. For me, a pause, a lovely
slow tempo that rested and refreshed on a pressured day.

Wednesday, May 12th

HOW SLOWLY one comes to understand anything! I am
these days sometimes a muse for other poets. I remember
well what it was like to be suddenly seized and shaken by
a presence around whom everything crystallized. I have
written about that side of it in *Mrs. Stevens.* But I had not

perhaps ever quite understood how hard it is to respond to such poems and to such feelings and at the same time how necessary it is to make a response that can shelter and nourish a talent and not kill the impulse, not freeze the tender shoots. The time comes when there is an understandable need to meet the faraway muse who has inspired so much. And for me the time comes when I must take a stranger in and give at least a day or two to talking things over, to being there as a tangible presence. I dread the imminence. I do not want to be invaded, and try to balance someone's needs (someone I have never seen and who does not know me) against my own need for time to myself, time to think and, above all, now in May, time to drink in the beauty of this place and to do the work that has to be done to keep it beautiful.

The daffodils are lasting because we are having very cold weather and icy winds. Yesterday afternoon I managed an hour to sow seeds, but the wind was so high the risk was that they would blow out of my hands. I got in only three rows; then UPS delivered two big boxes of perennials, and it was nearly six before I had unwrapped them. They come buried in those horrible little white plastic bubbles and have to be extricated patiently, one by one. Luckily they will be all right for a week or so.

Yesterday and the day before I wrote no letters and did not even write a line in this journal because the proof on *Anger* had to be mailed back yesterday to meet the deadline. It was very clean, and I enjoyed reading the book for the last time. When I think of the agonized struggle I went through in February and March to revise it, I am pleased now, and the immense effort is forgotten, just as women who bear children forget the labor pains, I am told.

On Monday my friend Phil Palmer, the Methodist pastor, came for our yearly invigorating talk. As always my compulsive anxieties vanished as we sat by the fire in the library (it was cold outside!) and I felt happy. It is moving to me to see how he has grown and how beautiful his face has become since he first came here seven years ago. The Coles interview was much on my mind, and once again I wondered aloud whether I should have given my life in some more obviously useful way than by writing books. Phil's response was immediate and definite. "You have a vocation and you have a ministry, and that is what you have been asked to do." Only he said it less piously and better than I have done here. It was comforting to hear that, and it had come out of his talk about vocation in general. A friend of his, a brilliant man and scholar, feels his vocation as a pastor is to live in a very remote parish on next to nothing and to do scholarly work.

That was always my father's dream—poverty and scholarly work—and we often teased him about it, saying he might have been happier as a monk! We all have our nostalgias for the giving up of "the world," I expect. But the people who act on it are rare. Karen Saum, who last winter lived here for half of every week, commuting to a job in Augusta, is one of those. As I think over this past year, I believe what has stirred me most deeply and given me hope is Karen's entry into the St. Francis Community, H.O.M.E, in Orland, down east from here, to devote herself to Sister Lucy's formidable and imaginative work among the very poor. She and Sister Lucy know all about being "God's fools."

Thursday, May 13th

IT WAS a spring-drunk drive to Wellesley and back, to see Eleanor Blair; a vision of spring at its most perfect. Along the thruways, I drank in the trees, with their marvelous flowering of strange mustard and emerald and orange and dark red making a tapestry of color on every side, and here and there, near houses, pear and cherry in clouds of white. Then, as I turned off Route 495 at Littleton to stop for plants, the distant vision came close in with purple lilacs, rhododendrons, azaleas at the peak of their flowering, no petals falling, and in Wellesley masses of pink and white dogwood that my mother loved, partly because it is not known in Europe and always seemed marvelous to her eyes. She was with me as I dropped in at various nurseries, looking for blue violas and dill and the red and white impatiens that did so well last year in a shady curve of stone wall. I found them all. Triumph! And sensed in myself again my mother's greed—is that the word?—when it came to plants for the garden. I had birthday money to spend, but she so often had to choose very carefully and then, like me, always ended by spending lavishly, come what would later on, and for the same reason as mine, that she got out to nurseries so rarely (she and my father had no car).

It was a glorious day, with a brief visit to Marguerite Hearsey (Keats away) and then lunch with Eleanor. We had sherry in the garden, sharing our joy in her beautiful trees and the lush, thick row of very blue violets along one border. Eleanor still manages to garden despite a broken hip and near blindness. How trim and beautiful everything looked!

It was hateful after lunch to be in a hurry to get home, and I left after Eleanor dug up a large tuft of Jacob's ladder from her big clump for me to put in the garden. Of course healthy plants from a friend's well-tended garden do far better than the spindly things one can buy! In exchange I left her some dill and the promise to come back in late June and spend the night so we'll have a chance for a really long talk.

Friday, May 14th

SINCE I GOT BACK I have been reading the proof of a stunning book on the relation between fathers and daughters, *The Wounded Woman* by Linda S. Leonard, and have at last written to the publisher, Swallow Press, to recommend it highly. I admire Leonard's courage in talking frankly about her relation to her father and combining her insights learned from patients (she is a psychotherapist) with her experience, so the book spoke to me with great force. Her willingness to speak of her own problem and vulnerability makes one believe her when she enters the realm of theory. She uses fairy tales to great effect. I marked the following passage. She is talking of Heidegger whom she calls her spiritual father.

CREDIT: ROD KESSLER

"I went out early to pick seventy-two daffodils"

Time is like an ever-moving spiral, he suggests. The
future continually comes toward us but it meets us
with our past at each moment of the immediate present. Each time this process happens, we are con-
fronted with mysterious new levels of our being. We
must meet the unknown future by bringing to
bear everything that has been shaped by us in the
past.

That is why we are never done with thinking about our
parents, I suppose, and come to know them better long
after they are dead than we ever did when they were
alive.

Reading Leonard devoured the hour I could steal
today, the day of Huldah's dinner party for me at the
Whistling Oyster. I went out early to pick seventy-two
daffodils of nine different kinds for the florist to arrange
for the tables in little baskets. It's a perfect May day,
marred only by the violent eruption of a red squirrel who
leapt out at me from a kitchen cupboard and is still perhaps somewhere in the house, a small terrified devil who
does not add to the gaiety of the morning. I have to complain about the squirrels, huge gray ones who manage to
climb into the big squirrel-proof feeder and eat five
pounds of birdseed in a few hours, small red ones who are
perpetually angry and, in their rage, bite into the thick
plastic of the Droll Yankee feeders if they find one empty.
The only virtue of these creatures is that they keep Tamas
young as he rushes out to chase them at the word "squirrel." Next fall I shall have to find a way to string a wire
across the lawn to see if I can circumvent their ingenuity.
They are charming to watch, but the red ones hang upside
down on the feeder as soon as I fill it, eating until there
is nothing left. So the small birds don't get a chance. These
days the goldfinches in their new bright yellow suits and

the house finches are an enchanting sight. And now I have
hung a hummingbird feeder on the ornamental cherry
where Bill Heyen saw one the other day.

Saturday, May 15th

WE SAT, fourteen of us, in an upstairs room at The Whistling Oyster, at four big tables set in a square, with four
baskets of daffodils from Wild Knoll set among us. Leonard's phrase "the future ... meets us with our past at each
moment of the immediate present" became vivid to me
as each of these dear friends, old and new, rose when the
spirit moved to remember where and when we first met.
I had quite forgotten that Rene Morgan had lunch with
me at Old France in Boston when I can't have been over
twenty and she perhaps twenty-four, fifty years ago. She
had dreamed of becoming an apprentice at Eva Le Gallienne's Civic Repertory, and that year I was director of
the apprentices. We became friends much later, but it
was delightful to remember that occasion when I had
seemed to her so much more sophisticated than I was.

Liz Knies, poet and youngest person among us, beautiful in a red dress with her Renaissance look, read a passage
from Shakespeare. Beverly Hallam reminded me of her
visit to Nelson with Mary-Leigh to pick up a monotype for
her retrospective show, and, as she talked, had the idea I
might come and live in this house—a pure chance, for, as
she suggested, if she had not had to pick up the monotype,
I would not have found my way to Maine. Janice made us

all laugh when she said that she was probably the only person there who had not wanted to meet me (out of shyness) but finally arrived one day with books to sign, and from then on we became friends. Lee Blair spoke most movingly of her recovery from a terrible automobile accident and months in the hospital where she had discovered my books, and then came to Nelson—how many years ago? For we are now woven into each other's lives and exchange the state of our souls by telephone every other day or so.

It was marvelous to see this galaxy gathered together, tall Martha Wheelock, tall Nancy Hartley, and tiny Heidi moving among us with her Polaroid camera, Anne Woodson and Barbara, so much my family—and marvelous that some of these friends could meet each other at last. Lee had driven all the way from Long Island, and everyone there knew of her but few had met her. Huldah, the presiding genius of the dinner, had suggested drawing our places by lot, and I was happy when it turned out that she sat on my left with Lee on her left. She had engineered this final and most glorious celebration of my birthday, and the heavenly menu was her choice, of course. Heidi offered the champagne.

All I could do was bask in the loving atmosphere and go to Yeats to express what I felt:

> Think where man's glory most begins and ends
> And say my glory was I had such friends.

I must say that hardly a day passes here without those lines running through my head.

And among all the presents, one stands out this morning. Lee brought it yesterday, photographs of two of the pieces she has been working on, carved out of birch, with a lightness and elegance that seem unbelievable, wrested from such resistant material. They are birds reduced to essence and to the elegance of flight, four or five feet tall. Lee has been having hard times financially and is living a life without luxury now. This is her luxury—to be able at fifty to do what she has always dreamed of doing, and doing it with grace. Once more, through physical pain (she has had several operations on one knee and is never not in pain) and loneliness and anguish, the work of art finds its way out.

"In the midst of winter I discovered that there was in me an invincible summer," as Camus said.

And as I looked around the table, what struck me hard was that, none of us young, we had all managed to become our true selves, that none of it had been easy, and that all of it has been built on dedication and on love.

The missing person was Karen Saum who, while we drank champagne, was way up north felling trees, building houses, teaching, helping in every possible way the very poor. For her I have put on the record Betsy sent me of "Chariots of Fire," for it is about love and dedication, the long haul, and the fire that makes it possible.

Sunday, May 16th

"OUR REVELS now are ended." The silence flooded in as Lee left this morning early, Huldah yesterday afternoon to take a plane to England. I am alone in my life with Tamas, Bramble, and all the daffodils and must get to my desk, overflowing with letters, and try to resume my self.

It is natural that the moment is one of depletion this morning, but if I can accomplish a little before lunch and get out into the garden this afternoon, all will be well. The emptied-out feeling will change and the well begin to fill again. I am reminded of the poem "Mud Season," which I read rather often on the trips in April, and of the line "What we are not drives us to consummation."

Keeping a journal again is a real comfort and joy. I had to smile at a paragraph quoted the other day in the *Times Literary Supplement* in a review of Robert Pinget's "Monsieur Songe" (shades of Valéry and M. Teste). Pinget, John Sturrock says, "uses Songe to ruminate with a measure of impersonality on the lot and the needs of the writer, delving wittily but at the same time searchingly into the paradoxes of authorship." Sturrock then quotes this paragraph, which I translate into English:

> The great difficulty when one writes one's journal, says Monsieur Songe, is to forget that one does not write it for others, or rather not to forget that one writes it for oneself, or rather to forget that one does not write it for a time when one will have become someone else, or rather not to forget that one is someone else in writing it, or rather not to forget that its only interest must be for oneself immediately, which is to say for someone who does not exist since one is someone else as soon as one begins to write.

And that is to say that moods change, but that it is the business of the journalist to record a mood as it comes, as exactly as possible, knowing that life is flux and that the mood must change. Today I am suffering from deprivation in spite of all the friends who made my birthday memorable, suffering because there is no central person. I laugh about it and say that the sea is to be my final muse, but one cannot fill a well with an ocean.

And that is the problem. A life extended in a thousand directions risks dispersion and madness. A kite can fly only when it is held taut by a string in a hand and then catches the wind. Today I am a kite entangled in a tree, and there is no one to free me for flight. Let us hope the garden will do it!

Monday, May 17th

IT WOULD be fine if now, after two weeks of it, the east wind that has been coming in every afternoon, cold and enervating, subsided. Later on in summer it is a blessing, and we are often ten degrees cooler than the town of York, but now when the ocean is still icy cold, the wind comes like a death blast and shrivels some flowers—though not the tough daffodils—and blows the seeds out of my hands. I did get in three rows yesterday and planted a box of Chinese and Connecticut Yankee delphiniums in the terrace border, because they never grow to great heights and should work well there. I'm also trying blue erigeron, but these plants are so small, the chances are slight that they will take hold. I just keep on ordering in the middle of winter in an intoxication of hope.

Every day now something new is happening in the woods when I take Tamas on our morning walk. The

"I did get in three rows yesterday"

wood anemones are full out, shining like stars above their delicate shower of fine-cut leaves, so that each one is a tiny bouquet in itself. I hope the nymphs are happily transforming themselves into dragonflies, for the mosquitoes have already begun to buzz in my ears and the horrible blackflies are back. At least the east wind does keep them down when I am working outdoors these days.

Peace flows in, now there is a little less pressure. But I must write letters.

I begin to feel the fatigue of the runner when a race is over, but I am quite pleased that I managed that month of public appearances, and all that has happened since because of my birthday, and felt happy and more or less in control. I am far better able to cope at seventy than I was at fifty. I think that is partly because I have learned to glide instead of to force myself at moments of tension. It doesn't always work, of course, but I am far less nervous before a poetry reading now than I used to be and so enjoy doing it. I used to be in a hard knot of nerves for days.

I realize that seventy must seem extremely old to my young friends, but I actually feel much younger than I did when I wrote *The House by the Sea* six years ago. And younger than I did in Nelson when I wrote the poem "Gestalt at Sixty." Those previews of old age were not entirely accurate, I am discovering. And that, as far as I can see, is because I live more completely in the moment these days, am not as anxious about the future, and am far more detached from the areas of pain, the loss of love, the struggle to get the work completed, the fear of death. I have less guilt because there is less anger. Perhaps before I die I shall make peace with my father and be able to heal the wound that Leonard's book has forced me to think about again.

Tuesday, May 18th

MARCIE HERSHMAN is meeting me for lunch to do an
interview for *Ms.* I always like seeing her. We are real
friends now because we have been able to share some
painful experiences in our private lives. But I feel like a
turtle today and wish I could stick my neck into my shell
and not be available to probing questions, however kind
they may be. Inevitably on poetry-reading tours I talk
about myself and finally feel overexposed. I am touched
by the real caring and interest people show, but after a
while the instinct is to close the door and turn inward.

Why is it that people who cannot show feeling pre-
sume that that is a strength and not a weakness? Why is
it common in our ethos to admire reserve, the withhold-
ing of the self, rather than openness and a willingness to
give? To show vulnerability remains suspect. Marcie and
I are in agreement about this. We have each suffered from
people who cannot give because that is too dangerous,
people for whom self-protection becomes a way of life at
the expense of growth. It is rather a relief now to be able
to speak of these things, not out of pain but from detachment.

I have been meaning to go back to the Robert Coles
interview, because I thought of what he said about Flannery O'Connor when Phil Palmer and I had our talk and
because it is one answer to the writer's fear that he is not

useful enough to justify his withdrawal from the world. The following passages are at the end of the interview with Ellsburg:

ELLSBURG: "You are an admirer of Flannery O'Connor's stories. So many of them take place on a kind of battlefield of belief and doubt in which the antagonists are, on the one hand, children, trying to hold on to a sense of mystery in life, versus the adults who would deny that mystery."

COLES: "Christ was once a child. And I think what Flannery O'Connor tried to show in some of her children was the true nature of innocence, which is an earnest moral and spiritual inquiry and search that has yet to be undone by the kinds of 'mature' rationalizations and self-justifications that the rest of us have learned to take so seriously."

ELLSBURG: "Is that what Christ meant when he spoke of the need for us to become like little children?"

COLES: "I think he meant that unless we recognize the radical nature of Christianity, which means shedding the imperatives of the secular world and taking with extreme seriousness the imperatives of God, we are kidding ourselves. I think we are meant to do as that child of the wealthy Florida family I described, who took seriously what Jesus had to say and worried about it, and didn't just worry about it in the abstract but worried about it concretely in his own life and the life of his family.

"His family feared that he was turning everything upside down, but I think that's just what Jesus intended for us to do— turn things upside down, look at things in the strangest and wildest ways. It's very hard for us to do that. And psychotherapy is not going to help us to do it. I am not sure that political activity is going to help us do it.

"Flannery O'Connor wanted to help us do it by writing those stories, because she saw what the Bible was getting at. In all her stories she confronts secular self-satisfied twentieth-century liberalism; she confronts it with Christian radicalism. It makes for a social, intellectual, and spiritual confrontation of the most dramatic kind."

I must ponder this, partly because I associate "innocence" with my father. I saw, when I was still a child, that innocence can be a paradox, delightful if one does not have to live with it, but cruel, a kind of indifference toward the needs of others, if one does.

The wood pigeons are cooing insistently. They always make me think of Virginia Woolf and *The Years* where they are a leitmotiv. The writer, perhaps, may be concerned with defining innocence but cannot afford to be an innocent. But then what about William Blake?

Thursday, May 20th

AT LAST we had some rain last night, and all the bushes and plants must be feeling a lot better. Yesterday was a lost day, that very rarest kind, when I am too tired to enjoy anything. Eleanor Perkins was here cleaning (she comes twice a month, so there is much to do). The basin in my bathroom had clogged up, so the plumber was here late in the afternoon just when I sorely needed an hour to get a quick sandwich before being picked up to see a new play about Sarah Orne Jewett in South Berwick. And I had got very little done at my desk. Then I wasted time watering in case it did not rain.

Today Kelly Wise comes to take photographs, but I think tomorrow will at last be a clear day, a day when I can resume my self, write, and garden in peace. "Peace" is putting it a little optimistically, because the garden at this season is more than I can handle, and I feel more driven than a Datsun, but maybe I can get in the sixteen miniature roses Edythe gave me for my birthday, now it is warmer. Until last night, the nights have been cold, forty often, and the east wind would blight these delicate greenhouse-grown flowers.

I did have a half-hour of pure bliss while I was eating my sandwich on the chaise longue and watching a rainbow of birds come and go. During that time, the cardinal and his mate were there and a flotilla of goldfinches, several jays, the rose-breasted grosbeak, the nuthatches, house finches in their rosy hoods, and the male pheasant! The chickadees have gone into the woods for the summer. But, oh dear, the ground was soon covered by starlings, grackles, cowbirds, and redwing blackbirds, while a red squirrel took over one feeder! I listened to the wood pigeons cooing "peace, peace," and refrained from rushing out and chasing this unwelcome crowd away. Instead, for about fifteen minutes I looked on a magic congregation of birds—red, blue, purple, rosy—topped, of course, by the half-moon crimson in the grosbeak's white breast. What a stunning bird he is!

And all of this takes place in the branches and around an ornamental cherry, now on the brink of flowering, still in crimson bud.

Friday, May 21st

I CHEERED myself up a couple of days ago by sending a check to get myself on a list for a retirement community in Bedford, Massachusetts. I am thinking of making the move in five years when I shall still be able to cope with

clearing out this house and disposing of papers. I sold
some of them to the Berg Collection at the New York
Public Library before I left Nelson, but there are still
many unsorted letters and manuscripts. I don't want to
leave that horrendous job to the executors of my will, and
perhaps in the end the idea of moving out will force me
to get it done before I am seventy-five, and then I may
decide to stay here after all, all neat and tidy. Who knows?

The reason that act of planning ahead cheered me is
that I am a little overwhelmed by my life here. It "com-
poses the mind," as Marynia Farnham used to say, to
imagine order in a time of such chaos. This week has
slipped away with the interview for *Ms.* on Tuesday, the
Nicholas Durso play on Wednesday, and Kelly Wise here
to photograph yesterday afternoon. What an ordeal being
photographed is! I think I must copy out an old poem I did
not put in the *Collected Poems* and send it to Kelly, because I am reminded of it today and thankful that my
feelings were expressed long ago. It is fun to rediscover an
old poem and find it a comfort.

Frogs and Photographers

The temperamental frog,
A loving expert says,
Exhibits stimulation
By rolling of bright eyes
(this is true frog-elation);
But in a different mood
Withdraws under a leaf
Or simulated bog
(This is frog's sign of grief),
Closes his eyes to brood.
Frogs do not weep, they hide.

The camera makes him cross.
Eyes glaze or tightly close;

His whole expression's changed.
He will not take a pose.
He has become estranged
Who was so bright and gay—
"Hysterical," they say,
As subject, total loss—
Burrows himself away,
Will not rise to a fly:
The frog is camera-shy.

A form of lunacy?
But whose face does not freeze,
Eyes shut or wildly blink?
Who does not sometimes sneeze
Just at the camera's wink?
Withdraw to worlds inside?
Invent himself a bog?
And more neurotic we
Than the spontaneous frog,
Sometimes cannot decide
Whether to weep or hide.

A Grain of Mustard Seed

It was calming after Kelly left to do some watering, put
a roast of lamb in the oven, and resume private life. Janice
came to have dinner with me as she does once a week, my
only steady visitor. She brought in fifty pounds of sunflower seed from the car, and then we sat out on the
terrace for the first time this spring—how green the field,
how blue the sea!—and had a postmortem on The Whistling Oyster dinner last week. Janice rather characteris-
tically came into my life three years ago when she heard
I needed fireplace wood, and she and her friend, Priscilla,
brought me a truckful and unloaded and stacked it for me.
After that we slowly became friends, went for walks and
picnics. Finally, last year, she came with me on the QE2
when I was on my way to France to see my cousin, So-

lange Sarton, in Brittany and she was on her way to
England. We discovered then that we felt a perfect accord, and since then she has become part of my extended
family. I treasure her for many reasons, for the caring
work she does in the Public Health Association of Portsmouth, for her gaiety (how often we laugh together and
how happily!), and perhaps, most of all, for her balance
and wisdom. Nearing fifty, she is asking herself all the
important questions about what one gives up to make a
human life. In her case, it meant a year ago deciding not
to take an important job in a hospital and settling for less
than half the salary in her present job so she would not
have to live her work, day and night. She settled for living
her life, for having time to see friends, to garden, to read,
to listen to music, to be "available." In a society where
success and money both mean so much, where people are
judged too often by "what they make," it takes character
to make the choice she did.

The other day I said to her, "With you I feel at peace."
I am fond of a great many people, but I would say that to
very few. No wonder Janice is precious.

Sunday, May 23rd

LAST THURSDAY, that rushed day, I saw Mr. Webster, the
plumber, for the first time in a long while. His wife has
cancer, and the last time we met was by accident in the
hardware store. When I asked about her then, he was in
a state of grief and panic and said with tears in his eyes,

"We have four children, you know," and I could feel his despair. On Thursday when I asked again about her, he simply beamed and told me chemotherapy had helped, but the "message" that came through was not about a physical state but simply that they have decided to do now all the things they had planned to do "someday," and they were just back from a trip to Florida to see her parents. Webster glowed. I suppose I have always believed that one must live as though one were dying—and we all are, of course—because then the priorities become clear. Such a pure love shone out from that man. How he has grown. How much he has learned since that day last winter at the hardware store! Later someone told me that his wife has been active at the hospice in York and is greatly cherished for her work there.

When Webster was here last winter he asked me shyly whether I would be willing to give him a signed copy of *A Reckoning* in exchange for the work done. I told him he was getting the lean end of the bargain, but he insisted the book would do it.

In the same order of good happenings, Bob Johnson at the florist's left a round planter filled with spring plants, a hyacinth, two yellow primroses, and some lilies on the terrace, this time with a note to say how he felt about *Recovering.* What do critics matter when workmen and florists are moved to respond with their gifts to mine?

I sometimes imagine I am the luckiest person in the world. For what does a poet truly want but to be able to give her gifts and find that they are acceptable? Deprived people have never found their gifts or feel their true gifts are not acceptable. This has happened to me more than once in a love relationship and that is my definition of hell.

Yesterday I found my balance at last, and it was because, waking in the night to the undone, I decided not to write in the journal but instead to concentrate on a few letters that have been much on my mind. Somehow that broke the awful tension of the last three weeks, and for the first time in a long while I was able to put on a Mozart record. Nancy Hartley came in the afternoon yesterday and that helped too as we got a lot of work done outdoors.

Wednesday, May 26th

ON MONDAY I had a grueling day. Kay Bonetti and her technical assistant, a silent young man, came here in heavy rain (poor dears, they had hoped to see the place) to record parts of *As We Are Now* and parts of *Journal of a Solitude* for the American Audio Library. They were half an hour late, and for me the tension rose. I wondered whether they had had an accident. I didn't dare come up to my study as I can't see the driveway from here, paced about, and finally looked at a television talk show. When they did arrive, some of my primary energy had been siphoned off, and I found the reading an excruciating effort. Going back into *As We Are Now* was painful. For some reason I became too aware of how I speak, the New England accent, which may sound elitish, the exact diction, which works well with an audience because every word comes through clearly but sounded self-conscious as I sat in an armchair in the library. After an hour of so of reading, there followed an hour of interview. Bonetti was well prepared and asked cogent questions, and I think my answers were not feeble-minded, but I have had to talk too much about myself and my work lately and had a strong wish to be silent, an inappropriate wish under the circumstances! Finally, at nearly two (I had had my breakfast at five), I took them to Spice of Life, the York equivalent of Alice's Restaurant, and by great good luck, lobster and avocado salad were on the menu. My Scotch and Kay's martini got the social juices flowing. But when I finally came home at nearly four I was so tired that I did not know what to do with myself. I couldn't rest and couldn't garden because of the rain. I was agitated because I found a huge box of plants from White Flower Farm when I came in the door. I have been pushing so hard in the garden these days, these constantly interrupted days, that a big job landing on me just then created panic.

About 3 A.M. yesterday I woke and decided the only thing to do was to break, for once, the inexorable routine and go out in the garden right after breakfast. It turned out to be a perfect day for planting, cool, the ground beautifully wet and soft after the rain, no bugs around. And it is such fun to plant plants—far less exacting than sowing seeds. The border below the terrace is newly open and free now that the euonymus has been torn off the lower retaining wall. It had grown to two feet high, so plants were choked, lacked sun, and it was impossible to get in there and weed. Now there is a chance that I can make of it a real English perennial border, and I am so intoxicated by the prospect that I ordered perhaps too many plants to stuff in there. But then there are always losses. I planted columbines, anchusas (that wonderful blue), blue erigerons, a purple centaurea, and lots of other things, even some butterfly weed for Huldah's sake as she loves it.

I had lunch with Heidi, went to the dentist, had a short

rest with Tamas, and then did another two and a half-hours' planting. Quite a day! But at the end of it, I was happy—tired, yes—but such a different tiredness from the nervous exhaustion of the day before.

This afternoon I hope to finish the job. The rain was a real blessing. Everything is shining and healthy after it. The white viburnum is in flower, and the delicious scent flows out in waves—I keep wondering what it is and then remember.

What is hard about my life now is not only that it is overscheduled for comfort but scheduled so far ahead. Even October is already marked off with two guests arriving, and, of course, the Ware lecture for the Unitarian Assembly looms at the end of June. July is chockful of people. But it is only when one is dying, like Laura in *A Reckoning,* that one is allowed to shut life out and concentrate on "the real connections."

Friday, May 28th

WHAT A WILD SCRAMBLE of a month! I can't believe it is nearly gone, daffodil deadheads almost all picked off, and iris and peonies on the way in the garden now. The blue spires of camassia, which I have never tried before, are stunning. "Why make so much of fragmentary blue?" Robert Frost asks. I don't know, but it is a fact that any blue flower seems precious, and among those I have been planting these last days, quite a few are blue—a rare blue salvia from Japan, Little John anchusas, and some asters.

The low Biedermeier columbine I planted last year are now the glory of one border, not spindly like some columbine but thick and luscious with a crown of soft blue flowers bending down. For some unknown reason, naming flowers makes my mouth water!

These days I am reminded of my mother, who, as she grew old and felt ill so much of the time, nevertheless indulged in what she called "Colonial Expansion" (taking over the end of the dead end street in Cambridge) to make a new border and expanding the garden when she had little strength. That is what it is to have a passion for something!

This garden is really too demanding for me at this stage in my life, but I know I shall never be able to restrict myself there. It has to be accepted that gardening is a madness, a folly that does not go away with age. Quite the contrary.

Pantheon sent me a book in proof that has been a real joy, Anne Truitt's *Daybook: The Journal of an Artist*. It has been, in the first place, an immense pleasure to read a journal so deep, succinct, and illuminating. The style is as pared down and elegant as her sculpture appears to be as she writes about it. How rare to find an artist who can talk about her craft as she does! It reminded me of Delacroix's *Journals,* which were a revelation to me years ago and which I took over to Quig when he was dying. I remember how his face lit up when he came upon a portrait (was it Chopin?) and sat for a long time looking at it. There is much here I recognize. When she talks about David Smith's death, she says, "After his death the studio felt lonelier. I came to understand that David's essence for me was that while he was alive he was working. And, if he was working, I was not alone." I felt this kind of loss acutely when Virginia Woolf died and realized there was no one left whose opinion of my work mattered a hoot to me. But that was different, for we were not intimate friends, and at that time I had published only two or three books. But I did sense her as in some way "kin," as far as work went.

I marked another page in Truitt.

> Last winter, during the course of preparation for the retrospectives, I found myself on the crest of an unspeakable loneliness. Stopped, I told my children that I would like a day to myself and went to the National Gallery. . . . I went straight to the Rembrandt self-portrait, painted when he was fifty-three, my age. He looked straight out at me, and I looked straight in at him.
>
> There is a sort of shame in naked pain. I used to see it in my patients when I was working in psychology and nursing. They found it more seemly, more expedient to pull over themselves thin coverlets of talk. There is wisdom in this, an unselfish honor in bearing one's burdens silently. But Rembrandt found a higher good worth the risk and painted himself as he knew himself, human beyond reprieve. He looks out from this position, without self-pity and without flourish, and lends me strength.

It is that kind of honesty that I have been after in the journals, but I envy the painter who does not have to use elusive, sometimes damaged, often ambivalent *words.* Still, I find that keeping a journal again validates and clarifies. For the hour I manage in the morning at this task I am happy, at ease with myself and the world, even when I am complaining of pressure.

I sometimes feel old these days when I am suddenly made aware of the little time *ahead.* It came to me with

a sharp pang when I found myself saying, as I have done
every spring for years, Housman's

> And since to look at things in bloom
> Fifty springs are little room
> About the woodland I will go
> To see the cherry hung with snow.

But I have at most ten or fifteen springs! Is that possible? Almost a lifetime gone. On the other side though,
what I do have is seventy springs in my head, and they
flow back with all their riches now.

Saturday, May 29th

I AM FEELING a bit dismal this morning in a wild, wet
nor'easter because yesterday afternoon when I came in
from planting the last of the plants I saw feathers by the
bird feeder. When I picked up one and saw the shiny
blue-black with a white tip, I knew Bramble had caught
the rose-breasted grosbeak. All evening, as I got my supper and watched the news, I waited, hoping that he would
turn up as he has every evening without fail, a kind of
secret treasure. How can I bear that Bramble could tear
this glory apart? I had noticed that he was unusually tame,
not flying off when I filled the feeders but waiting in the
flowery branches of the cherry. It is awful. "Nature red in
tooth and claw," I find, is Tennyson, not Emerson as I had
thought. I mourn the grosbeak, a solitary, without a mate

"Bramble's demure walk"

apparently. I mourn the havoc everywhere we can do nothing to stop. And last night I even thought of getting an indoor cat when Bramble dies. She is a savage hunter, I fear, with her fixed, concentrated look, her eyes as cold as stones. Yet an indoor cat is a tiger in a cage.

And how I shall miss Bramble's demure walk every morning, keeping her distance about twenty yards behind Tamas and me, then, when I wait for her, coming to wind round my legs and purr. And she is exceptional, I think, in her dependence on and love for Tamas. When she finally comes home after a twenty-four-hour absence and I am worried sick, she runs first to Tamas to lift up her head to his nose and be greeted. He, on the other hand, is quite mean to her and jealous when she gets attention from visitors! And Tamas is just as savage when he catches a squirrel (rarely), just as "red in tooth and claw." The first time I was aware of that I remember being deeply shocked, for Tamas is such a gentle dog.

I suppose we all have this ferocity buried in us. Weakness of any sort arouses sadism in most people. But if we are to love anything well, we have to accept it as it is. "We love the things we love for what they are...." At least that is the wisdom I have been aiming for lately. And these cogitations bring me to a paragraph in Truitt's *Daybook* that I want to keep in my mind:

> Unless we are very, very careful, we doom each other by holding on to images of one another based on preconceptions that are in turn based on indifference to what is other than ourselves. This indifference can be, in its extreme, a form of murder and seems to me a rather common phenomenon. We claim autonomy for ourselves and forget that in so doing we can fall into the tyranny of defining other people as we would like them to be. By focusing on

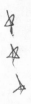

> what we choose to acknowledge in them, we impose
> an insidious control on them. .... The opposite of this
> inattention is love, is the honoring of others in a way
> that grants them the grace of their own autonomy
> and allows mutual discovery.

Monday, Memorial Day

AND STILL it drizzles on—such a gloomy Memorial Day
weekend, without a gleam of sunlight. I am reading the
fourth volume of the Virginia Woolf diaries, laid aside
earlier for more urgent matters. This is the period of the
last pages of *The Years* and seems more of a catchall than
the earlier ones. She disposes of Bowen's Court rather
meanly, I feel, for despite its shabby splendor, it stood
there as a haunting presence, a real presence, and I
sensed when I was there that for Elizabeth it was pure
poetry and perhaps even her muse, a difficult and demanding muse that ate up all the money she made but
which she served well. I suppose what I envy when I read
these diaries is the Woolfs' friendships with writers, real
friendships, not mere acquaintance.

There was that one extraordinary period in the thirties
when I went over to England every spring and by a series
of lucky chances met the Julian Huxleys, the Woolfs,
Bowen, Basil de Selincourt, Koteliansky. But I was in my
twenties, unknown, and was meeting them as "great writers," way beyond me, and the charm was just this, to be

included in a, to me, fabulous world that I had in no way earned. Now I do know a few writers who are in the position I was in then, who look up to me, and I treasure their friendship and try to help them in any way I can.

I miss Louise Bogan and also Doris Grumbach, who is not dead, thank goodness, but has vanished in a cloud of creation as she is writing both a novel and a critical biography of Willa Cather. With whom can I talk about craft? George Garrett, that most generous of men, is just across the river, but we meet very rarely. Perhaps it is my fault. I have shied away from my peers, partly because writing, as a trade, is so competitive, and I am a bad loser. Any meeting with a successful writer opens wounds.

When I really am honest with myself I believe I may have chosen nonwriters as intimates because I wanted to know "real people," people at work in the world, people who can tell me things I could not otherwise know, and people who are not congenitally prickly pears as any professional writer is, and heaven knows, as I am myself.

Yesterday on an impulse I called Eva Le Gallienne to see how she is and told her about the grosbeak. Her bluebirds are back. I forgot to ask about the raccoons, nine of whom came every evening to be fed when I saw her last three summers ago. We laughed about not being able to believe our respective ages, hers eighty-three, mine seventy. She told me that it is possible that her marvelous production of *Alice in Wonderland* may be revived with the original Richard Addinsell music this fall. And such memories welled up, for I was Le Gallienne's understudy when we took *Alice* uptown and played at the New Amsterdam, and I had the enormous fun of playing the White Queen there when she took a week off. I can still remember the wall of laughter that greeted every line and the exhilaration of hearing that!

Now I am going to give myself a present and get together a small group of poems for Bill Ewert who wants
to do a chapbook.

Thursday, June 3rd

BEFORE CLOSING the curtains up here in my study, as
sunlight dazzles my eyes on a page, I looked down and
saw the shadow of a bird crossing the lawn, then the bird
itself flying at the level of these high windows. The sun is
out, and the birds have shadows again. That is the great
news this morning as the blue ocean and the green field
sing together, and the ocean that was silent in the rain
murmurs in the distance.

How marvelous that the sun did come out yesterday
after lunch! Eleanor Blair and Elyse Rotella sat on the
terrace wall dangling their legs and drinking in the garden, soaking in the warmth. After an hour, Eleanor and
I stretched out on the chaise longues while Elyse went
down to the ocean with Tamas.

We had Mary-Leigh's champagne before lunch by the
fire and a cozy talk. Eleanor spent a few minutes really
looking at the plant window, which is rather fine these
days, since I centered it with a standing blue and red
fuchsia and bought some orange-red geraniums and pale
pink ones. A blue streptocarpus is in flower and three of
the white ones, so it all looks rich and airy—it was Eleanor
who suggested that I turn that bow window into a green-
house, so she has a proprietary interest in it, and I'm

amazed that, despite partial blindness, she appears to notice everything.

Maple syrup on coffee ice cream was a great success. When they left, I dressed in jeans and went out to plant the tomato plants and had just started when UPS drove up and delivered the eleven lily bulbs I had ordered last week—it's a joke that nearly always when I think I am in the clear some such event takes place. But we are promised this day (rain tomorrow and Saturday), and it's perfect weather for planting, so I intend to get them in this afternoon.

Then Raymond came after a long absence, as usual recounting various disasters; the emergency brake on his truck had to be replaced, and both his rototillers are out of commission, so I can never complain, but when the litany is over and I have commiserated, he gets going on a piece of work that would take me days to achieve. Yesterday it was to clean out the rose bed, plant the white rose Maryann gave me for my birthday, and then move several other roses that had survived partly because they were hidden in the shelter of the rugosa. Six roses died this winter. I could hardly believe how neat and flourishing it all looked when I went out after my bath. These days I do without Raymond much of the time, but when he does come, what a difference it makes! Courage flows in. Work gets done. He promised to come back today, cut the terrace grass, and do some trimming.

The garden is an obsession at this season, and I'm afraid there is little else in my head. But why not be obsessed by a garden? Both the gambler and the puritan in me are satisfied within its limitless expenditures and failures and by the hard work it entails.

And when it gives pleasure to my friends, such as Eleanor and Elyse yesterday, my cup runneth over.

Friday, June 4th

HOW DOES ONE contain it all? Yesterday I heard from Belgium that Eugénie Dubois is dying. And now I have been silent after writing that sentence, listening to Kathleen Ferrier singing Mahler's *Der Abschied.* More than anyone I have known that cry *"Die Schönheit!" was* Eugénie, a radiant spirit, torn by life but always responding to beauty as my mother did, having the power to choose and take the path toward elevation rather than despair. She sowed light in all her friends and in her two children and her grandchildren and, before that, in the children she taught, sowed light like some miraculous seed. Always in our relationship she brought me back to the essence. I suppose her greatest gift was that of accepting people *as they are.* How few people are capable of that! Her marriage had never been easy, but in the last years those seeds of light she had sown in Jean, her husband, came to flower, and they spent the years of old age in perfect accord and peace. It was she who kept the household together, cooked, gardened, made everything *happen,* while Jean became more and more a child to be looked after, but never did I hear a word of resentment. "He has become so beautiful," she said to me more than once. That was Eugénie. And at the same time her door was always open to friends and their friends, to strangers, to her family, always ready to listen in such a wise and endearing way to the problems and joys of others. After Jean died, she was very much alone, struggling in silence to accept death. Oh, how I hope it comes gently to her, that she simply goes to sleep! It is strange how *dépaysée* I feel with this news in my heart, how lonely and in exile I feel. Europe, my Europe, the heartland, will have almost gone when Eugénie goes.

How to contain it all? That mail brought a letter confirming a trip to Vancouver and Victoria in early November. And also a powerful request for help in fighting for clean air, clean water, and for the endangered species, all about to be done in by the Watt demands. I sent a check, but with a sinking feeling. Where will it end? So much is being destroyed that cannot be recovered.

There was also a request to see a young scholar from Saudi Arabia who adores my father. George Sarton is a hero in the Middle East because of his great work on the Arabian mathematicians and astronomers of the eleventh century, the bearers in their era of intellectual light to the world. God forgive me, I had to say that there is no space this weekend. At what point is one justified in closing the door to strangers? I pay a heavy price when I do, but is there to be no time for mourning? For poetry?

I set aside all this turbulence yesterday afternoon and planted the eleven lilies needed to replace those the chipmunks ate last winter. It was good to forget everything else and feel the good damp earth in my hands, the great restorer! Today it looks like rain again, disappointing as Nancy was to have come to help me weed.

Sunday, June 6th

"RAIN, RAIN go away. Come again another day." We are
in a deep green well, endless downpour battering the
windows. Perhaps the wind will blow it all away. Nancy
and I did get two hours last Friday between showers and
managed to weed and mulch three or four rows in the
annuals bed. What a treasure Nancy is! It is fun to do
things with someone; everything seems easier, and we
laugh a lot. Living alone, I find shared laughter is one of
the things I miss most.

I have been meaning to speak of the television play on
Golda Meir that was aired sometime last week with Ingrid
Bergman as Golda. I saw only the second part. It is good
that we are forced to remember the absolute peril that
Israel has been in from the start, for it explains what often
looks like intransigence. I was moved by all of it, and by
Bergman's authentic, honest performance. The only trouble is that part of Golda's power was in her worn, lined,
very plain face and grizzled, untidy hair. Bergman is too
beautiful. So I missed the real face—it had in it all the
suffering, tension, and courage demanded to overcome
impossible odds that made Golda what she was. Neither
she nor Eleanor Roosevelt was beautiful, but in both the
spirit triumphed over plain features and shone out. So
why do we worry about lines in our faces as we grow old?

A face without lines that shows no mark of what has been lived through in a long life suggests something unlived, empty, behind it. I think of Lotte Jacobi's face, a mass of wrinkles, now she is well over eighty, but so full of wisdom that *that* is what one sees, and she is still enchanting.

Still, one mourns one's young face sometimes. It has to be admitted. I now use a night cream for the first time in my life. At the same time, as I went over photographs yesterday for a children's book of biographies in which I am included, I felt that my face is better now, and I like it better. That is because I am a far more complete and richer person than I was at twenty-five, when ambition and personal conflicts were paramount and there was a surface of sophistication that was not true of the person inside. Now I wear the inside person outside and am more comfortable with my self. In some ways I am younger because I can admit vulnerability and more innocent because I do not have to pretend.

Several deaths have come to this house lately. One I want to record here, that of Dave McKay Wilson's grandmother. Dave has become a real friend these past years as he makes his way as a reporter, a feisty reporter. It's rather rare when a grandson is able to celebrate his grandmother as he did in the Litchfield *Enquirer,* which printed the words he said at the funeral. By a piece of luck Dave had gone to live with his grandmother in the last seven weeks before her death while she looked for a housekeeper, so they had time to become true friends, and he spoke of her with a twinkle of pure enjoyment in his eye. I especially liked the first paragraphs:

"We are here to celebrate the life of my grandmother, Charity Elizabeth McKay Wilson.

"The matriarch of Peaceful House, she died last Wednesday after ninety-three-and-a-half years on the upbeat. My grandmother touched seven generations with her loving kindness, her quick mind, her girlish laugh that came as she cocked her head and smiled an impish grin.

"Since Easter I've stayed at Peaceful House in the room she lived in during the 1930's. Until her final day she was vital, inquisitive, opinionated, healthy, and willing to take risks."

And now, thinking of old age at its most splendid, I must write to Camille Mayran, who is also ninety-three, in Strasbourg. We have been corresponding for almost thirty years.

Tuesday, June 8th

YESTERDAY it seemed that the deluge would never stop. It has been extremely frustrating not to be able to garden, and the gray world outside (no light, no shadow through the leaves) made me feel gray inside. But I did manage to rough out the big speech I am to give at the Unitarian Universalist Assembly on June 25th, and that took me over the hurdle of panic about what had begun to loom. What I want most to convey is that, in spite of the baffling state of the world around us—war in the Falklands and in the Middle East, poverty, recession, racism at home—it is still possible for one human being, with imagination and will, to move mountains. The danger is that we become so overwhelmed by the negative that we cannot act. I am going to talk about H.O.M.E. (Homeworkers Organized for More Employment), Sister Lucy's community in Orland, near Bangor. I hear about it very directly from Karen Saum, and it has been for me a point of light for the past year.

Sister Lucy, like Mother Teresa, left a contemplative order because she saw so much need outside the convent wall. Ten years ago she began to build and to attract others to help her build a center for helping the very poor in that poverty-stricken part of Maine where lumbering is just about the only employment.

She began by creating a center where women could learn a craft, or if they had one, teach it to others, and sell the products. At present, ten years later, five hundred people have been able to make a little money in this way. But in ten years the project has expanded to include most of life. The people at H.O.M.E. cut wood and see that the old have enough for the winter; they take the sick to the hospital or to a doctor; they help alcoholics to join AA and get them to the meetings; they teach night classes so people can get high school diplomas; they teach reading and writing to illiterates; they are finding ways to improve livestock and plan to breed workhorses themselves. But the most amazing achievement is that they have built five houses, solar-heated, for five families who needed shelter, and built them with mostly volunteer labor. How all this has been achieved on next to no money only God knows.

The community is doing more than helping the poor, for at the same time it is giving hope to the young volunteers who troop up in summer from schools and colleges, helping them to understand what life is all about, helping them out of the apathy or depression of wondering what is the matter with the United States these days, creating in microcosm a true democracy of the spirit, which is also a practical democracy. Things get done at H.O.M.E. Impossible things get done.

Karen gets up at five in winter, builds a fire in the stove and writes me letters, so I feel close to the joys and problems. There is no running water in the main house. They drag it up from the lake, bucketful by bucketful. There is no electricity, so Karen writes by lamplight. At half-past six the resident priest offers Mass, and at seven they have breakfast. After breakfast Sister Lucy plans the day and may announce, "Well, I think I'll chop down three or four trees this morning," and goes out and does so.

That is only the start of the tasks they handle and the crises they meet every day. A family is found living in an automobile (temperature 30° below!) and the family scheduled to move into the next new house gives it up so the automobile family can be housed. A prisoner is released from prison with nowhere to go and is taken in. It is a little like being God in the middle of Creation, although I'm afraid the people of H.O.M.E. do not rest on the seventh day!

I look forward very much to sharing this with the Unitarians. They will understand what H.O.M.E. is all about. I shall end with the last lines of my poem "To the Living."

Speak to the children now of revolution
Not as a violence, a terror, and a dissolution,
But as the long-held hope and the long dream of man,
The river in his heart and his most pure tradition.

That was written in 1944, thirty-eight years ago. Poems do last.

Friday, June 11th

WHERE HAVE the days gone? On Wednesday I went to Portsmouth on a big expedition to get birdseed and liquor and to lay in food for Betsy Swart, who arrived yesterday in the afternoon. The sun is glorious, but we have an icy breath of wind, so I was alarmed when she got off the bus in a summer dress! Yesterday morning I made Carbonnade Flamande after breakfast and later went to Finest Kind fish market for salmon and cooked it while I had my lunch. Two days just flew away!

Betsy is doing her dissertation on my novels and is at the moment in her room reading the typescript of *Anger*, and I am up here at my desk madly trying to catch up on correspondence and gather myself together for the day. I have been playing the Mozart Piano Concerto in E-Flat Major no. 9, which Betsy brought me, and writing a long letter in French to Pauline Prince, the last of the great old friends in Belgium, now Eugénie is dead. I have leaned on her wisdom and been restored by it for more than forty years, and as long as she stays alive (she must be close to ninety) I still have a root, a taproot, in Europe. My dictionary defines *taproot* as "the main root of a plant, usually stouter than the lateral roots and growing straight downward from the stem." That root, I expect, is the root of infancy, of the language of infancy as well as the land of infancy, and Belgium is that for me, and Pauline is that for me. I did not know her when I was a child, but we have been nourished by the same things, literature and art and passionate attachments. She was a professor at the École Normale for many years and one of Jean Dominique's *fidèles*. In some ways she knows and understands what I am all about better than anyone else still alive. Her brilliant intellect and lucidity (I revel in the pure French style of her letters) are warmed and tempered by modesty and her faith as a Catholic. And all this comes down, as I consider Pauline, to the fact that people who have the intellectual power to judge and to pass judgment on others always refrain from doing so! Nothing in Pauline asserts "I am right and you are wrong." She has passed her life in quiet meditation on the values of literature (she is reading Flaubert's letters again, she tells me) and on divining the essence of those she loves or admires through a penetrating sensitivity that absorbs and relates to, rather than judges. She has been, for her students, and for me, a civilizing influence. Yes, a taproot.

It is always rather frightening to receive as a guest a person one has known only through letters and, in Betsy's case, for a short time. I was nervous about her visit. But here she is, tall, beautiful, with red hair, and forty years younger than I! Tamas makes the bridge, as usual—he is the most loving of hosts and greets anyone who comes here with delight, like a long-lost friend. I am taking the three days as a kind of holiday. It is lovely to share the beauty of this place with someone who comes into a known territory and recognizes everything because she has read the books.

Sunday, June 13th

IT WAS A GOOD VISIT, as we finally got on the beam together after a rather strained twenty-four hours. I feel my
age when I am with such a young person, not because I
feel old but because, in the forty years that separate us, I
have deeply grooved my life in one direction and to do
that have had to be the opposite of an adventurer, have
had to be rather practical. I envy Betsy her capacity to
abandon a thesis that was half finished because she discovered my books last October and decided that they were
what she wanted to study and write about—there is something grand about such spontaneous combustion, grand
and courageous. She reminded me in some ways of myself
at her age, the extravagant gestures toward those I admired, in spite of very limited means. She arrived here
without a coat or raincoat but with a bottle of horribly
expensive champagne, a recording, and a few books for
me to sign as presents. I gather she and her friends eat
almost nothing, no breakfast, rarely lunch, and live on
granola, I suspect. In contrast, how old and bourgeois I
have become!

We had a lovely hour clearing out weeds along the
terrace wall before the eternal rain began again. Betsy
was brought up in the country and said she had forgotten
the pleasure it is to get down to earth again. That was a
companionable time without strain. What is exhausting

for me is to talk about the books and try to respond intelli-
gently to cogent questions while looking at my watch and
remembering to get the water boiling for the potatoes—
in fact, to be a housekeeper, cook, emptier of ashtrays,
getter of drinks and at the same time be Sarton, the
writer, whom she had come to see. But the cook is necessary, too! The constant remaking of domestic chaos into
the order that keeps a house alive and peaceful takes a lot
of doing. When I'm alone here I enjoy that side of things
because there is no tension, and I can think as I water the
plants, but when I have a guest it is all done under pressure, and I begin to feel rather put upon. That is my
failure, of course. But by the time Betsy left today, she had
begun to help me, so we washed her sheets and remade
the bed together.

I was touched when she asked for Jean Dominique's
books and spent this morning before she left copying out
poems she liked. So here is Jean Dominique being discovered by another ardent young woman, as I discovered and
read her forty-five years ago!

I am maddened today because I put a new ribbon into
the typewriter but it apparently is not working, does not
move forward or backward.

Monday, June 14th

WELL, we have broken all records for rain in June, and the
month is only half over! It's pouring again, so my little
holiday to see Lotte Jacobi on Star Island seems ruined.
Perhaps it will clear later on. And it will be a saving grace

to see her on the dock. For ten years I have been aware
of the Isles of Shoals, southeast from here. Sometimes they
seem to float in the air as the Greek islands do, floating on
a band of light. Sometimes they are very dark and sharply
edged. Sometimes they are not there at all, those magic
islands I have not yet, in the ten years I have lived here,
set foot upon. So it will be an adventure even in the rain.

Wednesday, June 16th

I HAD SUGGESTED to Edythe, who came here for the
night, that it might be fun to treat the trip to Star Island
as though the *Viking Sun* were the *QE 2*, so she drove me
to Portsmouth, and we had lunch at a riverside tavern
looking out at a huge freighter called *Bulk Queen* (what
an ugly name for a ship) and the three resident tugs, one
of which is called *Bath of New York*, God knows why. To
have a delicious lunch, topped off by chocolate cake, in
the presence of three tugs is a distinct pleasure! The one-
hour trip was very rough and very cold, so it seemed even
more of a journey.

The island looked rather forlorn in the icy wind under
gray skies as we approached, but Betty Lockwood, who
runs the bookshop, greeted me warmly, and waiting for
me on the porch of the nineteenth-century hotel was
Lotte, looking like a benign troll in a Peruvian cap with
a point on top. I was feeling rather queasy, so it was startling to discover that somehow "it would be nice" if I read
poems at five and signed books at five-thirty during the
sherry hour! I had come, longing to get away from letters

and interviews, to have twenty-four hours "away"! I settled for a rest in my room in one of the small houses
attached to the hotel, opposite Lotte's room. At once,
taking it in like an animal in a strange place, I sniffed
around feeling cold. How chilled it was!—and strange.
The room felt rather as a room in a Shaker community
might feel, pale-blue walls without a single painting, an
immaculate bedspread, a stand with a jug of cold water in
a basin and a slop pail below. A narrow bureau, and that
was it. I pulled the shades down and borrowed a blanket
from Lotte and wondered whether I would ever be warm
again. But I liked the bare, peaceful, spotless look of
things. And after reading the mail Edythe had picked up
for me, I did finally fall asleep.

Lotte came to wake me at quarter to five, and I stumbled out like a person waking from a dream, still disori-
ented, still wondering what the magic of the place was,
still there only to be with Lotte, who was suffering from
the cold too, she told me. But as I looked out on the flat,
rocky, almost treeless landscape, the paths like goat paths
between tall, wet grasses and over rocks and stone—all
surrounded by ocean—I remembered Patmos. Star does
have something of the quality of a Greek island.

Then I was swept into a room in the hotel where forty
or so people had gathered. I read—since this third week
in June is Art Week here—poems inspired by music,
painting, and poetry. Then we walked up a goat path to
the small, low stone house where the daily sherry hour
takes place, and I sat down at a long table and signed
books.

After supper in the immense, noisy dining room, some
of us gathered again in the small parlor where I had read
to talk about our lives as women. There was only time to
go round the circle and introduce ourselves, but the vari-

ety of experience was amazing. The leader, a young woman who runs a day-care center in Acton, did talk a little about her problems, lack of funding for one, and there was some discussion about whether it is possible for women with full-time jobs to bring up small children well, leaving their care to a center during the day. One of the most interesting women said she had suffered from a chronic, debilitating disease that was cured finally by a holistic approach, and she has now become a therapist, helping others to get well in the same way. She appears to have an intuitive understanding of what each person needs and spoke of several patients who had been totally incapacitated but now lead normal lives.

After that I went to bed, comforted by an electric blanket Betty Lockwood kindly lent me. With only the thin blanket provided, it would otherwise have been a cold and sleepless night.

I woke at five to discover we were clothed in a dense, clammy fog! By breakfast time at eight it was lifting, and the warm, sunny day we had been promised looked not impossible, after all. At a breakfast of tomato juice, pancakes, and coffee, I sat next to a Mrs. Harris, who was related to Myra Harris and Bessie Lyman, who inhabited the parsonage almost next door to my house in Nelson. We talked about Nelson and about Shelties for, like me, Mrs. Harris had fallen in love with the Shelties at the Frenchs' farm in Nelson and purchased one called Duncan, a cousin of Tamas's. That is a real bond, and we glowed. This brave woman had had an appendectomy a week ago but was determined to come for Art Week as she has done for several years. The first time was after she had had three babies in quick succession, and her husband, sensing exhaustion, had sent her off to Star for a week of renewal and solitude. She talked about what it had meant. At first she went off by herself, sat on a rock, drank in the ocean spells, and then gradually joined in. Opposite her sat a minister and his wife, and she had had the same experience. She had saved to come and thought it would be once only as it seemed too expensive an indulgence to repeat, but there she was for the fourth or fifth time because it had become a necessity.

On an island—I used to notice this at Greenings Island with Anne Thorp when Judy and I spent days there together every summer—the world is distanced. We did not talk about the war in the Falklands or the war in Lebanon. That was a rest in itself.

After breakfast Lottie and I set out to explore. The sun was out. The sea was suddenly blue and calm. The island seemed to be floating. I pinched a bay leaf and drank in its spicy smell and felt joy rising and peace rising. Lotte in her old age has become an astonishing beauty. She so obviously enjoys being herself, being the center of a great deal of attention, being "the wise one" and the mischievous one too, for she is a great tease. We slowly progressed along a goat path, stopping to look out at the blue all around us, stopping to talk by an old rowboat filled with small white flowers and nearly buried under the tall grass, until we came to what must once have been a barn and there found two nuns teaching an art class in simple design. We stayed a while. Lotte made a sketch, using words in a pattern, as had been suggested, and I had a great wish to spend an hour or two drawing rocks. At that moment I knew I would have to go back next June and stay the whole week, truly "get away," so the magic was working.

*with Lotte Jacobi, "the center of a great deal of attention," on Star
Island*

Saturday, June 19th

THE SUN CAME OUT for Elizabeth Roget, and how amazing it was to have tea on the terrace, to look out on a hazy blue sea, to see light and shadow on the azaleas, which are in full flower—those lovely de Rothschild ones I planted, four or five feet tall, airy, with huge separated heads of bloom, apricot and white (that one is highly scented, pungent and honeyed) and one flame-colored just coming into bloom. The tree peonies are also in flower in the most subtle variations imaginable, one yellow—dark gold with greenish highlights—and one dark red. The white one I loved best died last winter.

Elizabeth is a joy. She is now eighty-three and has just finished a novel, her second. I know her through Louise Bogan, and we have corresponded for years across the continent since she lives in Bolinas, California. So it was a happy chance that we could make connections, and here she is, downstairs, immersed in Virginia Woolf's *Moments of Being* while I work.

It is a pleasure to be with someone who says that the eighties are her happiest years and who is silent while we drive around because she wants to concentrate on what she is seeing. That is wonderful for me because I am the same kind of being. I want to do one thing at a time and give it my whole attention. Most people, I find, use driving as a time for talk!

Like all good writers, Elizabeth is very observant,

"takes everything in," from Tamas to the azaleas to the wild flowers in the field, and contemplates all with keen delight. I feel at home with her partly because she was born in Switzerland, so her roots are European, and also because I admire her resilience and toughness. She is very realistic and not afraid to be blunt. It is refreshing to be with someone so direct and so detached.

But I am beginning, nonetheless, to feel like a camel in sore need of an oasis. The oasis is silence. I woke up in the night starving for silence, for time alone here, but there is none in prospect. And what *is* in prospect? The Ware lecture for the Unitarian Assembly next Friday, and it terrifies. Oh, how relieved I shall be when it is over!

Meanwhile, just when I need music so much, the player has something wrong with it, and God knows when I can get to Portsmouth to find a new needle as that may be the trouble. The typewriter too does not move the ribbon properly. I ordered an electric pencil sharpener that works on batteries, and it buzzes away but accomplishes naught. Things, machines, are my enemies. And when I am tired they become exasperating.

Sunday, June 20th

AT FIVE when I got up it looked like rain, and I felt outrage—the fourth weekend of rain in succession. But now the fog has cleared away, the sun is out, and hope is in sight, as Nancy Hartley is coming to help me attack the weeds in the picking garden this afternoon.

Elizabeth leaves in an hour. It has been a good visit, and I wish she lived nearby, for again I take strength and joy in the friendship of someone older than I. It is a rest to be with someone who has made her peace with life and enjoys everything so much. I am keenly interested in the young women who come here with their fervors, their problems, their hopes, who come to me, I suppose, to reaffirm a vision of life or a way of living that appeals to them. But they cannot know what such a life costs. They take so much for granted, and when I look back at myself at twenty-five or thirty, I am newly aware that so did I. Youth is a kind of genius in itself and knows it. Old age is often expected to recognize that genius and forget its own, so much subtler and gentler, so much wiser. But it is possible to keep the genius of youth into old age, the curiosity, the intense interest in everything from a bird to a book to a dog that I have witnessed these past days in Elizabeth Roget.

Wednesday, June 23rd

I AM TRYING to create a design, a shape in my mind, that will make these days devoured by visits viable. It occurred to me as I was out in the wet grass (rain again!), picking a few flowers to replenish the bunches in the house, that I might imagine each day as a whole year long. Then it would not seem impossible that only a third or less can go into work at my desk—a third of a year is four months! What this might do is expand my compulsive sense of time passing. So here I am at my desk for four months before the children form the Acton school arrive at half-past eleven.

Yesterday, for the first time in ages, I had a day to myself. It was wonderful to walk Tamas, without hurrying for a change. In the woods one or two lady's slippers are still bright pink, although most have turned brown and disappeared into the lush green.

The pheasant is the marvel of this spring, but I still mourn the rose-breasted grosbeak.

After a rest, I went out into the garden and worked hard and blissfully, staking up the peonies, which have grown very tall for lack of sun and are about to flower. I discovered some perennials I had planted in May hidden under other bushy plants and brought them forward. The de Rothschild azaleas are still in flower, so the garden is dotted with white and pale orange, and just under the arch at the entrance and along the fence the first clematis have burst into song—a host of pale-purple flowers with a scarlet line down each petal. When I first came here the clematis were the great glory of the place, but they have suffered. A garden is always a series of losses set against a few triumphs, like life itself, I am thinking, as the sun comes out! And the sea at once changes from miserable gray to heavenly pale blue.

The Acton children and Mary Jane Merrill, one of their teachers, who brings them and also supplies a wonderful luncheon for us (I supply root beer and ice cream), have been coming here for years, the first time—when they were in third grade—because they had read *Punch's Secret*, then because they love the stuffed animals and rush to find their favorites as soon as they arrive, and because they love Tamas and the place and to run down to the rocks and make collections of shells and stones and to

© ANNE CHAPMAN TREMEARNE

"one or two lady's-slippers are still bright pink"

climb the enormous oak—and because I have become
their friend. They turn up as though by magic whenever
I read poems anywhere near Acton. They write me letters, and today we are celebrating Midori's imminent de-
parture for Japan where her father goes on a Fulbright.
I have put together some books to give her, and maybe
there will be time for me to read some of the Japanese
poems.

Was it twenty years ago that I spent a month in Japan,
in March, when the plum blossom was out? It feels like
yesterday.

Thursday, June 24th

SUMMER HAS COME. Today is sunny and there is no wind,
so I am basking in the warmth and taking it easy because
of tomorrow. The children piled in yesterday, Midori so
tall and grown up I didn't recognize her at first. We had
a feast of beef fondue, salad, chocolate ice cream, and my
third or fourth birthday cake, and all was as it always is
when these delightful beings come. Maura collected
stones and part of a lobster pot; Jennifer picked Indian
paintbrush and daisies and goatsbeard; Midori wandered
off by herself; and after we had got things in order and
lunch was ready, Mary Jane and I sat out on the terrace
with a drink. Then, when the children came back with
their trophies and Tamas, panting after a good run with
them, we had a few moments of real talk in the library,
about Japan and the world in general. It is amazing to see

what happens in seven years when one is very young.
Now Midori has written a paper on two of my novels; they
discuss their teachers in a very grown-up way; and we all
agreed that Prince Charles was extremely lovable when
he described being present during the birth of his son as
"a rather grown-up thing."

After they left I lay down with Tamas and did not even
garden. Tomorrow looms.

Sunday, June 27th

AT LAST a real June day—fresh cool air after rain again
yesterday, a serene blue ocean, no wind. I have put out
the cushions on the terrace.

I feel disconnected from my self and from my life as
though the triumph last night—and it really did go well
under rather difficult circumstances—had dispersed my
center. I guess it will take a day or two without people to
recover it. And when will that be, dear God?

The Ware lecture took place in a huge gymnasium at
Bowdoin College, so the audience was very wide in front
of me and flat, since, of course, there was no rise as in a
theater. Two high balconies on each side were also filled,
but I couldn't look up because of intense spotlights there
as they were videotaping. The atmosphere in the hall
resembled that of a political convention. While I was test-
ing the mike and arranging books and talking to people
on the platform, the audience was anything but quiet.

People kept rushing down to take pictures. Friends came up to speak to me, and I wondered whether I could ever get it all focused and quiet, but by then I was in the saddle and eager to take off. The poems did ring out, and I could feel the silence and the attention lifting me up. The best moment was after reading "Dialogue," when a great wave of laughter from two thousand people really raised the roof, I had deliberately put it in the middle of the reading to break the tension, and it was good to see how well it worked. I haven't read that poem, much anthologized, for years.

The president introduced me as "our poet," which was a beautiful beginning. I feel that the Unitarian Universalists are a community I can happily feel at home with. In that huge gymnasium there was so much intelligence and concern, such good, open, caring faces, so many men and women I longed to know. I am proud to be called their poet.

So it is over, the last of the ordeals until September! And little by little I shall be able to pick up the pieces and put them together and feel like myself again.

How touched I was in the afternoon (when I also read a few poems) to be given the UUWF's Ministry to Women award. I have not thought of myself as ministering to women, but I am happy that they feel I do. It is good to be seventy and honored in such a nonacademic way for more than literary achievement, as a human being. I wish I could wander around thinking about it all, picking the peonies suddenly in full bloom, not pressured. But my desk is a clamor of "things to be done." It is not exactly a letdown today but rather another race, so maybe I'll put the music from *Chariots of Fire* on the player.

Wednesday, June 30th

OF COURSE it rained all day on Monday, Janice's fiftieth birthday—the white rose at the terrace step is bowed down with all the wet, so guests have to creep under it, but it has the most delicious scent, so one creeps through sweetness, an old-fashioned rose with a crumpled face. After seeing so many strangers here, it was a rest to be with Janice and her friends Maryann and Priscilla. We had a fire in the library, gave Janice her presents, and then I read the poem I have spent three mornings trying to get to "come out." It now has two final stanzas, and she will have to choose between them. Reading it, I had a lump in my throat thinking of Janice's fifty years—all she has given to life, how imaginatively kind she is, and how successful in her public health career. Like many great women, she seems to be at the same time a mother and a daughter and brings those two very different roles together in a whole. The poem was partly about that and partly about coming to a place where life has grown more important than ambition and what she longs for is the self she is becoming and time to experience its needs and joys. Will she manage to get it?

Yesterday Judy Rutherford came on the bus from Boston in a deluge of rain, her first visit to America. She has been writing to me since she discovered *Journal of a Solitude* in England, and there she was in blue jeans and with a duffel bag to stow away. It was raining so hard we could barely see out the car windows, but what she needed was a real home for a night, after four days in New York, and that she found here. We had a good talk by the fire and lobsters and apple pie for supper, as I wanted her to taste this country as well as see it. At twenty-nine, she is making a transition from theater in London, where she has been a stage manager, to writing as a career. I tremble before the hazards involved. Now this morning the sun is out. The pheasant is screaming his pleasure. The fat gray squirrels are, as usual, destroying the bird feeders in their greed, and the peonies have been beaten down again by the hard rain. It is time I went down. It is also time I had a day off, and that will be tomorrow.

Yesterday morning in the gloom I forced myself to correct and annotate a badly written, carelessly thought-out short biography of me for a children's book about literary women. I just hope that Willa Cather, Emily Dickinson, and Maya Angelou will have been treated with a little more care. I am shocked that a publisher would consider such poor work. It offends me to think of all the talented people I know who fail to find publishers while this young woman gets a chance and then permits herself such lazy work. Writing is, after all, a craft as well as an art.

But as an art I always come back to my belief that what a style transmits is a vision of life, and this will come through to a reader whatever the subject may be. Last night I finished reading a novel in manuscript that deals with a lesbian love affair. The subject is treated with sensitivity and tact, but what is absent is a style that communicates more than plot and does more than tell a story. Still, I admire the writer, for it still takes courage to write on this subject.

Friday, July 2nd

YESTERDAY, a perfect summer day, for a change, cool, clear, with a dark-blue ocean shining in the distance. And at last a day to myself. It was pure bliss to sit down in the picking garden in the afternoon and for two hours pull out weeds, which are now a thick carpet strangling the frail young annuals.

Priscilla Power, Janice's friend, came at three, and while I worked she cut the grass on the terrace, which was covered with clover flowers and looked very raggedy indeed, as though no one lived here except, perhaps, an old witch. Priscilla can come for a few hours every week, and that will make all the difference. There is so much to do, so much more than I can ever do alone, that I felt rescued like a drowning swimmer about to go down for the third time when she said she could come for the rest of the summer.

Sunday, July 4th

I WOKE THIS MORNING thinking about the strange chances that rule lives. Had it not been for the German invasion of Belgium in 1914, I should have turned out to be a Belgian writer with French as my language! I am so happy to be an American. For me, as for my father, it was a lucky disaster that forced us to leave Belgium; for my mother (twice transplanted) less so. I do feel that English is the best language for poetry, with its weaving together of Anglo-Saxon and Latin words, so it is both earthy and lucid. Even the difficulty of rhyming in English makes for a certain tension and toughness; in French it is a little too easy.

As an American, I am proud that we have become one country out of such diverse peoples, languages, backgrounds, that the dream was large enough to include many, many separate dreams, in spite of our failure to absorb and our continuing inability to heal the wounds of the blacks, brought here under duress as slaves. How I rejoiced the day before yesterday when the Supreme Court backed the boycott of white stores in Mississippi and reversed the state court's decision that the blacks should pay an immense sum to the white-owned stores involved. This is the first time in ages that we have seen justice done to blacks and hope for their cause. It is the best news when nonviolent protest again proves that it can work.

Charles Barber was here overnight on Friday. We haven't had a chance to talk for years, immersed as he was in the theater in New York. He was nineteen when I met him. He is now twenty-nine. *Unbelievable!* And he is now having to face some of the hard facts about a life in theater and is turning back to the other string to his bow, writing. We met when he was a student at Ohio Wesleyan and I was Carpenter lecturer there for a month, and he brought me poems he had written to celebrate Virginia Woolf. Good poems.

Life has not been easy on that innocent face, for Charles once had the look of a Blake angel. But it is a troubled face now. I have been thinking about innocence

these past days, because I am reading a novel published
years ago in France, Camille Mayran's *Histoire de Gotton
Connixloo*. In it, a young girl, seduced by a married
farmer who leaves his family to live with her, has to pay
a terribly severe price for her loss of innocence—ostra-
cism by everyone in the village, loneliness, and, finally,
when she has no child, the fear that God is punishing her.
Yet we have to lose our innocence to grow up, although
there is always grief and sometimes remorse in the loss.
We are not meant to be angels but human beings.

> For Mercy has a human heart,
> Pity a human face
> And Love, the human form divine,
> And Peace, the human dress.

Charles has sent me back to Blake. The problem is perhaps that innocence has a fatal attraction for those who
are drawn to what they have lost, and then they corrupt
it. They manage to destroy the very thing they love. But
it is also perhaps true that one has to lose one's charm, the
charm of the child, and make something sterner if one is
to survive as an artist.

This summer I have not been stern enough, have made
myself available to too many people. I am well aware of
it. It is quite a joke that I conceived of this journal as a
peaceful, reflective one, and instead it is the record of a
runner who never catches up with herself, although that
self is the real goal. Yet each person who comes here and
with whom I talk as openly as possible brings his own gifts,
problems, joys, and I learn much from each one.

Charles read me some passages from his journal, after
he had eaten his first lobster (what fun that was!), and
hearing him read brought back in a great wave of recognition and astonishment what I went through at his age. I

too was meeting famous people, people far beyond me on their life's journey. I too was dazzled by other people's fame, a heady excitement.

Thursday, July 8th

I NEVER FINISHED that idea four days ago, but under all that has been happening since—including our first hot, humid days this year, which breed mosquitoes, dry the garden, and force me to water—I have been thinking. I am severe with Charles because I respect him and his talent and because I recognize some of the traps I fell into when I was his age. The move to Nelson, putting down roots in a small, lonely village where I knew no one, did, after fifteen years, season and toughen me. There began my real life; from then on I did not need to know "famous people" and had a hunger for people like myself who had to struggle to keep their heads above water and bore no resemblance whatever to "the beautiful people." They were my kin, I felt.

Last night Martha Wheelock and Marita Simpson came for a showing at the Barn Gallery of their new film *Kate Chopin's "The Story of an Hour"* and another showing of *World of Light,* their film portrait of me. It is a jump from a documentary to a dramatic story, and I was eager to see what they had done. What a joy to see with what tact and expertise they created the historical past in Louisiana and one woman's tragic moment of freedom to be herself! What I loved was their willingness to hold

silences for long seconds, to let us witness "things happening in the psyche," and, as always in their work, a marvelous capacity to present lyrical images of nature, a spring
in Louisiana, in this case. The music is quite wonderful in
the ways in which it helps create suspense. And Gwen
Coleman does a fine piece of acting.

But the financial problem for young filmmakers is immense and the time needed immense too. M. and M. have
been working on this half-hour film for a year! I wish I
could give them a year, but to accomplish that one would
have to buy the lucky ticket in the Maine or New Hampshire lottery!

Yesterday I walked Tamas down to the sea on the path
between the tall grasses, with flocks of daisies and Indian
paintbrush on each side. I have not been down there
lately as Tamas and I usually walk through the woods. But
because I did, I had a marvelous vision as I looked back
at the house, over the starry foreground of daisies, to wind
moving through long grasses, that elusive wave on wave
of rippling motion, impossible to capture, though I have
tried to do it again and again in a poem, and once almost
succeeded—in "June Wind." The field is at its most seduc-
tive now before it is cut.

In the afternoon Priscilla came and did a job of prun-
ing and tidying up behind the house. It is hard to measure
or quite believe the relief it is that she is willing to work
for me. She is expert, quick, and a joy to have around.
Tomorrow Nancy Hartley will come, so at last the garden
may begin to have its formal shape and cease to be the
jungle I look upon with a kind of fear, for I no longer have
the strength to do it all alone, and Raymond these days is
elusive. All the bushes need clipping now, but he does not
come. And I cannot complain because I know he is always
behindhand (like me with the letters) and full of guilt.

Saturday, July 10th

I WAKE UP HAPPY these days, enchanted by the summer weather at last after so much rain, by the lush green world and, as I look out on the field, by the tall grasses turning a soft dusty pink as they go to seed. It is hot, and that makes it easy to be lazy, to say "Why do it, after all?" when I contemplate a corner of the garden choked with weeds. But then "Why not do it?" is the answer, so yesterday afternoon after a delicious nap with Tamas, I cleaned out the terrace border and clipped back the creepers that begin to strangle everything in July. I worked in the shade and did not hurry and, meanwhile, had set the revolving hose to freshen the border below the terrace that gets burned up with reflected light from the wall. The peonies are almost over. How quickly it all goes! Now they have lost their form and those that remain have shaggy too-abundant heads, flopping all over the place.

I am happy for the old reason that I have given so much money away lately, yet I feel a twinge of anxiety. It just happened that I told several people I could be a bank in time of need, and several, all at once, *were* in need. No wonder, these days of lost jobs and scary futures! One ingredient of happiness at my age is to have a wide enough margin so that one can be a bank. Giving money away is pure pleasure. I use the word "pure" advisedly. It happens that just as these requests came in I was buying a new car, turning in the Escort, which has been uncomfortable though efficient. Generosity saved me from a Buick, and I have settled for an Escort station wagon with air-conditioning and am off to get it this morning. It would not have made me happy to buy the Buick. I never feel real happiness when I spend money on purely material things, whereas, in a different sphere, happy that I had spent less on the car, I bought a lithograph at the Barn Gallery the evening of Martha and Marita's movie. Ah, extravagance of this sort is happiness! for who could love a machine as one loves a painting?

But the real happiness yesterday had nothing to do with giving or buying anything but came from solitude, an unhurried day, the silence unbroken except for the pheasant's cry. Even the ocean, silky blue and absolutely calm, was silent.

Among other things that have come into the house lately was Mary Barnard's stunningly fresh translations of Sappho. We have corresponded because she has written in her new book a description of the poetry readings I organized at the New York Public Library during World War II, inspired by Dame Myra Hess's free concerts in London. It was thrilling how many great poets, including Marianne Moore and W. H. Auden, agreed to read for nothing, so it became a feast of poetry, and people thronged in to listen.

Mary Barnard questioned a line in "My Sisters, O My Sisters":

And in renouncing passion did Sappho come to bless.

M.B. says in a letter to me

The line really amazed me. We know so little about her that when we talk about her we are usually speculating, but I didn't find anything in her poems to suggest, even remotely, that she ever renounced anything, and certainly not passion. I am glad that you feel my translations have lifted a fog that obscured her. I was a long time groping my way through that fog to get to her.

Years ago I read C. M. Bowra's essay on Sappho in his *Greek Lyric Poetry* and it was a revelation. He makes the point that Sappho's life was devoted to the worship of the goddess Aphrodite, and that she was teaching the girls who came to her school in preparation for their eventual marriage. Into that fact I read "renouncement," because she knew she had to let them go.

Tuesday, July 13th

I READ the Bowra essay forty-six years ago, and it had the good effect of helping me come to terms with the fact that women alone inspired me to write poems. It was troubling, but the seizure, when it came, was so commanding I could not doubt its value. I could not believe I was wrong or aberrant. It gave me courage to be myself and not to allow the ethos of the times to blur my vision.

But Sappho, I now see, should have been brought into the end of the poem as the true precursor of what we now feel and wish to be, "In the pure light that brings forth fruit and flower / And that great sanity, that sun, the feminine power." That is what Sappho tells us and always has.

Forty-six years later I have come to see this with Mary Barnard's help.

Yesterday was one of those days of "things that have to be done," a mizzly day of fog and rain. I left the house at seven to go to Kennebunk for the plates for the new

car; then when I got home I had a call saying my typewriter was ready, so after lunch I dashed off to Portsmouth to fetch it and spent the rest of the afternoon
answering letters. No gardening, but on Sunday afternoon
Nancy Hartley came and we had an orgy of weeding in
the annuals bed, rescuing four rows that were almost
obliterated by weeds and mulching them. It looks almost
like a rational garden now at last.

It is order in all things that rests the mind. And I marvel that I am able to work at all these days when my desk
and this whole room are as cluttered as they are. But
tidying up, which takes place about three times a year,
means hours of what feels irrelevant compared to rescuing the annuals or writing to a ninety-year-old woman
who writes that her first book of poems will come out this
year or to Mary Barnard whose *Collected Poems* have
given me sustenance these past days when I have been
reading them at five in the morning.

So what is the inward order that makes it possible to
shut out the chaos around me as I sit here? Perhaps a
strong sense of what my priorities are—first friends, then
work, then the garden. If I died suddenly, how bitterly I
should regret work undone, friends unanswered. As for
the garden, that is my secret extravagance and one has to
have one! I learned when my mother died that a garden
dies quickly without a loving gardener to keep it alive. In
a year, hers had become a jungle. So the garden is perhaps
irrelevant as an ethical compulsion. No one but me really
sees this garden, suffers when there is drought, rejoices
when a rose I had thought dead suddenly flowers or the
tree peony, which looked quite "gone," shows a spray of
new leaves and a sudden renascence. The garden is where
my madness lies, and that is a more useful madness than
drunkenness or a tantrum. The garden takes care of the
daimon very well these days.

Saturday, July 17th

WHERE HAS THIS WEEK GONE? Into a limbo of fetid heat
for one thing. And then a lot of bothersome time-consum-
ing things of no great moment. The new car refused to
start yesterday and I had an appointment for lunch and
then for an X-ray (part of the semiannual checkup for
cancer that also took me to Maine Medical Center on
Wednesday). With the help of Priscilla, who was doing a
huge gardening job, and Heidi, with whom I had lunch,
I was driven here and there and finally got the car back
at four and came home under my own steam. Then I
began watering. It is ironic that after a month of rain in
June, we are now in a drought, not a drop of rain for
nearly three weeks. Never a dull moment in New England, but hardly a day without anxiety about the garden
for one reason or another.

It is quite necessary for Huldah to come here two or
three times in a summer because then things get done. I
had not seen Raymond for weeks, and when he finally
came, a little sheepish, I teased him because he has been
giving all his time to neighbors who were to have the
Garden Club first and then a big party. I suggested that
if I could tell him the King of Rumania was coming he
would get to work. He came the next day and I *could* tell
him "not the King of Rumania but the Queen of Tennessee." That is what he has always called Huldah, and her
imminent arrival on Monday with her daughter, Leslie,

had a galvanizing effect. At last the hedges are clipped; awful brown patches in the large juniper bushes that frame the grassy path to the sea have been cut out; the terrace grass has been cut; the old-fashioned rosebush at the entrance has been pruned and tied back so it no longer scratches my face when I come in with parcels, and, much to my amazement, the paths to the wild garden have been trimmed "in case the Queen of Tennessee walks down there."

But when, I ask myself, shall I get to work? One of these days I shall reread the two hundred pages of "The Magnificent Spinster," the novel about Anne Thorp that I laid aside two years ago because it had gone dead on me. There were two reasons for that. One was that I had been reading all her letters to her great friend, Anne Almy, and had got bogged down in knowing too many small facts, so the imaginative channel got clogged. The other reason was harder to surmount since Anne and I had had a rather serious misunderstanding at one time and I found an upsetting letter about it. But after two years the sediment had fallen into the unconscious, been absorbed, I suppose, and I feel ready to start writing again.

Monday, July 19th

IT MUST HAVE BEEN 95° here yesterday. We are in a true heat wave, but up here in my study in the morning it is only 80°, thanks to the air conditioner. When I go downstairs at eleven I open the door into a solid wall of hot air and rush out to turn on hoses, for the garden is burning up, and in the house flowers fade in a day. I am glad I got the new air-conditioned car in time for this assault. It makes going out to get the mail a real pleasure, and it made possible the drive to North Parsonsfield on Saturday.

I was struck, as I drove along the familiar route, by the shriveled look of fields and pastures. The corn is only a foot high. Normally it would be about ready to pick. A hard year for farmers because of the cold and rainy June, followed by this drought. And when I got to Deer Run Farm, I saw at once that their vegetable garden has suffered, too—especially hard for Anne and Barbara who count on "living on" the garden all winter through.

But, as always at the farm, there are innumerable delights to see or to be told about. The bluebird Anne rescued last summer as an infant has come back with his mate and they are nesting in one of the nesting boxes in the field—last summer he came "home" every evening at eight to be fed and then flew away in the autumn, so it was a great joy when he came home after the winter away. I have never seen a bluebird here. They are getting very rare. Meanwhile, this spring Anne found a miserable baby robin pushed out of the nest, soaking wet, probably dying, and he is now a pet named William and talks a lot in the house and out, not shy at all.

Of course we walked around the garden to see all that has been done since my last visit ages ago. And there in front of the new grape arbor I saw *Persephone,* a sculpture I had commissioned from Barbara. It is beautiful, fluid, graceful—Persephone emerging from the ocean and her long winter with Pluto. I can hardly wait to see it placed on the terrace wall!

Anne has been making a whole series of cement bird-
baths (with clay from the place) to set flat in the grass, and
these are going like hot cakes. I brought three back with
me for various people who had asked for one. Like me, A.
and B. are inundated with visitors in the spring and summer and also by people passing by who see the sign and
come to buy eggs or a birdbath or herbs and then are so
enchanted that they stay on and on, unaware that they are
stealing time from two women who have work to do. At
least no one comes here uninvited, though at Nelson they
used to, and I'm afraid I was less welcoming and less
patient than Anne and Barbara are.

But, without being aware of it, Anne and Barbara are
great teachers, and everyone who comes to the farm
learns something about how rich life can be without any
of the usual *things* most people find essential. People are
moved by what they see but have very little idea of what
it costs in energy and skill to live such a life.

Last night Royce Roth and Frances Whitney came for
supper, for what has become our yearly ceremony of lobsters and champagne when they have a holiday at Dock-
side. I love these continuities; they are restful. Over the
years Royce and Frances have become true friends. I was
pleased that they felt at once that Tamas is in fine fettle,
"looks younger" than last time, and Frances even
managed to coax Bramble, who had gone to lie with her
back turned to us, down off the wall to be caressed and to
purr. By a miracle a slight breeze from the ocean started
up a half-hour before they arrived, so I sat out on the
terrace while I waited, basking in the cool wind. As always, time flowed away as we always have so much to talk
about and exchange after a year, and when they left, the
field and lawn were pulsating with fireflies, all lit up by the
soft points of light like notes in music through the velvety

dark. The fireflies at least love the moist heat and become extremely amorous. "Here I am, where are you?" the signals flash out in hundreds and thousands. By then, at nearly ten, the wind had died down and the heat, too, pulsated.

But I was exhilarated by the good talk, and both Tamas and I slept well in the enclosing whir of the big fan in my bedroom.

Wednesday, July 21st

LIFE IS APT to come in wild bunches, and Monday was indeed one of those days when too much happens and one feels, at the end, like a hen with her head cut off.

In the mail *May Sarton: Woman and Poet*, the National Poetry Foundation book, that Constance Hunting edited, came at last. It seems I have waited for this event for years, the first time the whole body of my work has been considered, with essays on the poetry, the memoirs, and the novels. What an event! All I longed to do was sit down and consume it page by page. Instead, there was the plumber to call, for I could get no pressure in the revolving hose, and by noon it was 95° here, and the garden was burning up. At the post office the car again made a strange noise when I started it. I managed to get it back here, but then it stalled and would not start at all, so I had to call the Ford place and arrange for them to come and get it. Huldah and her daughter, who has not been here before, were coming to take me out for lunch.

Thursday, July 22nd

I HAD TO STOP where I was yesterday to take Tamas for a walk through the woods, the first in days. On Tuesday the heat wave was broken by a blessed rain, and yesterday the air was clear at last. It was wonderful to walk through all the wetness, brushing through tall tasseled grasses as we went down the path, everything with that after-rain sheen on it. Bramble came too, walking very precisely, as she does, then suddenly darting up a tree. In spite of a luncheon engagement yesterday, I felt able to resume my self for a change.

In the afternoon while I did some happy weeding (the weeds easy to pull from the wet ground) I roasted a chicken and picked the first calendulas in their silky bright orange and gold petals, some white nicotianas, and even a crimson spray of phlox. The cosmos are almost in flower, so at last Nancy's and my arduous work down there is bearing fruit. I also picked a basketful of sugar-pod peas and had them with my supper. Altogether a fine day.

Saturday, July 24th

I WOKE before five, just before sunrise, to delicious cool air and an orange glow in the sky. And I woke eager to get up, do a laundry, pick two great white lilies with petals backed in green that are just out, capture them before the sun did, and then come up here for a quiet morning. I am feeling happy today for several good reasons. Yesterday in the mail came a photograph of my namesake, little Sarton, who is now two and looks out at me with a shy smile and a rather determined and victorious look, a solid character already. Her parents came here once for a talk before they were married; we do not know each other well, but here is Sarton, a joy to behold! She is now on my desk beside Camille Mayran, who is ninety-three. They make an absorbing diptych.

One of my nightmares is not a nuclear holocaust but the taking over of the earth eventually by the insects. When I took Tamas for his walk through the woods yesterday morning, the deerflies were everywhere; the mosquitoes buzzed in my ears, and the walk was extremely uncomfortable. Tamas stops at such times about every ten steps and stands there, head bowed, waiting for me to drive the deerflies off with bracken fronds, but Bramble will have none of that, and I don't know how to help her. Usually she takes refuge under the ferns and bushes. I cover myself with anti-mosquito stuff and wear a cap, but it is no fun walking in the woods these days. So this morning we'll go down to the ocean instead.

Sunday, July 25th

I HAVE NOT MENTIONED the war in Lebanon here because, like everyone else, I find it hard to be clear about what is happening. It does seem evident though that the PLO is winning the public relations battle. There are endless photographs of bombed-out families in poor battered Beirut, but rarely, if at all, does anyone mention that Beirut itself is a hijacked city where the PLO has captured millions of people and really holds them as hostages. And from Beirut the PLO has been attacking Israel for years and making retaliation impossible, because it would involve killing innocent people. For the third time we have prevented Israel from winning "for the sake of peace." The Arabs, as part of their policy, have deliberately kept the Palestinians in refugee camps for propaganda purposes and made no effort to resettle them. So one has to have some sympathy for the Israelis, who have always been willing to negotiate with the PLO if and when it recognizes Israel's right to exist.

After I had written this yesterday I saw a long piece in the *Times* headlined "Lebanese Tell of Anguish of Living under the PLO."

Wednesday, July 28th

IT IS RAINING, good news as we need it badly, but the promised cool has not come. It is heavy, wet air and I feel knocked over the head. But yesterday was one of the two or three perfect summer days we have had, and a charming thing happened to cheer me on my way back from a yearly examination at the optometrist. I stopped first at the splendid bakery I have discovered and got an apple pie for Peg Umberger, who comes tomorrow for a few days from upstate New York; then I swung round by a farm produce place at York Beach to see if they had raspberries. No raspberries, but something even rarer, a huge bunch of blue and purple and violet salpiglossises. Now and then I have managed to grow a few among the annuals but never with such magnificent results. The girl sold them to me for fifty cents because they were a day old, and I came home feeling as though I had found some marvelous treasure—the same sense of joyous incredulity experienced when I was nine and found a five-dollar bill in the snow outside our house in Cambridge! That time my mother made me go up and down the street ringing doorbells to be sure it had not been lost by a neighbor. No one claimed it and I was able to buy Kipling's collected poems, a lovely edition on India paper in a red binding, which I still possess. This time I came home and arranged the velvety striped flowers in a Venetian glass my mother loved. But the best was still to come. Rita Nathanson, who had written to me from Camp Manitou where she is teaching boys to do pottery, was coming at four for tea. She brought as a present a most beautiful iridescent turquoise and dark-blue raku jar that she had made. It was perfect for the delicacy and brilliance of the salpiglossis. What a happy chance that one day here brought two such beauties together! Of course, after that the door was open for a good talk. I liked her and her decision to work as a waitress three nights a week rather than exploit her talent by taking large orders that would mean repeating the same pot many times. That takes courage and also a sense of what being an artist is. These days Route 1 is filled with shops that advertise "handcrafted gifts," but these are mass-produced and have very little to do with art—or true craft, for that matter. It is sad.

Rita is one of the few people who have come to this house who was excited by the two old Japanese pots my mother bought at an auction years ago. Most people do not even know what they are.

After tea we sat out on the terrace—how rarely that has been possible this summer! And then at half-past five I suggested that she might like to walk down the grassy path to the sea with Tamas, as I had a long-distance call to make. The grasses are so tall now that the path is visible only from the upstairs window.

I had it on my mind to telephone my adopted daughter, Georgia, who had called while Royce and Frances were here. I had checked in with her at ten, after dinner, but by then she was too tired to talk. So this was the time to communicate at some length. My life sometimes amuses me it is so packed with such a variety of things that summon me out of myself. While we talked, I heard loud scrabbling and thumping in the cupboard where I keep

"Rita Nathanson . . . was coming at four for tea"

birdseed. A red squirrel, of course! Almost every day one
turns up somewhere in the kitchen to scare the daylights
out of me, as they are lightning-quick and stop the breath
as a snake does:

> But never met this fellow
> Attended or alone,
> Without a tighter breathing—
> And zero at the bone!

So Emily Dickinson says it. I am proud to see how Georgia
recaptures her composure after times of stress and how
well able she is then to analyze herself and come to terms
with the very real anxieties she has to handle. We are on
the same beam, each needing to say things out in words,
and she is a true pelican, nurturing her two small children
as I hope I am nurturing a lot of people I hardly know. So
we call ourselves the Pelicans and can laugh and weep
together. But all the time we talked the noises erupted in
the cupboard, and I knew I would have to cope with this
unwanted, terrified stranger as soon as I hung up. I did it
finally with a broom. The streak of lightning fled down the
cellar stairs, maddening! Had he chosen to turn left he
would have been outside and safe. But the cellar is huge
and I suspect has holes in the walls, and there has been no
sound since.

The phone rang again as I was getting supper ready,
a little flustered by then, and anxious to sit down with a
drink and watch the news. It was Marcie Hershman to tell
me that *Ms.* will run her interview with me in the October issue, good news indeed, for both of us. She had some
cogent questions to hand on from the editors; and there
I was seeing potters, chasing squirrels, listening to
Georgia's problems, and suddenly asked, "How did you
do it? Go on writing for fifty years? What kept you going?"

What kept me going was, I think, that writing for me is a way of understanding what is happening to me, of thinking hard things out. I have never written a book that was not born out of a question I needed to answer for myself. Perhaps it is the need to remake order out of chaos over and over again. For art is order, but it is made out of the chaos of life.

Thursday, July 29th

WHAT IS MORE BEAUTIFUL than a bright morning after rain? Everything shines today, every plant has been given a good drink, and I won't have to water while Peg is here. I put on rubber boots at six and went out to shake heavy water off the phlox and get them standing up again, to pick a small bunch of flowers for the guest room, and to cut off the faded day lilies from each stem. There are six different yellow ones behind the house, such crisp strong forms, although they do fade in a day. But they light up the jungly greens back there and will go on flowering for weeks.

I had a letter yesterday from Catherine Claytor (so she calls herself since her divorce from David Becker) with the good news that at last she had begun a drawing. "I have not been able to do anything creative for a year and a half," she tells me. "Now a drawing is slowly coming into being. To work is to feel whole. To work for long moments unselfconsciously is grand. To still all other voices and to work, just quietly work."

Reading it, I thought about the *Ms.* question. If you are
a writer or an artist, it is work that fulfills and makes you
come into wholeness, and that goes on through a lifetime.
Whatever the wounds that have to heal, the moment of
creation assures that all is well, that one is still in tune with
the universe, that the inner chaos can be probed and
distilled into order and beauty.

In the mail I found a letter from Barbara Rex about
Anger—this is the first response I have had to the book
except from a few friends who read it in manuscript. Rex
is hugely generous, so whatever happens, she gave me
some moments of pure joy and relief that I shall not forget. At the end she says, "This book is new. It speaks to
women. Yes, and to men. It says things that no one has said
before."

Can I rest on that? No, I am getting ready to think
about "The Magnificent Spinster" again. After Christmas
I mean to get at it and plunge in. So it simmers on the back
of the stove, waiting for me to have clear time ahead.

Sunday, August 1st

PEG UMBERGER arrived early in the afternoon on Thursday and left this morning at seven. She is one of the few
of my friends who can laugh at me (gently) and we had a
good time. The good weather held, which was a blessing.
She is a wife, a mother, and a grandmother and works
very hard, so I enjoyed spoiling her a little, enjoyed

watching her walk down to the sea with Tamas, sitting on
the terrace with our drinks—hers V-8, mine Scotch—and
doing a little driving around to see the sights during the
day. While I worked up here from eight to ten, she read
the manuscript of *Anger*. But only this minute did I remember the journal and that I have let it go for two days.
No gardening has been done. Letters have piled up, and
I feel rather emptied out and tired. But in many ways a
three-day visit is a good length of time. Less hurried and
intense than a short visit, for the guest begins to find her
own way around and to be able to help too. Yesterday Peg
braved the deerflies and took Tamas for a walk in the
woods. Why then, with such a beneficent presence here,
do I get up so exhausted? Because the inner life comes
to a complete stop. The self who writes, thinks, gardens,
the solitary compulsive is temporarily absent. And I miss
her.
    This afternoon I hope to meet her again when I do a
job of weeding behind the house, and by clearing out that
bed of perennials almost smothered in weeds, to clear the
senses again and compose the mind.

Monday, August 2nd

I DID GET OUT into the garden yesterday afternoon and
replenished the flowers in the house, but I was too tired
to enjoy it. The mosquitoes were ferocious in the muggy
heat. I could feel them biting through my shirt as I cut

back the smothering grapevines and freed the perennials from weeds. In the end I was glad I had made the effort and cleared some space out there and in my mind. August is the dead end of summer, when everything goes to seed or becomes too lush, and there is a special August silence in the heavy air. The birds do not sing. The ocean sighs in the distance. The whole tempo slows down.

Lately I have been reading Alyse Gregory's journal sent to me by a friend in England. A large part of it is about her consuming love for her husband, Llewellyn Powys, and the anguish she suffered when he fell in love with a younger woman, Gamel Woolsey—a love she accepted and learned to live with until Llewelyn's death; she became his comforter and support through his despair when Gamel married Gerald Brenan and through his own long illness. The journal is chiefly the record of her own suffering, and I suppose it became her comforter, for she confided in no one else, apparently. It has had a strange effect on me. It has made me see once more how destructive passion is, how cruelly single-minded. For Llewelyn never seems to have been aware that his confiding in her caused continual pain and that to ask his wife to listen to his passionate involvement with another woman, to talk about her incessantly, to demand pity under these circumstances is very cruel. To take her understanding for granted when she is being horribly hurt seems quite intolerable, and here and there is a cry of anguish.

I was struck to the heart by the tragedy of being so wrapped up in one human being that nothing else exists or gives life. That was Alyse's state. She loved Llewelyn to the exclusion of everything and everyone else. "I must be self-sufficient. I live like a stunted tree in the shadow of a mountain, the warmth never reaches my branches." And another entry ends, "Llewelyn saw a stoat chasing a rabbit today and clapped his hands to frighten the stoat away. The rabbit was too frightened to run. I too remain stationary from fear."

All through my reading of this book I have felt immense relief that I am not attached in that way to anyone. For so much of my life I was, but now I am free of passion, I see that it is a great blessing not to be in its thrall.

Sometime after Llewelyn's death, Alyse writes:

> I went out, my heart destitute, longing only for death, knowing that love alone has reality, that our words have meaning only when there is another to give them value. Blind with suffering I walked through the streets, and suddenly saw a very old, very ragged man chopping sticks with knotted shaking fingers, doing his wonted task as best he could. A dog with a blind eye came to him to be stroked, a shy dog with a silky coat, half spaniel, half hound, and the old man gave it the affection it asked for, calling its name and caressing it with gentleness; and this scene took the sorrow from my heart, and I knew that our misery comes too often from the foolish claims we make, and that if we can contemplate existence with a pure heart, seeing everything in its process of change, objective and compassionate, we can cast away misgivings.

I can say amen to that, but I know, just the same, that when one is "objective and compassionate" one is not a poet. And when one is no longer moved deeply by a single face, the only one, the centering one, wisdom has been bought at a high price. And of course Alyse Gregory knew it, too, and that knowledge is the scarlet thread through the whole journal.

Thursday, August 5th

ON TUESDAY I drove down to Weston, Connecticut, to spend the night at Eva Le Gallienne's, the first time in years that I have seen her alone there in her house hidden in the woods, settled beautifully against a wall of ledges where she has made a series of gardens, so one looks up at lily of the valley in spring, day lilies and hostas in summer. One goes in through a little path past the rose garden, and as I walked it, a host of house finches flew up from the feeder. The atmosphere has always been of a haven from public life, and this time I was touched once more by its silence and secretness and by the beauty she has created there and, at eighty-three, still works very hard to keep alive. But of course it keeps her alive, too, Franciscan that she is, for whom flowers, birds, and the raccoons and skunks who come every night to be fed after dark are the most rewarding joys.

Inside, the house is so full of life, of all her lives, that one is stopped at every turn by a photograph of Madame Duse or Sarah Bernhardt, and the walls in the library, "the Blue Room," are lined with books, many of them having to do with the plays she has acted in, and, in the case of Ibsen, translated herself. There are portraits of L'Aiglon (which she played after the Civic closed) and of her father, the poet Richard Le Gallienne—a recent acquisition, the famous Max Beerbohm cartoon of him—and

of her Danish mother, for many years the London corre-
spondent of a Copenhagen newspaper.

It is a very European house, and I suppose I mean by
that a house where nothing has been artificially designed
for show or to be in fashion but where every object, book,
and piece of furniture has come naturally to rest as the
outward manifestation of the rich experience of life itself.

I always feel happy in the Blue Room where Le Gallienne stretches out on a chaise longue and I sit opposite
her in a wing chair, and we talk. We have been friends for
fifty-three years, since I joined the Civic Repertory
Theatre as an apprentice when I was seventeen and often
was permitted to sit in her dressing room while she made
up as Peter Pan, Hedda Gabler, Juliet, Masha in *The Three
Sisters*—and so many others. There was a lot to catch up
on, and after I had a short rest in my room upstairs, letting
the rush of travel die down, we dived into everything.
Foremost of course at the moment is the imminent resurrection of the Civic Repertory production of *Alice in
Wonderland,* which will open on Broadway before
Christmas. This is a small miracle in itself and is happening because an Astor saw the original production when he
was ten years old and has never forgotten it. He met a
producer who has also dreamed of bringing it to life again,
and so it is going to happen.

But what a monster the New York theater has become
because costs are so high! All that was needed to keep the
Civic Repertory alive in the thirties was $100,000 a year
for putting on at least three new productions, a repertory
to draw on, at the end, of twenty-six plays, and eighty
people employed full time. To bring *Alice* back will cost
a million and a half at least! It makes one's hair stand on
end. We talked about that and how awful it is that tickets
are priced so high that the people who care most (the

really intelligent responsive audience) cannot afford to come. It all seems topsy-turvy. But then occasionally a fairy tale happens like this revival of *Alice* all because a small boy was entranced by it fifty years ago!

All good artists have to endure frustration of one kind or another, but few actors have had their lives cut in two as Le Gallienne did when she was nearly burned to death in a furnace explosion in the Connecticut house when the Civic was at the height of its glory. For a year the theater was dark while she healed herself from the terrible burns and suffered several operations on her hands. She came back in triumph with one of her great successes, *Camille.* But no one, I suppose, can imagine what it cost, what sheer courage, determination, and what undying flame that would not be put out, it took to make the comeback. The most cruel stroke of fate one can imagine.

Monday, August 9th

I HAVE BORROWED Janice's electric typewriter to see if I can get used to the buzz. It has been a daily frustration to have the Olivetti continually stick, even after I took it back twice in July to be fixed. Rain today, much needed, but unfortunate for friends coming some distance to take me out to lunch. Fatigue is the enemy now, as the lack of time and solitude begins to blur the edges of perception. Then I wonder what on earth I am doing to have allowed such a pileup this summer. Besides, the gremlins have been active. On Thursday *Ms.* called to arrange for a photographer, and the phone went dead in the middle of the call. I ran over to Mary-Leigh's and got through to them, but it was agitating. Luckily the phone got fixed just after five—how literally "cut off" I am without it! A charming photographer, Sarah Putnam, came on Saturday morning to take pictures. She worked outdoors with the terrace border as background, or the field, but the sun dazzled me and made me feel weak. And when she left I felt as empty as a flat balloon. Meanwhile, there were the lobsters to cook and prepare for salad for Eleanor Blair's birthday yesterday. That calmed me down.

Then I had a nap and got ready for Doris Grumbach who was coming at five-fifteen. I have not seen her for a year and we had a lot to catch up on, as we did for an hour and then went out to dinner, a peaceful and stimulating exchange. Doris is a stunning example of what an intellectual life can be. She looks glorious, brown from long hours of reading on the beach where she has taken a house with one of her daughters for the month of August. I was entranced to contemplate her day. It begins with a two-mile walk on the beach at six, followed by an hour and a half of study with her scholar son-in-law, comparing the Hebrew text of Isaiah with the Greek. My father would have enjoyed doing that, but I would not have the patience, I fear. After that and perhaps a little talk with her adored grandson, Isaac, Doris settles on the beach and reads for most of the day, taking a swim when she feels like it. She has two strings to her bow, the critical biography of Willa Cather and a novel based on the Ladies of Llangollen, and of course she still reviews now and then.

All this made me feel like an old Chinese poet entertaining a luminary from Peking—an old poet whose life goes by in a dream, far from the center of intellectual life, far from the literary world, an old poet who spends too

much time observing flowers and birds and too little
working, drunk on the natural world. It made me see,
with a pang, what a lazy life I lead, although it seems to
me a terribly driven one! The laziness becomes productive when there is time to think and write quietly from
the center of myself—yet how can I not wish and need to
share this beautiful place? And how not rejoice that so
many people want to come here and share it with me?

Yesterday I got up earlier than usual to pick a bunch
of flowers for Eleanor, then mixed the salad and laid it on
a bed of lettuce from the garden in a lovely bowl, sur-
rounding it with bags of ice, for it was going to be a hot
day. The bunch of calendulas, cosmos, sweet peas, and
phlox looked too thick and somehow unpunctuated until
I remembered the veronica in the terrace garden and
picked a few blue plumes of it. That did the trick. I
changed my bed as it was Sunday, and finally, at quarter
to nine, set out through the misty, thick green world of
August to go to Wellesley. I enjoyed the pause of the drive
and on the radio heard a beautiful pastorale by Stravinsky.

It was a day of celebration. First a half-hour with Keats
and Marguerite, for it was M.'s ninetieth birthday. She
looked absolutely beautiful—Oh, to look like that at
ninety! Such a glow she had about her in a lovely soft,
blue-green silk dress as she recounted the luncheon for
her former trustees, professors, and students from Abbott
Academy had arranged the day before. I was given to
read aloud a delightful ballad that managed to include
most of this great educator's life. I told her what an inspiration she is and she asked why—that people said so but
she did not see why. I believe—and said as much—that it
is because she has combined to a rare extent warmth and
intellect. That, in my experience, is uncommon. Neither
Eva Le Gallienne nor Doris Grumbach, whom I had in

mind as I had just seen them both, has this warmth, though *all three* are great women and each in her own way a great giver to life.

After that visit I went down the street to Eleanor's house, The Beehive, for the celebration of her eighty-eighth birthday. I found her full of love and joy, admiring a most beautiful bunch of flowers a friend had sent— daisies, yellow lilies, and orange-pink roses in a delightful round vase. Eleanor is nearly blind, but when that friend called, I heard her describe the bouquet like a painter, every detail had been seen and appreciated. The day was given a special sheen because her young friend, Elyse, had come from Indiana (where she is professor of economics) to engineer everything—from blowing up flotillas of balloons to, at the moment I arrived, finding the right nails to hang the stained-glass poppy she had brought with her in a window, to ordering the superb chocolate torte. Elyse, round, relaxed, and extremely efficient, beamed upon it all like some guardian angel. And soon we had a card table up in the garden, found the right chairs and a cloth, and set out the lobster salad and an exquisitely arranged plate of fruit, all cut up in a pattern that Elyse had created. I opened one of the last of my birthday champagne bottles and we drank. To what? To getting ready for a ninetieth birthday celebration not far off! There in the garden we talked, among other things, about trees. Eleanor told us she had planted the tall willow as a tiny seedling and had transplanted an immense elm to the edge of the garden when it was only a foot high. It was moving to think of all the years of growing that have found such a vital image in these two trees. I thought of Lugné-Poë who planted trees one by one for his best friends in the garden at Avignon—I wonder how "Paul Valéry" is getting on!

Wednesday, August 11th

I SPENT YESTERDAY morning getting a new typewriter.
And at last I can write fast with a light touch. It is a
Smith-Corona portable, not electric. I had begun to feel
as though I had lost the use of my hands—but just now the
carriage would not stay put and I have been fiddling with
it for about half an hour! These are such pressured times
that endless frustration with a machine is hard to bear.
But it is one of those days, hot and muggy. A guest arrives
at three, for overnight, Bobbie Geary, who has been writing me poems for a year and comes to meet the muse. I
have so often been on the other side of this state that I feel
for her, but I have learned that it is a more joyful thing
to be the writer of such poems than the recipient.

Yesterday was a free day and I did get out at last and
cleaned up the gone-to-seed border below the terrace.
And I saw that the beautiful turquoise snake, very dead,
that I had hesitated to touch, is being taken care of by
nature itself, has turned gray and almost vanished in the
grass. I feel badly about this creature, so beautiful and yet
menacing. A family of snakes lived in the wall of the
garden in Nelson, and I welcomed them as friends, as
lares, and here too there have always been snakes in the
terrace wall. But I have never met such a brilliant fellow
before, pure bright turquoise like a jewel.

Thursday, August 12th

A GRAY SKY, a gray ocean this morning, and it feels autumnal. I have put the electric heater on downstairs for Bobbie. As I think of our five or six hours of talk yesterday, it seems to me that all went well. The best was walking down the grassy path and sitting with our legs dangling over the edge of the rocks with Tamas beside us, just listening to the ocean and watching the waves breaking gently on the rocks below. It was high tide. One gull stood on a promontory, but this year there are few here at Surf Point. Not a duck to be seen. And I told Bobbie how I remember my father pointing out more than once a whale spouting in those golden summers we spent at Ogunquit sixty-four years ago. There were seals on the rocks then. It is painful to realize that we live in a diminished world.

What Bobbie brought me yesterday were three books in manuscript, the result of her seizure by a great creative energy six months ago. They are two books of poems and a short novel. It is not kind of me, I suppose, to have reminded her that the present is my reading them, not her giving them to me to read. It takes a long time for anyone possessed by the joy of creation to realize that asking a writer to read your work is always something of an imposition. Bobbie is an endearing young woman, and

I hope her novel will get published. I read fifty pages last night but was too tired to judge.

Saturday, August 14th

I REALIZED YESTERDAY when I was picking a tiny bunch of roses, phlox, and sweet peas for the guest room, and putting books of poems on the desk there to welcome Karen Buss, dear friend and former student of mine at Wellesley, that the trouble this summer has been not so much too many guests as too many admirers I had not met before. Then the visit becomes inevitably an exhausting effort to communicate with and understand a stranger. Also, since so much is expected, I get nervous imagining what a disappointment I am sure to be. Strangers who have come to know a person only through works of art have to meet a plain human being, full of folly, conflict, harassed by domesticity, not always kind. Fatigue can make a monster of me.

But there was Karen, on the bus from Boston, looking beautiful, and oh, I was happy to see her and at last to talk! We write long letters and have done so for years, but she lives in Texas with her husband and children, so we meet rarely. When we do, it is an event. Karen is the best poet I have ever taught. I am certain of her genius, in spite of the hard time she has had placing poems, in spite of her periods of such self-doubt that she has tried to cut the poet off—as well try to keep the moon from rising!

Sunday, August 15th

BECAUSE OF A TRAGEDY in her family Carol Heilbrun
can't come tomorrow for the three days we had planned.
I had looked forward to seeing her, but for me it is a
providential gift of time. Now at this moment Mozart (the
Piano Concerto in G Major no. 17) is pouring energy into
my spirit like a cordial.

Down in the garden, Priscilla is cutting back the over-
grown vines along the terrace wall. This summer when I
have failed to do a thousand things in the garden that
should have been done, her presence is a true blessing. I
have never had such a quick worker here before, quick
and with high standards, higher in many instances than
my own.

Often I feel that tending the garden is a selfish occupation, since I do it primarily for myself, but then when a
guest like Karen Buss comes and sits watching the goldfinches at the feeder and speaks of the beauty of the house
indoors, I realize that keeping things up is, after all, often
a shared joy. And when I complain of too many guests,
and ask myself why I invite so many, I do realize that
"staying overnight" has a real value. It gives a guest time
to go down to the ocean and sit on the bank, looking out
to sea and gradually feeling the world fall away and the
long sighs of the waves take its place. So it is a gift of

timeless time, and that could not happen if the visit was simply for an hour or two.

Monday, August 16th

HAROLD BLOOM in *The Breaking of the Vessels* brings to light an amazing passage from a review T. S. Eliot wrote a few weeks before the famous "Tradition and Individual Talent" appeared. Eliot writes:

> There is a kind of stimulus for a writer which is more important than the stimulus of admiring another writer. Admiration leads most often to imitation; we can seldom remain long unconscious of our imitating another, and the awareness of our debt naturally leads us to hatred of the object imitated. If we stand toward a writer in this other relation of which I speak, we do not imitate him, and though we are quite as likely to be accused of it, we are quite unperturbed by the charge. This relation is a feeling of profound kinship, or rather of a peculiar personal intimacy, with another, probably a dead author. It may overcome us suddenly, on first or after long acquaintance; it is certainly a crisis; and when a young writer is seized with his first passion of this sort he may be changed, metamorphosed almost, within a few weeks even, from a bundle of secondhand sentiments into a person. The imperative intimacy arouses for the first time a real, an unshakable confi-

dence. That you possess this secret knowledge, this intimacy, with a dead man, that after few or many years or centuries you should have appeared with this indubitable claim to distinction; who can penetrate at once the thick and dusty circumlocutions about his reputation, can call yourself alone, his friend: it is something more than encouragement to you. It is a cause of development, like personal relations in life. Like personal intimacies in life, it may and probably will pass, but it will be ineffaceable.

The usefulness of such a passion is various. For one thing it secures us against forced admiration, from attending to writers simply because they are great. We are never at ease with people who, to us, are merely great. We are not ourselves great enough for that: probably not one man in each generation is great enough to be intimate with Shakespeare. Admiration for the great is only a sort of discipline to keep us in order, a necessary snobbism to make us mind our places. We may not be great lovers; but if we had a genuine affair with a real poet of any degree we have acquired a monitor to avert us when we are not in love. Indirectly, there are other acquisitions: our friendship gives us an introduction to the society in which our friend moved; we learn its origins and endings; we are broadened. We do not imitate, we are changed; and our work is the work of a changed man; we have not borrowed, we have been wakened, and we become bearers of a tradition.

In my own life I recognize this as having happened twice, perhaps more. But two such passions altered my ideas about transforming life into art. The first was W. B. Yeats. His severity toward his own early poems, his ability to change his style from sensuous and diffuse to clear and rocklike forced me to clean up my own poems. To condense, to be willing and able to revise almost indefinitely. He also taught me, whatever Louise Bogan said to me to the contrary, that a poet has to be responsible and that political poems could be more than empty rhetoric. Mauriac had a profound influence on the novels. I saw, through reading and studying him, that what I must do was cast aside the "poetic" style (for which I had been praised) and to embed the poetry into the substance, that poetry in the novel is something that lives between the lines. I worked then toward a style that would not be noticed, precise and clear.

When I was in high school I became enamored of Edna St. Vincent Millay, as so many of my contemporaries did, and this brings me back to those who have found a muse in me and in my work. The danger, when the passion aroused is for a living writer, is that one confuses life and art. At the height of her fame Millay resembled a movie star. A movie star can hardly be a role model; instead, she magnetizes her audience into a fantasy world, and that, as far as creating literature goes, is dangerous and unproductive. I was saved perhaps from trying to *be* Millay by a wise friend, Giorgio de Santillana, who said, "Don't imitate Millay, go back to what influenced her," and so I read Donne and Marvell.

I identified on a much deeper level with Virginia Woolf and that influence shows itself in the second part of *The Single Hound,* but I think not again. Because the Woolf style is so much the exact communication of a sensibility, of a vision of life, it cannot really be imitated or borrowed without becoming a simulation, thus, not *authentic* for the imitator. You are Virginia Woolf or you are not Virginia Woolf. It is as simple as that—and as elusive.

Wednesday, August 18th

FOR THE FIRST TIME in weeks I have three whole days to myself, and it is heaven not trying to take in and commune with someone else. And to catch up with all the neglected things that range from remembering to put saucers of beer in the plant window to catch the snails, to writing letters that have been on my desk too long, to reading Bobbie Geary's novel, which I finished last night. This afternoon I am going to have an orgy cleaning up the picking garden, which is a mass of self-sown nicotianas and poppies.

Yesterday was a heavy day, ending in thunderstorms. But today the air is clear and the place looks clear too, as a man came to prune the trees and bushes yesterday. What a difference it makes when the feverish growth of August is at last cut back and the ornamental cherries rounded off again, the French lilac a neat, clipped hump of green instead of what looked like a giant Struwwelpeter!

I have been thinking about people and relationships, about giving and receiving. It came to me this morning, as I lay in bed after breakfast for an unhurried think, that we all have illusions about what we give each other, and we rarely realize that receiving is also giving. I suppose that in the end the only gift, the most important, is simply to be there for each other. There is a popular song that says "No one stays in one place any more" and the people who do, who can always be imagined in a certain house, in a certain garden with a certain view, and who are *"disponible,"* as Gide used to say, give their friends the comfort at least of a still point. I hope I do that now, as Céline did for me for so many years and as Edith Kennedy did. On the other hand, it is not always possible to respond. Here the telephone is sometimes an imperative interruption at a crucial moment, and I react with anger. That is not good. It breaks a thread of trust, but then the thread of my concentration on this journal or on a poem or letter has also been broken. Can anyone be absolutely present to another all the time and any time? I think not.

Sunday, August 22nd

I LEFT HERE early Friday morning for the University of Maine at Orono, for a luncheon organized by Carroll F. Terrell—Terry—who is responsible for the National Poetry Foundation series. It was to honor the book in the series devoted to Sarton, and to honor Constance Hunting who edited it. I spent a night with Connie to catch up on things and then, on Saturday, drove to Orland for my first visit to H.O.M.E. The conjunction of such different, almost opposed parts of my life, leaves me split wide open. But the drive took me over hill and down dale through rural Maine, "the happy autumn fields" (for autumn is in the air) dotted with Queen Anne's lace, every kind of goldenrod, and black-eyed Susans, all so rich, so redolent of summer and the turn to fall. It is always a poignant moment of the year. Suddenly in spite of the heat and the bugs I want summer to stay a while and I feel the slight shiver of apprehension the fall brings with it in a northern climate. But I enjoyed the long drive from York to Orono mightily. I enjoyed being swung between worlds, without responsibilities, enjoyed seeing farms and cows in the fields, for they are rare around York.

What pleasure, then, to walk into Connie's kitchen where so much happens and where I feel so much at home in its lively disorder and then, for a moment, to go out on the porch where the huge orange cat was snoozing on a bench and let the journey quiet down as we talked, she and I, about all that has been happening to each of us since we last met months ago. The view from that side porch of the big Victorian house struck me again as a vision of the essence of New England. A plain white church spire stands high above the next-door house, and that afternoon there were dramatic clouds shot through by sunlight, setting off the starkness and strength of the spire. In the foreground we looked out on a high wall of birch logs that Rob, Connie's husband, had cut, and the extraordinary garden he has made in a small area by using space in highly original ways—for one, a barrel of potatoes. All one can see is one large potato plant at the top, but potatoes are actually growing, layered all the way down—I wish I could be there for the party they will give when the barrel is finally opened.

It is hard to say in a few words how grateful I am that Terry wanted to do the critical book on me, and how lucky I am that Connie was chosen to edit it. It is a major event in my life as a writer. But social occasions around such events are apt to be rather awful, partly because people are shy and do not know what to say. I felt like

Elinor Wylie's "camelopard at a party," longing to be
approached but apparently unapproachable. Neither
Hugh Kenner (who was visiting Terry) nor a Professor
Hayman from the University of Wisconsin showed the
slightest interest and it was horribly embarrassing to be
asked to sign books for them. I longed to vanish like a
witch in a puff of smoke. The food was elegant, but elegant food does not require conversation. It was lovely to
change into blue jeans and a shirt after a nap and settle
in to a homey evening with Connie. Rob had to go to a
party so we were alone to eat, drink, and be merry as we
did in full measure, with swordfish and delicious vegetables from the garden, and champagne I had brought from
my birthday case.

After supper she took me into her study where manuscripts and journals are piled on the floor in a positive
ongoing disorder that I recognize and enjoy because it is
so like my own disorder up here. Out of Connie's disorder
come the poems (her collected poems come out this year),
a novel in progress, her work as editor of Puckerbrush
Press, her teaching and her poetry series on Maine radio.
But in her study are a Franklin stove, two piles of logs,
and, generous Connie, more than one chair! There we
settled in for another hour.

My father had a theory that some of the best work in
the world is done by ugly ducklings, those who turn into
swans in the end but get started late. Connie was never
an ugly anything, but she calls herself a late bloomer because she was for years absorbed in bringing up a family.
Now Rob has retired and their roles are at least partially
reversed. He sometimes gets the dinner, for instance. And
Connie is coming into the realization of considerable
powers. How enlightening and exhilarating it is to be with
someone so clearly "immersed in the constructive element"!

Monday, August 23rd

THE NEXT DAY was one of the most memorable I have ever experienced, my first visit to Orland. After writing that sentence I paused for ten minutes, overwhelmed by all there is to recount, wondering how to communicate it. Karen Saum met me in Bucksport and took me first to see two of the houses H.O.M.E. has built almost entirely with volunteer help. We drove in through a rough dirt road ("What happens in winter?" I asked. "Lucy plows it out," was the answer). and pretty soon I could see the two roofs over the brush and small trees, a distinguished outline against the sky. The owners gradually pay off their debt at $175 a month, and these solar houses, each with a small greenhouse built into one wall, cost only $12,000 to build! The idea is to help the people who have them become as independent as possible, so around one of them, Jack's house, were a vegetable garden, hens in a cage, rabbits, and a milk cow that provides manure, of course, as well as milk. I have been dreaming about these houses, the sheer miracle of getting them built—a miracle partly realized because the one professional carpenter happens to be a genius at teaching—and it was marvelous to see the reality. The families were not there, so we didn't go inside but continued on our way to H.O.M.E. itself, where at least some of the money needed for building is raised through a craft shop.

The center is right on Route 1. What I saw first was the

two workhorses out in the pasture, with a tiny Episcopal
church behind them and an old farmhouse painted red
alongside it. But only when we turned in did I "take in"
the extent and variety of what has already been accomplished here in six short years. There is a building for the
weavers and another for the potters, who have only recently come to join H.O.M.E. The red farmhouse is for
offices, but what astonished me was to see two large buildings beyond these. They look extremely professional and
well built. They contain the classrooms (H.O.M.E. teaches
and can give a high school diploma now) and the lovely
day-care nursery that is open year round, freeing many
young mothers to take jobs, no longer imprisoned at home
all day, cut off from any sense of community. One of the
buildings also has a big loft still being "fixed" as a dormi-
tory for the students who pour in to help, not only to work
but to contribute tools and building materials, such as $50
worth of lumber. These volunteers come from all over the
country and occasionally from abroad. I was struck by a
poster on the wall that said "Things Take Time." One has
to place the slow, hard work that has gone into just one
of these buildings against the speed in another sense with
which a small area of human life among the very poor has
been transformed in a mere six years! Our last stop was
the craft shop, an immensely successful project that not
only sells amazing quantities of the craftwork done here
but also employs older women on a part-time basis to do
the selling and packing. I dived into this Aladdin's cave
and came away with two handwoven white and green
place mats, some Christmas cards, and a charming blue
and white cereal bowl. Standing in line to make my pur-
chases, I was behind a woman who had just spent $175
for various items, including a quilt. And here again, as I
had felt seeing the houses, I realized that the quality of

what has been produced is very high, astonishingly so.

I wanted to get some cheese to take to the Mandala Farm where I was to have dinner with Karen, Sister Lucy, a priest, a Sister of Mercy, and two young people who live there. So we stopped at the community's cooperative food store, which is run by two sisters who live next door and take in families in acute need for months at a time.

Finally we set out down an interminable, very rough road ("Does Sister Lucy plow this too?" "Yes.") to the settlement that is the heart of H.O.M.E. We left the car beside a barn that the community had been roofing that day. Karen explained that they work for H.O.M.E. all week, clearing pasture, chopping down trees, and doing a thousand other chores and tasks, but that on Saturday they work for their own community, and this was Saturday. But Karen had been given the day to show me around and be with me.

Rough as the drive in had seemed, it was nothing compared to the clifflike descent on foot to Sister Lucy's house at the border of the lake. I found it hard going and simply could not imagine what it must be like in winter when every single thing has to be carried down and laundry and tools carried up. Water must be fetched from the lake, too, by hand! And the wood for the stoves chopped! But there was Karen beside me looking so well and happy, so much in her element, the beautiful proof that it may be a hard life but it is an invigorating one.

Once on the wide porch of the house, standing high over the lake, and then inside the big living room, full of light, I sank into a chair and felt the silence and the peace of it, and how necessary such a haven must be to come back to after the long demanding days and all the human needs that pour in, in a never-ceasing flow.

Sister Lucy stayed to eat a grilled-cheese sandwich

"but there was Karen beside me"...

...and Sister Lucy "getting on with the roofing"

with us and then went back up the hill to go on with the roofing. She is not what I expected. She has brought all this to life, this highly organized work, involving hundreds of people, and I had imagined a powerful presence, a commanding person. Not at all. The impression she gives, her still, dark eyes, her gentle smile, her way of listening, is quite the opposite. It is here perhaps that faith enters. She is grounded so deeply in faith, it would seem, that she can take the crosscurrents, the endless problems, disappointments, demands, needs, into an absolutely still center. There seems to be no tension, even that caused by a guest when what was on her mind was finishing the barn roof! And when she did leave us, it was with no sense of pressure or hurry.

I curled up with the kitten and had a long quiet time then, talking with Karen and alone. That evening the community would gather at five for Mass and to share dinner with me. It was to be a feast, I knew, as Karen went out to fetch fresh herbs from one of the tiny plots she has made between rocks and rubbed them on the roast of lamb she then put into the oven. About sixty percent of their food comes from gifts. When a neighbor kills a lamb or steer, meat comes to the house. And of course at this season vegetables are plentiful. No one seems to worry, although Karen and Lucy live on next to nothing. But the essentials are there—mother cat and kitten, the old white dog, the daily *New York Times* on the table, books everywhere, and the shining lake and its gentle lapping just outside. It was good to lie down for a while and think it all over. I felt at home in the silent house. I felt at home with myself. There was blessing in the air.

At five we sat around the low, round table, Sister Lucy, Karen, Peter, Norm, the young priest, and I, waiting for the others to join us for Mass. I felt a little apprehensive.

Would I be able to share truly? Would I feel overwhelmed, as I so often am during a church service, by the
sense of being forever an outsider? But Karen had asked
whether I would be willing to read a poem during the
Mass, and we had decided on "Night Watch." So I had
already been "taken in," and the book lay open before
me. That was a help.

On the table there was a piece of brown bread from
an ordinary loaf and covered pottery bowl. And when the
others joined us, it all became very simple. We read an
ecumenical prayer aloud together; Norm recited the
Mass; we said the Lord's prayer. And after I read the
poem, there was a long silence. Then Sister Lucy read a
short passage from St. Paul's letter to the Corinthians.
And it was time, time out of time, to break the bread and
share it and to pass the little bowl and sip it, as it went
from hand to hand, "the Body of Christ, the Blood of
Christ." Amen.

I was close to tears, tears of relief, tears of praise and
love, tears of communion at last.

Then while Karen carved the leg of lamb and set out
the two casseroles of vegetables that Peter and the Sister
of Mercy had brought, we talked about the poem. Sister
Lucy had been moved by it. So were they all. And what
had not happened at the academic luncheon yesterday
happened in a beautiful way. It was Peter who asked—
because I had said at some point earlier on that I felt a
kind of awe at their lives, awe before what they were
doing—whether I had meant that, and whether I had
been honest about my conflict about my work, whether it
had been worth doing, whether I had made the right
commitment. And so I said that no artist can ever wholly
believe that he is doing what is most useful or good, that
I go through that conflict between art and life every day.
And that it had been far worse when I was younger, that

now, because of all the letters and all the lives that pour into mine through the work, I feel better than I used to. And I talked a little about the responsibility toward a talent.

We had second helpings of the marvelous feast and talked on for an hour or more, and then before dark so I would not stumble on the steep climb up into the world, it was time to hug Sister Lucy and to say good-bye.

Karen took me to my motel, which seemed absolutely unreal and strange, impersonal, too comfortable and somehow revolting after the reality of the long learning and feeling day.

Friday, August 27th

I DROVE DOWN to Harwich on Wednesday in a violent rainstorm for three days of real rest at Rene Morgan's little house set among the pitch pines so characteristic of the Cape and so reminiscent of Japanese paintings with their tall, twisty trunks and branches in irregular clusters. It is perhaps only here that I have a sense of holiday, bliss. And what is a holiday? For me now, first of all, sleep, turning over at five and going back into a dream instead of wrenching myself awake as I usually do—having no responsibilities about meals, no letters to answer, no garden to water or weed, an open day stretching out before me when nothing *has* to be done. All summer Rene creates this magic for one guest after another and then drives to Albuquerque for the winter where perhaps she gets a rest herself.

A holiday is time to read. I brought two books with me and they have proved to be a fruitful combination, Alan Paton's new novel, *Ah, but Your Land Is Beautiful,* and Gilean Douglas's *The Protected Place* about her life on an island. I shall be going to Vancouver at the end of October to do some readings and book signings and Cortes Island is near there. Douglas has divided her book into the months of the year. Just now I opened to August and found a paragraph that speaks to my condition about my least favorite month. She says,

> Too few birds apparent and too many people. Too little silence and too many boats and boaters screaming. Too puny breezes and too great heat. Flowers fading in fierce sunlight; well dry and sea opaque; beaches littered and daylight shortening. Then one morning the smell of autumn on gnat-filled air. Oh, a raucous, arid, feverish, swarming month altogether, with no "r" for oysters in it.

I could add to that list the battle to get rid of red squirrels in the house. Last Tuesday, having seen one run out in the laundry upstairs and knowing how terrified Edythe Haddaway is of them, I finally called Mary-Leigh and we went to work. First two men came and went over the house and cellar inside and out, and they did find three holes under the porch and mortared them up. Huge relief. Then, of course, a few hours after they had gone, I heard violent scrabbling in my bedroom wall, the usual squeaks and uproar. The next step is exterminators—the whole business is hateful, but squirrels are dangerous and destructive. I tried a Havahart trap weeks ago, but they were much too clever to venture inside it! The problem has to be solved by winter and I expect it will be, but this time getting away from squirrels is also what "holiday" means.

Yesterday after the rain we woke to a washed clean, cool, sunny day and spent a leisurely morning wandering around Chatham to find me a winter raincoat—such pleasure to be on the Cape in no hurry, taking byways, and rare fun for me to be with an old friend who knows every shortcut and delightful hidden road, to savor it all together, and even to find the exactly right raincoat at the end of the rainbow. Rene tells me she loves to "solve problems" such as this, and I try to believe her.

But of course the climax we had been moving toward was coming home to make a picnic—ham sandwiches, cucumbers, a tomato each, and some Gourmandise cheese, grapes, and white wine to top it off. Then we set out for Paine's Creek, the site of many a picnic over the years. Low tide. Great waving green splashes of beach grass, low-tide pools, then immense white stretches of sand, and finally a band of brilliant blue ocean below paler blue sky. The scene opens the mind, sets it at rest, and, in my case anyway, floods it with a kind of ecstasy of atavistic memory of the Flemish lowlands that are in my blood. All this breadth is punctuated by a few human figures, dragging sand pails and beach chairs out to the farther sands —an immemorial scene. Rene and I sat with our backs to rocks and I wanted to sing "Holiday, holiday . . . this is it!"

Holiday went on all afternoon as I sank onto my bed and into a deep sleep after reading a chapter of Alan Paton. Even here it is not possible to shut out suffering or the world, but I can read this book only a chapter at a time, so complex and terrible are the strains and conflicts it brings to vivid life.

When I woke up I began to sort out this summer in my mind and discovered that another point about a holiday is that it gives one a chance to look backward and forward, to reset oneself by an inner compass. I have been too busy living lately to know what is happening. But yesterday, lying there suspended in time, without pressure, I began to see what a rich summer it has proved to be, a litany of friends old and new, a few great events like my reading at the Unitarian Assembly and the appearance of the book of criticism and my visit to Orland, a constant ebb and flow of life coming and going—and, not the least, three birthdays to celebrate, Eleanor's eighty-eighth, Marguerite's ninetieth, and Laurie's ninety-first, three great women all in full possession of their powers—seventy is not old, after all, and if I can be like them at the end of two more decades I shall have reason to be happy.

What better way in fact to celebrate a seventieth year than with a feast of friends? And if I had imagined this year as one with time for reflection, it is always a mistake to try to order one's life in such an arbitrary way. Time for reflection will come when time is ripe. And right now I realize that just three days' rest and holiday are all that I need to reset my course, as happy and free as a sailor putting out again into the ocean after anchoring in a sheltered bay.

Next week, adventure! My first sight of Monhegan.

Monday, August 30th

THE SQUIRRELS are silent this morning. What a relief that is! And I am savoring three days alone. It is pure pleasure to go down to the picking garden, a thick mass of flowers, and make four or five bunches for the house, as I did on Saturday when I got back from the Cape. The sweet peas are flowering, though not in profusion; a very few scent the air when I bring them in. Zinnias are all over the place and calendulas; the asters are beginning, puffballs of lavender and white that go well with a summer bulb just flowering, a white, long-stemmed, lilylike flower with a purple throat. The grasses in the field have gone from pinkish-bronze to pale gold. It was 40° this morning when I got up and feels like autumn, but there are no red leaves yet, even on the swamp maples, so the idea that it is autumn already because of the icy air is an illusion. We need rain. Yesterday, reveling in the lack of mosquitoes, I watered the terrace and the tuberous begonias under the pine trees. It has become a pleasure instead of an ordeal to walk Tamas through the woods.

Yesterday the *New York Times Magazine* had a good piece in it about Milton Avery that made me realize that a painter must have not only talent but also a critic to recognize and publicize it. Avery for years had fallen between the fashion for abstract expressionism and the later fashion for realism. At that time, Hilton Kramer says in the *Times,* "It was not uncommon for even knowledgeable people in the art world to be indifferent to Avery's achievement. It could not quite be fitted into any of the handy categories by which contemporary art tends to be judged. It belonged to no 'school,' it generated no controversy and the artist who created it was definitely not a 'personality.' It was therefore assumed—mistakenly—to be not of major importance." Then in the 1960s Patrick Heron, the English critic, was taken to see Avery's work and he was bowled over. "Why hasn't anyone ever told us about this marvelous painter?" he asked, and promptly arranged for his dealer, Leslie Waddington, to show Avery's work in London. Now he is dead, Avery is beginning to be recognized as a major American painter at last.

The same thing is true for a writer like me. The other day I had a letter that asked me to what I attribute my success. Of course, I do not have "success" in the ordinary definition of that word, but I answered, "A talent, persistence, and luck." I was thinking that my luck was those years in London before World War II when Koteliansky persuaded Cresset to publish my poems and my first two novels, and when they were reviewed by people I knew, Elizabeth Bowen, James Stephens, Stevie Smith. Here in America I have never had a cluster of critics on my side. But it was luck that brought my first book of poems to Conrad Aiken's attention. Houghton Mifflin sent him the manuscript and decided to publish after his warm response. And it was luck, thirty years later, when Carolyn Heilbrun discovered *Plant Dreaming Deep* and came to see me. But the fact that I have no existence in the literary establishment is simply that so far no other important critic has "discovered" me.

Like the painter Avery, I belong to no school and have never been in the avant-garde. Yet there is a lot of meat in my work for critics, as the National Poetry Foundation book makes clear.

Tuesday, August 31st

IT IS MY FATHER'S BIRTHDAY. I have been thinking of him a lot lately, partly as I draw nearer to his age when he died so suddenly on his way to give a lecture in Montreal. I understand how driven he felt and how tired he was in the last years. All his life he had been climbing an Everest of scholarly endeavor, knowing that he would never reach the top. That would be for others to come, yet he never ceased for a day the enormous effort that work entailed. Always generous in his answers to scholars, always *"disponible"* when it came to that. From him I learned that impatient patience that drove him on, learned what routine can do, learned not to give up on any day, and also perhaps to go my own way. I think, too, of his beaming smile, so boyish and innocent. I am glad he is not here to see Lebanon torn apart and Beirut destroyed, a city he loved and knew well, as he and my mother spent a year there when he was learning Arabic. He was never dispassionate, never took on the detachment and noncommitment fashionable at Harvard in the thirties. He cared, and it showed in everything he wrote, so Professor L. J. Henderson, who did not care, could call him "sentimental."

He loved the sea, and some of my happiest memories of my parents are of being with them during the summers they spent at Rockport in a little cottage near the Straitsmouth Inn, where Daddy sat for hours, smoking a cigar and looking out at the ocean. Cloudy, the beloved gray half-Persian cat, used to follow him down to the shore when he went swimming and meow loudly with fear and distress when he disappeared into the water!

I was grownup then, but there are also happy memories of summers in Ogunquit when I was five to ten years old, and Lucy Stanton generously lent us her studio behind the old High Rock Hotel each August. How old was I when I haunted the public library, still there unchanged on Shore Road, and took the Waverley novels out one by one and read high up in a pine tree? It is very odd that reading in a tree, uncomfortable at best, seems to be an atavistic longing children have.

"my father's . . . beaming smile"

If only my parents could see this place! How my mother would love to walk down the grassy path and look out, how my father would have enjoyed sitting on the terrace smoking a cigar! He has been dead for twenty-five years. And my mother for thirty, a long growing time of my life without them.

But they will be with me when I go to Monhegan tomorrow. I feel rather like a child going to camp, as Linda Kilburn, who will show me around—she knows the island well—sent me a long list of things I should take, including a flashlight, rubber boots, long johns, extra shoes, bug killer, gloves, soap, tea bags, raincoat, sweaters. My luggage looks formidable and Monhegan begins to seem like the moon. It will rain, they say, but I don't care. It is an adventure and the wind is rising in my sails.

Sunday, September 5th

HOW GOOD that for once this Labor Day weekend is fine, warm, sunny, the last days of summer for so many people, and for me, too. Good news, as Georgia is here until Tuesday morning, working away on her dissertation on *King Lear* while I am up here in my study, catching my breath in the whirlwind of time. Autumn is in the air. We sat out on the terrace for an hour yesterday and the crickets were singing loudly—that regular rhythm so like a heartbeat, the heartbeat of autumn.

It has taken twenty-four hours for me to begin to sort out the Monhegan days. Linda Kilburn had asked me a

year ago to let her show me that island that has become
a haven and heaven to so many people and is her promised land. When I accepted the invitation, I did not know
what a full summer of people this would be, but actually
it was splendid to get in the car on a misty morning and
shoot away at half-past six. The drive down from Thomas-
ton to Port Clyde, where one embarks, was new territory
for me, lovely rural country with every now and then a
glimpse of ocean and pine-topped small islands in the
distance. I was there in good time and sat on the rocks
watching a flotilla of ducks swimming about, and a flotilla
of people, most of them dressed by L. L. Bean, arriving
and dumping bags and rucksacks on the dock beside the
stubby open boat. Then I saw Linda walking toward me,
slender, boyish, smiling, and looking ready for anything,
in a heavy shirt, sleeveless jacket, and boots. And soon we
were off and away, very glad to be outside, sitting against
the port wall, and not stuffed into the tiny enclosed cabin
for an hour's chug across mildly heavy seas, "rocked" in
fact "in the cradle of the deep."

The first view of Monhegan, the port, astonished me
because I had not expected so many houses, a big hotel,
and such a crowd to meet us at the dock. Our bags were
taken up to the Trailing Yew where we were booked, so
we had an unencumbered walk along a rough dirt road.
We landed finally in a small room with only a double bed
and two straight chairs and began to stow our gear away.
For a moment I panicked at the lack of privacy and wondered what the forty-eight hours would turn out to be.
Gray skies, rain pending, did not help, and I was drowsy
and felt heavy-headed as I had taken a pill for possible
seasickness. What we both needed was a hot lunch and a
sleep. But the people at the Trailing Yew had given up
providing lunch, and we had to settle for a paper bag with
a chicken-salad sandwich and a piece of cake in it. Linda

did manage to get hot water, so we made tea and sat on the porch eating, talked for a while, and then flopped on our bed and went fast asleep.

Where was I, I wondered, half awake at three or so? It was not at all the wild island I had expected, apparently. Earlier, as we ate our sandwiches on the porch, a handsome dark-haired woman had passed by, then came back, wide-eyed, to ask whether I was by chance May Sarton. No hiding place on Monhegan!

But after that nap, I was eager to explore. Linda led the way in a light drizzle, and we were soon on a woodsy trail that came out after a half hour or so to rocky coast, a huge rusting ship that had floundered on it years ago, and the open sea. Just across the way Linda pointed out Jamie Wyeth's house. We passed one solitary old lady also out exploring. No doubt she knew the trails well, for it soon became apparent that there were many aficionados who come back year after year, many solitary men and women for whom this island is potent magic.

The first day we were rarely silent, for we were, after all, not only exploring a trail but also ourselves.

By evening I had become a little homesick for Greenings where, as long as Anne Thorp lived, Judy and I spent ten days or so every summer. There we met only family, if anyone at all, on our walks. Privately owned, it was less accessible and therefore a secret paradise. The terrain there is less spectacular than the high cliffs of Monhegan, but both have the same lovely jumble of firs and spruces and hardwoods, the same areas of brilliant moss, and, as I was to discover the next day, the same solemn "cathedral woods."

The weather did not help during the forty-eight hours. I think we both felt cooped up, although, little by little, long silences became possible. I found the meals exhilarating because Monhegan draws like-minded, liberal people and the talk was good. The dark-haired woman who had recognized me and her niece, on her first visit to the United States, made me feel at home as the European-born always do. Why is it? We talked about that, what it is that makes the European draw on a deeper loam, seem more alive, more aware than most Americans appear to be.

It was a little like being on shipboard. It became clear that almost everyone comes to Monhegan to recover from something, if only city life. Linda had had a dramatically hard year and would be going back to teaching flute, clarinet, and saxophone after the weekend. I was recovering from too many guests this summer, but when I got home on Friday afternoon and went out to pick flowers to welcome Georgia, I was very glad indeed to be here and nowhere else. Adventures may be for the adventurous, but home is where the real things are sown and reaped, where in the end the real things happen.

They are happening now, for way off, in the distance on the rim where the field drops down to rocks, I see two heads and guess they are Georgia's and Tamas's sitting side by side and drinking in a shining ocean and gentle autumn sunlight on the soft grasses.

Labor Day, September 6th

IT IS PEACEFUL HERE. For the first time in ages I feel the blessing of the house, what it is to be here, the beautiful silence, a little time to collect myself, and that is partly because Georgia feels it all so deeply and looks visibly rested after twenty-four hours. It is wonderful to have her

here. It does not happen often, as she lives in German-
town, near Philadelphia, and can rarely leave her husband and two small children. But when she comes the
house is lit up by her sensitive presence. It was so homey
and comfortable to fold the sheets together after I did a
laundry this morning, and when she needs a break from
her morning concentration on *Lear,* she tells me she will
clean out the refrigerator! That is one of the innumerable
things that do not get done these days. It was chilly this
morning, so after breakfast I lit the fire in the library, and
there she is working away with Tamas beside her, waiting
to be taken for a walk.

What is wonderful for me is to be with someone whose
vision of life is so like mine, who reads avidly and with
discrimination, who goes deeply into whatever is happening to her and her family and can talk about it freely, so
it feels a little like a piece of music in which we are playing
different instruments that weave a theme in and out, in
almost perfect accord. I had this experience always with
my mother when I came home and we could talk. And I
feel so happy that perhaps I can be that kind of mother
for Georgia. I wish she lived nearer and we did not have
to depend so much on the telephone, that imperious and
sometimes intrusive form of communication. But at least
we can keep in touch that way, and we do.

Wednesday, September 8th

YESTERDAY was a humdinger of a day but, in a strange
way, peaceful and rewarding, although I was on the run.
I drove Georgia to Cambridge to be picked up by her
sister, Deborah, and Georgia's little daughter, Johanna,

and had suggested we meet away from traffic in the Mt. Auburn Cemetery. It is an island of tranquillity and beauty, an arboretum as well as a cemetery, designed like a park with ponds here and there, a tower on a high hill in the middle, and many Victorian mausoleums and gravestones. Judy and I used to walk there and sometimes take a picnic along when the dogwood and azaleas were out and also in the autumn, sit on a bench by one of the ponds, and watch the ducks. I had the feeling of coming home as we turned in and parked the car near a fountain and formal garden; then Georgia went off to explore while I soaked in the sunlight and peace, and thought about Judy whom I planned to visit on my way back after lunch.

My mother and father are buried in Mt. Auburn, their ashes mixed. Judy was with me that day, and Aunt Mary Bouton, dear old friend, and I always remember how moving it was that some of the ash was blown upward on a light breeze, such a delicate kind of burial—no heavy coffin to be lowered—that death itself seemed ephemeral. Anne Thorp is buried at Mt. Auburn, and Mary Bouton too. It felt like a communion between the dead and the living to be there with Georgia, the richness of life, always for me now enriched by memory. So what had seemed like a hassle turned into a beautiful pause.

I loved driving Georgia slowly around the winding roads and parking where we could sit on Judy's and my bench and watch the ducks. There was a great flotilla swimming toward us in hope of some bread, and one detached from the crowd, making a perfect V behind him, as he swam. I picked up some duck feathers on the grass and put them in my pocket—perhaps Judy would like their silky feel.

And then it was time to meet Johanna and Deborah

and to say good-bye. Not a sad good-bye this time, as it had been such a great time, a restful time, a time when we were in perfect accord.

From there I drove around the corner to have lunch with Cora DuBois and Jeanne Taylor, sit in their garden with a glass of wine and bask in the pleasure of being with them. I do not see many old friends these days and treasure the tranquil conversation, the autumn sunlight, and the not unhappy knowledge that we are all three in the autumn of our lives. So much does not need to be said, so much can be taken for granted.

But then I had to go shortly after lunch to drive to Concord to see Judy for the first time in months, since before Christmas. There she was, there she will be until she slips away, in her wheelchair, singing to herself. I know now that she will not recognize me, but I held her cold little hand and talked about old times. I gave her the duck feathers and reminded her of our walks at Mt. Auburn and for thirty seconds I thought she was enjoying the silky feathers, and perhaps listening, but then she put them into her mouth, and I had to try to take them away. She held on fiercely and only let them go when I gave her a brownie to eat. Her face is still so distinguished, the dark eyes, the cap of white hair, that it seems incredible that she herself is far away and what is left is a baby, for whom food is the only real pleasure. The truth is I go to see her for me, not for her. After a time I feel a strong compulsion to touch base, as it were. True love does not die.

The day had been planned to end there, but the night before Larry LeShan had called to say that Eda and he were passing through, and we had arranged to meet in York at six so I could lead them here for a glass of champagne and then go somewhere for dinner. I have so wanted them to see this place!

It was well worth the hurry when I got home to change and set glasses out, worth the fatigue, for I was happy and at peace and eager to be with them, new and good friends whose understanding and support came to me at a time when I needed it badly, the time of *A Reckoning.*

Monday, September 13th

I AM MORE AWARE than usual of the long rhythm of the seasons, and the recurring events become more precious as they structure the larger design of life itself, perhaps because this has been such an interrupted summer. So I basked in the return to Center Sandwich to spend two nights with Huldah, as I have done around this time for five years now, catching a glimpse of her daughter Leslie and Christina, her granddaughter, before they go back to Greece. We are having a warm spell, so it all felt like high summer. I passed fields of Queen Anne's lace and golden-rod and a few pale-blue patches of the first asters and reveled in the familiar route, especially after Wolfeboro when the road follows the edge of Lake Winnipesaukee, tranquil, since Labor Day is over and many camps and cottages are empty. A hazy day, so when I did get off the main road and was climbing up toward Sandwich I could hardly see the mountains, melted into soft sky. Such a holiday feeling with a day and a half of pure rest and enjoyment before me—except for the huge bag of letters I had picked up in York on the way. There is never any escape even for a day from those leaves off the human tree that appear to be always shedding in a perpetual autumn of feeling and connecting. And I would not have it otherwise, for what if there were no news from "outside"?

This was my first time of taking a picnic down to the lake at a house Huldah bought last year, really to protect a perfect cove, near her tiny lodge from which we used to swim off the float. This time, instead of skirting the Chalmers house, we went right in, to stand on the porch in a grove of immensely tall straight pines and look to the right at a high moss-covered bluff with beech woods on top that shelters the cove on that side, then out to the lake, the distant hills, and on the left—what glory! a point of flat rocks backed by pines. The only thing missing that day was loons! (For this is "Golden Pond.") The silence, the peace of it—only an occasional motorboat screaming past. Canoes drawn up on the half-moon sandy beach. I couldn't wait to get into that silken water. Huldah's big collies don't go in, but they stand in the water looking very noble, and Fawn wanted to follow me and gave hopeful barks but never did quite dare. For me, the first swim this summer was supremely delicious, clear water, just cool enough, and such quiet all around.

When we got home I had the unusual pleasure of sitting outdoors on Huldah's porch and reading for two hours. I wanted to shut the world out for a while. The mail had brought some bad news from a distant friend, news of a divorce, but I laid that aside and immersed myself in *Ah, but Your Land Is Beautiful.* What a joke to think one can shut the world out! This book is so vivid an evocation of the sickness at heart of South Africa, so full of the anguish and the humiliations of blacks and any whites or coloreds or Hindus who try to fight apartheid, that I had found it hard to read here in York. Now I was anxious to

finish it, more—to give it my full attention, to imagine
with Paton, to be for a few hours inside the agonizing
struggle. As in the Middle East, the fear and the hatred
have set up such blank, hard, high walls that one sees no
hope. What courage they have, those who stay and fight!
How lonely is the single brave man who follows his con-
science, his family endangered, himself always in peril of
being banned or imprisoned! The worst is that the hatred
feeds on the name of Christ, on what the rigid Afrikaners
insist is God's design that the races must be kept apart and
that they, who came as invaders, have a right to dispossess
and brutalize the black labor and the black world they
could not function without. What is to change hearts if
even religion is so twisted and misused? We see the danger here again in the Moral Majority, the same use of
fundamentalist doctrine to exonerate and permit hatred,
to set people up as more righteous or more right than
others.

Lonely, misused Christ, how can we ever come back
to You?

Today the Holocaust is being remembered in the Jewish communities, and we remember how far racism can
take a people, what hell on earth it makes possible.

All this was in my mind, the great good of having time
to think about it for a change, to let the sick world in for
a change, while Huldah was concocting a superb dinner
for us and her friend Dorothy Clay. Dorothy arrived at
eight, glowing with vitality and charm, ninety now, wid-
owed last year after, as she said, "the sixteen happiest
years of my life," in her late second marriage with Basil.
She is nearly blind and a little deaf, but who could guess
that? She is so alive and aware, such an inspiration of
courage and *savoir-vivre*.

So when I set out for home the next day I felt rested

and enlightened, and blest by two days' real holiday. At the moment, putting all this together in my thoughts, if someone asked me what is the single greatest human quality I would have to answer, "Courage, courage and imagination—those two."

Well, I came home to disaster, Edythe Haddaway telling me as gently as possible that there was no water! Not only that, but there is still a red squirrel at large in the house! The holiday was over.

Friday, September 17th

I GOT BACK from Connecticut yesterday, and this afternoon Marilyn Kallet comes for overnight, and I feel the pressure of my life building. At least there is water. It was good for me to be without it for twenty-four hours, to be without something I take for granted, enough water. It turned out to be the pump, and that has been replaced now, so all is well. Little by little the squirrels are being baffled, all holes stopped up. But the chaos on my desk makes me feel quite ill.

I have not given a public performance since late June and realize freshly just what such a sortie involves and how expensive it is. I want to do less of it from now on. What I enjoyed was the long drive through a hazy misty landscape, Connecticut so rich and tranquil, so very green, here and there a swamp maple flashing out red as I went past. I spent the night at Joy Sweet's and that is a perfectly peaceful place in Mount Carmel, an old house, rolling fields, a romantic pond—Joy was just coming in from a swim when I got there. She and Gordon, who died some years ago, created all this order and beauty through the years of their marriage, so it has all been growing and becoming more ample for a long time. I drank it in like an elixir and, as always, was enchanted by the space inside, the lack of clutter, the blue and white parlor where we sat and talked as the light went and night came on across the meadow. My eyes rested on a blue jar containing crimson cosmos and lavender Michaelmas daisies, color as brilliant and startling as a clash of cymbals against the white walls. And how restful and exhilarating it was to be with someone I have known for sixty years, so we talked in a kind of ocean depth of memories where magic fish swam past, as we evoked our parents and Joy's sisters, all dead now but with us for an hour in that exquisite room where time past and time present flowed together. Some of the memories were fresh and delightful, for Joy had been in France and gave me a glowing description of Monet's garden at Giverny restored to what it was when he painted there. Joy, too, has had a summer of guests, and we laughed about the way we are taken over and how impossible it is to say no to a friend and swore, as we have done before, that next summer will be different.

The next morning I drove to Willimantic, again through a misty landscape over a little-used road, and stopped to get two lavender chrysanthemums to perk up the terrace border and a bag of fresh spinach for my supper. This was the reading at Connecticut State University that had been scheduled for last April 9th when we had a tremendous blizzard and I was snowbound for forty-eight hours. Somehow I didn't want to talk about "Kinds of Renewal." That theme belongs to spring for me. But I read autumn poems and it seemed to work out all right.

It was a strange hall with a low ceiling and very bad acoustics, so I never could bounce my voice off the wall and had to force it to be heard, in spite of the mikes. But the atmosphere was so warm and welcoming, the two baskets of field flowers, Queen Anne's lace and goldenrod, so appropriate, and Parker Huber's introduction so loving that it all lifted me up. It is fun to read the poems and to hear them myself, like music that is hidden in a score until someone plays it.

Saturday, September 18th

I WANT TO PAUSE here for a moment to celebrate asters, the low pale-lavender ones that dot the field now, starry among the long pale-gold grasses, the tall white ones that line the road in the woods, the deep-purple ones I found here in the picking garden, and the cultivated Michaelmas daisies, as they are called in England, that I have planted over the years in the border below the terrace. Some of these are almost a true blue. One of my favorites (Frikartii) is bright lavender with large flowers. They come when the phlox is over and always seem like a special gift of autumn. Rare in color at this season, they light up the garden and make a splash with the oranges and yellows of zinnias and calendulas in vases in the house, a new spectrum for me, and delightful.

Marilyn is leaving on a perfect, still, sunny day. I can see her now, walking Tamas down the path to the sea before she takes off. Because I was really overtired I

dreaded her visit, but it has proved to be a blessing. She
looks beautiful, her serious, thoughtful face very white,
her glossy dark hair falling on either side. It is Rosh Ha-
shanah today, the Jewish New Year, and we celebrated it
last night by the fire by sharing an apple and honey before
we went to bed. That, Marilyn told me, is traditional. We
talked about anti-Semitism and about Israel and the war,
how badly it has been interpreted by the media, how
Arafat has manipulated public opinion, how peace will
ever be made. South Africa, Ireland, the Middle East, so
riddled by hatred, bitter memories, racial tensions, the
most ineradicable kind, for it has its roots in religious
fanaticism. If only people could come to believe as Gandhi
did that "all religions are true." But, as things are, religion
is the great divider, as it was in the dark Middle Ages, as
perhaps it has always been.

I have been thinking about hatred. The fact is, unfortunately, that hatred in the public sense makes people's
eyes bright, starts the adrenaline flowing, as love in the
public sense does not. People feel fine when they are full
of anger and hatred against someone else!

Love becomes a fire like hatred, fuels the soul only
when it is of a high order, when it can propel a saint like
St. Francis. But few of us reach this level, and I think that
is partly why so many still will not take in the Holocaust.
They are terrified of knowing what really happened, terrified because it is too painful to contemplate. So the worst
thing that has been happening lately is what feels like a
justified anti-Semitism because of the Israeli bombing of
Beirut. I sense a kind of relief that it has become "all
right" in some quarters to allow oneself anti-Semitism.

When Marilyn came up here to my study to say good-
bye, she handed me a page on which she had written first
in Hebrew, then translated for me, a blessing on the new

year: "Blessed art Thou, Oh Lord our God, Ruler of the Universe, Who has brought us to this season and enabled us to bless that which is new."

I take it to heart. I feel the blessing of it. And the need of it.

Monday, September 20th

I SLEPT BADLY after the excitement of the book signing in Ogunquit yesterday, and because I had coffee at dinner, but as I lay awake with Bramble in an ecstasy of purrs beside me, I rested in the idea that my life, exhausting as it is at times, and has been this summer, is wonderfully rich. This morning I got up an hour late, at six (it is dark at five). Now it is nearly ten. Before I got dressed I washed the sheets and made my bed up fresh, then after tidying up the breakfast dishes went out to the picking garden to pick two bunches, one all oranges and yellows for Mary-Leigh, one all blues and purples, lavenders and pinks for Beverly.

After that I packed up four copies of *Anger* to send off to friends. Every day I pack and send three or four and it does eat up time, but the real pleasure of having a book come out is giving it away, so this is a self-indulgence. If only the day were a few hours longer or I could function after supper! As it is I go to bed by nine and read. But writing a letter is not possible.

I have never signed books in a more beautiful and spacious setting, the big upstairs room at The Whistling

Oyster where Huldah's dinner for me took place in May.
This time it was in daylight, at four, and the view of Perkins Cove from the big windows was dazzling. I am
touched to think of how many people came, including a
woman in a wheelchair who had driven herself from
Staten Island, she told me. And there she was with a great
pile of books in her arms for me to sign. The trouble with
such occasions is that there is such a lineup that I hesitate
to talk as I would like to with each person. I felt badly
about it for the whole two hours.

One very young woman who was there at the start,
before the line got worrisome, told me she had graduated
from Emerson this spring. And what did she want to do
with her life, I asked. "Make money" was the appalling
answer. I am convinced that making money is a by-
product, and if that is one's chief aim, the chances are one
will never make a lot. She could work at AT&T, training
management people to speak in public, and that pays
well, she said. But, she added, "It would be boring." I
agreed that no amount of money is worth being bored for
eight hours a day! At present she is a waitress. It seemed
a sorry reflection on an "education" to come out with such
minimal aims. And, surprisingly enough, it was *Mrs. Stevens* and her love of that book, a very worn, much-read
copy, that had brought her to The Whistling Oyster! I
could not put it together.

As always, the people were a splendid mixture of ages
and backgrounds, and that pleases me.

At six it was over and Janice, Maryann, Nancy Hartley,
and I went down to the restaurant and had a lovely,
homey talk with much laughter around the subject of
Fonzi, the dachshund I had given Janice for her birthday.
He is growing to be a handful but is already greatly loved.
And so to bed.

Wednesday, September 22nd

STEADY RAIN today and it is a relief, as we need it badly.
I have had two whole days to myself, to enjoy the walk
with Tamas, following his nose close to the ground, his tail
swishing back and forth as he responds to a scent with a
kind of dance, growling low growls, then erupting into
sharp barks. I had hoped to find mushrooms after the
night's rain, but there are none, and that proves how very
dry the woods have been.

I wrote ten or more letters in the morning and then
hoped in the afternoon to get my desk into some sort of
order, as it is the wild piles that make me feel wild and
disorderly myself. It proved to be an impossible task, as
the more I dug into the piles, the more I was appalled at
what I should have answered weeks ago. Today I am determined to use the form letter Lee Blair had printed for
me several years ago, but which I find hard to use. Sweep
it all away and make a fresh start. Then I could perhaps
manage each day's mail right away, a mad hope. After all,
at seventy not only do I have many readers who want to
tell me their stories (always interesting) but, at seventy, I
have accumulated many friends. So the bulk of what is on
my desk is not "fan mail" but letters from real friends. I
suppose my address book has a thousand names in it, and
I write to every one at least once a year and often many
times more. So what is the solution? There is none. And

"to enjoy the walk with Tamas"

that is what makes me feel overcrowded and uneasy at the end of this much interrupted summer.

Yet always, in each mail, there is something that makes me rejoice to be alive and grateful that the books are reaching people and are proving useful. What does come through always is what burdens people carry, how hard any life is at best—any life where there is caring and sensitivity—and the need to reach out. I have been given a great deal by strangers; their letters have enlarged my heart.

I look out at the rain, the narrow winding path through the golden grasses to the gray ocean and rest in it. I am as close to heaven as I am to hell all these days as summer turns to autumn.

Friday, September 24th

SUN AFTER FOUR DAYS of blessed rain—fresh warm air, wet grass, and every plant and bush and tree refreshed. It's a perfect day for Anne and Barbara to come with *Persephone*. She will stand on the terrace wall, emerging from the ocean, and I can hardly wait to see her placed. I commissioned her months ago, and Barbara made several sketches before we decided just how it would be.

This morning after breakfast I set the table with wineglasses and utensils for eating lobsters and put a bottle of wine in the refrigerator, the ritual preparation for Anne and Barbara's rare visits here. In a little while I shall fetch the lobsters and make a salad. I also picked a glorious

branch of crimson-dotted lilies with five in flower and two
in bud to place in the bunch on the hall table. They make
it look quite splendid.

Yesterday I did three jobs that have been much on my
mind—brought in the four azaleas that have in a mad way
flowered all summer outdoors in their pots, pruned them,
nourished them, and set them back in the plant window;
cut back six amaryllises, which have also been out all summer, and set them in the cool cellar to rest; and, most
prickly, tore off the healthy side-children of the two very
pointed harsh tropical plants that came several years ago
from Florida wrapped in newspapers and have flourished
ever since. I throw away the parent plant and repot the
healthy children. It all looks a hundred percent better.
One has to be quite ruthless to be a good gardener, I have
discovered.

Saturday, September 25th

IT DID TURN OUT TO BE a perfect day, so warm that we
were able to sit out on the terrace with our drinks and
contemplate *Persephone,* now safely rising from the sea at
the end of the terrace wall. What I love is how Barbara has
achieved fluidity and motion in the stone, as she did also
with the *Phoenix.* Anne was delighted by the blues, lavender, and purples of the Michaelmas daisies, which she had
not seen before, and also that the felicity had one blue
flower and to know that the elegant plant that she
brought on my birthday has done so well on the terrace
all summer.

It's always a homecoming for me when they come here and set the seal of our long friendship on all that has been happening to all three of us. Anne brought me two dozen eggs from her hens, and for the first time in months I tasted a truly fresh egg with my breakfast this morning. Barbara brought leeks, such a bonanza, as I plan to make chicken soup this afternoon, and they are just what I need for it. That slightly smoky taste is the key to good chicken soup!

Yesterday the mail was immense, and I must get at it and also plan a short speech on writing fiction that I am to give at the Boston Public Library on Tuesday. Tomorrow I sign books in Portsmouth.

Mary-Leigh cut part of the field yesterday on her big machine. It has to be done to keep the growth down, but she knows I love the golden grasses so she waits till autumn. Before she began, I walked Tamas down to the sea and said farewell to the lovely blue asters and the thick white ones low on the ground that do so well in bunches indoors. Hard to say farewell, but that is what autumn means every year. And meanwhile overhead the leaves are beginning to turn, and we shall soon be in the glory of crimson and orange and yellow overhead.

The autumn of life is also a matter of saying farewell, but the strange thing is that I do not feel it is autumn. Life is so rich and full these days. There is so much to look forward to, so much here and now, and also ahead, as I dream of getting back to the novel about Anne Thorp and to good silent days here when the hubbub of this summer dies down. And right now there are hundreds of good letters to answer and hundreds of bulbs to plant. I do not feel I am saying farewell yet but only beginning again, as it used to be when school started.

Tuesday, September 28th

I SHALL BE GLAD when today, the last of the book signings for a while, is over. It's a rather pressured day, as I speak on fiction at the Boston Public Library at seven-thirty, then sign books from nine on at the Harvard Bookstore. And I have promised to read the continuity for a short film the Unitarians are producing on old age. They will come to the Copley Plaza at four to record that.

On Sunday it was exciting to arrive at the lovely old public library in Portsmouth (designed by Bulfinch) and, long before four, see people waiting outside and then piling in, some old, some young, and all with an air of expectation and delight that made it all seem easy and fun. The weather was good, and for once I decided to wear a new dress instead of my black pantsuit, which has become the uniform these past years for poetry readings. Since I live in pants, shirts, and blazers, I always feel rather dressed up in a dress and not quite at ease, but this one is going to work, I think. It is quite plain—gray with small purple geometric patterns strewn over it. A new dress or any new garment has to be gotten used to. And the first time it is worn should be on a happy occasion. This was a very happy one indeed, especially as at six Liz Knies and a poet friend of hers called Tanzi were making a fine dinner for seven of us, including the owner of The

Little Professor bookstore, who had organized the book signing, while the library contributed the space and gave two film showings of *World of Light*. That worked well, as the crowd dissipated to view the film, and since there was less crush by the table where I sat, there was a chance for some real talk, not just "How do you spell your name?"

I usually come home alone after these occasions, so it was delightful to have a superb dinner cooked for me and to relax with friends. But I slept badly from fatigue and excitement, I expect, and yesterday I felt abysmally tired. It rained all day, which did not help. But it did help to have Rene Morgan drop in, and we went out to lunch and caught up with each other. I was glad to have her with me to share in reading Dave Wilson's fine piece about me in the Boston *Globe*. Rene truly rejoices in any good things that happen here, and that is a help, for it is then that I long for my parents to know and sometimes feel rather an orphan. Not so, yesterday.

All these past days I have been reading James McConkey's *Court of Memory*. He often appears in *The New Yorker*, and one of these short pieces gave me such intense pleasure (I wept all through it for some reason) that I wrote to him about it. He affects me as Chekhov used to in the old Civic Repertory days when we did *The Three Sisters* and *The Cherry Orchard*, and I cried over and over again, overwhelmed by the truth, the tenderness, the poignance of that vision of life. McConkey uses as epigraph for the book St. Augustine: "All this I do inside me, in the huge court of my memory. There I have by me the sky, the earth, the sea, and all things in them which I have been able to perceive . . . There too I encounter myself . . . ."

Thursday, September 30th

A BEAUTIFUL sunny autumn day here, but I am too tired
to enjoy it, although I did enjoy going out early this morning in rubber boots (the grass is very wet after the rain
yesterday and the day before) to pick a few flowers. I have
been away for just twenty-four hours, but the chaos I had
almost tamed last week on my desk is back again as letters
about *Anger* and requests for recommendations, as well
as the usual mail, have piled up. I guess I had better plant
some bulbs to clear my mind and maybe I can this afternoon, although I must also cook Carbonnade Flamande
for Janice, who is coming for supper, and for Doris Beatty,
who arrives from California tomorrow evening.

I found being in Boston traffic, bewildered by one-way
streets, traumatic as I tried to reach the Copley Plaza day
before yesterday. When I finally managed to put the car
on a tow-away street and rushed in to see if they could
garage it and they said no, I felt so hysterical that I paid
them ten dollars to get someone to do it. It was an agitated
day for me. It was unlucky that my room turned out to be
a tiny one, dominated by a huge double bed, no space to
move around in, so all I could think of when six people
turned up for the recording was the Marx brothers in that
wonderful scene in a ship's cabin. The Unitarians persuaded the Copley Plaza to give us a larger room for a
half-hour, and off we went down long Kafkaesque corri-

dors to find it. I sat at a desk monitored by a woman who was not the recording angel but a martinet. She stopped me at each phrase or nearly because of a car horn or because I had stumbled myself, and when I thought I had done it perfectly, asked me to do it all over again! At that point the old donkey in me balked.

By then I was in no state to give a speech, but I did have a short nap, a bath, had fruit salad and cheese sent up, and gradually calmed down. No one can imagine how hard the last half-hour before a performance can be. Hotel rooms devour one's identity, and to hold still and stay oneself takes stamina.

But at seven-forty-five when at last I walked out onstage at the public library and was greeted, even before the introduction, by prolonged, happy, welcoming applause, all was well. The room was packed. Lots of people sat on the floor of the stage. I really only enjoy reading poems because analyzing things always seems so dry by comparison. The poems "happen" and that is another universe of discourse entirely. After the speech—I did sneak in four poems at the end—we all trooped over to the Harvard Café and Bookstore. It was unseasonably warm, and I was in a sweat the whole two hours of concentrated book signing under a low ceiling. But the atmosphere was so cordial and festive—even though the people with books had to stand for ages to reach me—that I enjoyed it more than usually. When I got back to the hotel after eleven, I was too excited and tired to sleep.

Monday, October 4th

IT IS a great piece of luck that the weather is so beautiful while Doris is here, and we have had two lovely days so far. On Saturday Heidi invited us to Barnacle Billy's in Perkins Cove for lunch. We sat outdoors in a delicious, cool air, with warm sun on our backs, and the whole atmosphere was happy and relaxed. I sank into the unhurried sense of arrival, of taking time, and drank in the familiar scene, of boats at anchor in the little harbor, people waiting to go out in the *Finestkind.* Heidi and I reminisced about our childhood summers in Ogunquit. (We must have been there at the same time in the twenties and would have loved being tomboys together had we met then.) After our lobster rolls, we sallied out to walk the Marginal Way and sit down frequently on a bench to watch a race of catamarans. Those sails banded in brilliant colors, red, green-blue, orange, against the dark-blue ocean looked like a Monet painting, and we might have been on the French coast. All seaside places have something of the same atmosphere, after all. Doris must have been comparing it in her mind to the spectacular California coast. This is a rather tame and civilized scene, but that is its charm, and it is always breathtaking when one emerges around a bend and there across the way is the immense stretch of white beach, five miles of it, that goes from Ogunquit to Wells. The rugosa roses are gone now.

I associate that walk with waves of their scent and also bayberry leaves squeezed to spice the air. But the fascination of the waves, curling in foam around the rocks, advancing and retreating in an endless dance, which always reminds me of Frost's "I Could Give All to Time"—that is always there. It was a just-about-perfect outing.

Yesterday was good, too, for we took a picnic to the field that opens out on the walk through the woods here on the place and did what I have long wanted to do, walked right into the field and out of sight over a knoll, spread out the rug under a big white pine, and, leaning our backs against its immense trunk, listened for birds. All that came were two pine siskins, making their intimate murmur as they went to and from among the branches over our heads. I had hoped for a thrush, but of course noon is not a time for thrush-song. I had hoped for a ruffed grouse, too. But what we had—Tamas lying in a soft place among the grasses—was the ineffable silence, the feeling of being far away and long ago, lost in time.

Janice came for lobsters at six bearing the film *World of Light* to show Doris, and after supper we watched it together in the library by the fire. I enjoyed seeing it once more, and it was fun for Doris to see it, now she knows the place. But the aftereffect was bad. I had an awful fit of weeping because the person it makes so vivid, the essence of what my life is all about, made me wildly hungry and desperate, for I have not been able to be that person all summer. And shall I ever again?

"The world is too much with us" these days.

Bramble did not come in last night and I am anxious about her. It is bird season and guns are about, the hateful murderous shots breaking the silence and arousing atavistic fear in me, fear and rage. I was so afraid the pheasant had been shot, but this morning I heard his squawk. And maybe that is a good augury and Bramble will come home.

Thursday, October 7th

I HEARD day before yesterday that Raymond, faithful Raymond, who gardens, takes the rubbish, and in general keeps things going here, is in the hospital, and I wonder whether he will ever be able to come back. I'm going to see him this morning while Doris packs and gets ready to leave. Two weeks of garbage and rubbish have piled up in the cellar. The fall gardening—cutting back the terrace gardens, hilling the roses, pulling up the annuals, putting salt hay on all the perennial beds—has to be done. There are three hundred bulbs to put in and I feel rather frightened. Some of it can wait till November when I get back from Vancouver. But what I have called a roller coaster all summer has now turned into a fast slide downhill. On the whole I am pretty resilient, but my head feels heavy and blurred I am so tired.

However, the last days have been splendid. Yesterday we went to Center Sandwich for a picnic by the lake with Huldah. The leaves are at their peak over there, and lit up by sunlight against a blue sky, they were beautiful. Autumn light on the white clapboard of the little houses along the way, often with a scarlet maple in front, always dazzles my eyes and heart, and I was happy to have such sights to give Doris on her first visit to New England at this season. She took me out to dinner at Spice of Life around the corner, so I did not have to cook and that was a help.

On Tuesday I took Doris to see Anne and Barbara in North Parsonsfield. As always, the serenity and beauty they have created in the old farm and all around it made it feel like paradise. But in bed that night I thought a lot about the *incredibly* hard work that has gone into making this heaven on earth and goes on every day. When guests come, the wood chopping is not done and the innumerable chores have been gotten out of the way. Anne has been putting in brick walls behind the two wood stoves and, really awful work, insulating under the peaked roof. For this she has to wear a mask. I came home with a little pouch of fresh dill, a little bottle of nasturtium vinegar (one of Anne's new inventions), and leeks from Barbara's vegetable garden. They were delicious with the halibut we had for supper. And Doris bought one of Barbara's small soapstone sculptures of a fawn.

Friday, October 8th

A DISMAL RAIN, but it is fitting perhaps, as I am feeling emptied out and gloomy, filled with dismay at my ups and downs these past days with Doris. She is a woman of great courage who entered a training program for women over fifty at the Bank of America a year ago and has been working there since she graduated. This is to help put her two still-in-school children through college and also help with care for her ninety-seven-year-old mother who lives with the family in Berkeley. I have watched Doris fight to keep alive since I first met her and stayed with her when I was teaching at Thomas Starr King School for the Ministry in Berkeley one summer. She has become an ardent bird watcher and goes out early on Saturday mornings, sometimes on all-day expeditions. When you work as hard as she does all week, what zest for life that takes! She is a great appreciator, went off with Tamas each morning, while I worked, and explored the neighborhood, was very sensitive about life here, said she loved the homey untidiness of the kitchen, and helped in every way possible.

But what has made this summer so difficult is moving very fast from one person's needs to another's with no time in between to recover my *self.*

It was wonderful last night to lie down with Tamas in the empty house, able to fall asleep listening to the wind, and no other sound, no creak on the stairs, no silence that might mean human distress nearby. I slept for two hours. When I got up I made tea and thought I was too tired even to freshen up the flowers, but I knew rain was on the way and finally did go out, so today at least the house resumes its peace and beauty. It would have been too sad to go down this morning to fading bunches all over the place.

It was an effort yesterday to go and see Raymond in the hospital. But he did cheer me up. He looked very well and handsome in an elegant robe and had a twinkle in his eye as he recounted, in answer to my query, what he had had for breakfast. To wit, sections of grapefruit, forty percent bran cereal, a waffle with maple syrup, a muffin, and cocoa! Anyone who could consume all that for breakfast must be getting well. And he said he would be home today and could come with a neighbor and tell him what to do and supervise the operation. Since there is a mountain of rubbish downstairs that was great news.

Mary-Leigh and Beverly are away on the QE2 on a

cruise. It is odd how lonely it feels when they are not here, though we meet so rarely. But when they are not here their house looks terribly closed up and I feel marooned.

Monday, October 11th

I AM BEGINNING to revive. Two days ago I felt that something essential had been taken from me in this summer without solitude and that I would never get it back. Primitive people, we are told, do not want to be photographed because they believe the machine will steal their soul. That is how I have felt, overexposed. I felt so tight and uncomfortable, so tensed up that I could not cry or feel anything except the kind of fatigue that will not permit rest, the kind that hangs there like a miasma. But three days alone have worked magic. Once more I realize acutely that solitude is my element, and the reason is that extreme awareness of other people (all naturally solitary people must feel this) precludes awareness of one's self, so after a while the self no longer knows that it exists. It is also, of course, that I am fully myself perhaps only when I am creating something. I don't know how I have managed to keep at this journal, a minor kind of creation, but that I have done, and today I have shoved aside the pile of letters, put them out of sight, after writing twenty-five yesterday and the day before and having to face once more that I can never come to the end, however hard I try. I must get back to my own life whether everyone gets an answer or not!

Yesterday was a great wallow of weather, a wonderful mass of dark clouds over a tumbled, rough ocean, with towers of spray flashing up at the end of the field, high wind, an exhilarating sense of autumn. And suddenly the leaves are at their peak here, and at every turn scarlet and orange and saffron light up the road. In spite of an hour's time given to a woman from San Francisco, I got out into the garden at four and sat down in the mud below an old apple tree to put in twenty-five daffodils. It meant tearing out various creeping bushlike weeds with long horizontal roots to make room. I enjoyed the tussle, the roar of ocean in the distance, the sound of wind rushing through above my head. Tamas lay in the tall grass, his ears pricked, thinking his own thoughts. What does he see, I wonder? Or is he chiefly smelling? His nose, round, black, shiny button, is almost never still. It quivers, alive to every passing scent on the air.

Tuesday, October 12th

THE FIRST FROST last night. When I went to bed the crescent moon was high overhead and the air was still. It felt like frost then, so I was not surprised to see a silver net over the lawn this morning. It means the end of garden flowers to pick, a sharp sense of loss, though I am prepared in my mind and can now cut down some flowering plants to see where there is space for bulbs. There is a glittering ocean of great buried swells so that from here it does not look rough as it did yesterday, but now and then I see a fountain of spray rise over the field. Those swells conceal turbulence, brought in from far away in the deeps of the ocean.

I felt anything but jubilant when I took Tamas and Bramble through the woods, lit up now by flaming leaves. We met two beagles, a bad moment as I was afraid they would chase Bramble, and Tamas becomes a raging dragon at the sight of another dog, his tail held high, his barks ominous. Luckily, the beagles turned tail, and after a while Bramble reappeared and all was calm once more as we ambled home.

I enjoyed the day without mail, lunch with Heidi like old times after these checkered weeks, but when I lay down with Tamas for a rest, I could not let go at all.

At five I had a last glimpse of Doris who came with her husband for a drink and to tell me of their adventures and brought a little orange tree for the plant window, which Doris must have noted was in sore need of bolstering up. It looks very healthy and promising among the leggy geraniums and the streptocarpuses, which have almost done with flowering for this year.

I told them that it had been hard to refuse their kind invitation to dinner, but that I have found that a dinner engagement takes the edge off the next morning's work. It seems absurd, but the fact is that good writing takes a certain kind of psychic energy. To summon it each morning, I must wake unblurred, rested, "one-pointed," as the Japanese say.

Doris and Jerry have managed to see so many things I have never seen that I felt dismayed by my ignorance. But it was fun to hear all about it and share in their discoveries for an hour—the Hamilton estate, for instance. Someday I must see that great house by the river near South Berwick and the gardens there.

But today I must puzzle out where I can find room to plant tulips and put some in. Such brilliant light outdoors. I can hardly wait to get into my jeans.

Sunday, October 17th

THE LEAVES are falling fast and it is suddenly much colder. The whole landscape is changing now every day. When I walk Tamas I note that the bracken, which had been a beautiful gold, lighting up the forest floor, is withering to dark brown. Overhead there is still brilliance, especially as the beeches are just turning that wonderful Chinese yellow, and some maples make splashes of crimson still against the blue sky. The other day I saw a ruffed grouse as I drove in with the mail. The pheasant has vanished, although I did hear that familiar squawk once last week. The egrets have left the salt marsh for the South. And I am on my knees every afternoon clearing out the borders and planting bulbs. On Saturday Nancy Hartley came and we did a huge job of tearing out annuals. I hope we can finish that up this afternoon. I am pushed to the limit of my strength now to get it all done before I leave for Seattle a week from today.

Houseflies buzz around. Where do they come from? And I am buzzing around too in the welter of mail and general disorder up here in my study. It will be a relief to get away from it for a while.

But the time is coming when I must manage to have my real life here and at whatever price in the not-done and the not-given.

Monday, October 18th

All Souls

It is God's honour on my head
That drives me forth to walk alone,
Among the lighter-footed dead,
Upon this hollow path of stone.

It is God's honour on my hands
That makes them cold in such a wise
That I must clench them; his commands
Thus mercifully stigmatize.

It is God's honour on my feet
That sets a nail in either shoe
To spur them down the common street;
This is the thing I always knew.

Elinor Wylie

Tuesday, October 19th

THAT POEM has been haunting me lately, as All Souls' Day approaches, and I finally felt compelled to copy it out. It has been in my mind also because I have been back in the country of pain since Sunday. It made me realize that pain forces me to the frontiers of being, brings me back by force to the inner world. Alive at the quick, forced to cope with my faults, and to respond to attack. Torrents of tears, lack of sleep, all back again.

Now it is seven, the sun just rising over a pellucid amber and pale-blue ocean, the field dark still and covered with frost. After the storm I feel composed, I mean the storm inside me, for we have had fair windy days lately. And the poor lobstermen have had a chance to retrieve their lobster pots from the rocky beaches here since the storm last week. They drive up in trucks every day.

On Sunday I got up very early, before five, and did a big stint on letters before a friend came to walk Tamas with me and tell me that she and her husband have decided to separate. This is the third friend of about her age, thirty-five, who is divorcing this summer or within this year. All made great efforts to keep the marriage in spite of radical misunderstandings and long suffering. All three have had to go trough the searing anger, the gradual letting go, and the moving toward autonomy and a new life. For Donna, it is easiest because she is in love.

After she left I rushed down to get the *Times* and, all unprepared (Fran Rosencrantz had promised to let me know ahead), came upon Sheila Ballantyne's review of *Anger*. It was a thoughtful and generous review, although she considers *Anger* a failure. I am grateful. But I had to face that by talking openly about the problems of a novel in the journal—in this case, *Recovering*— I expose myself. Ballantyne collates some statements in the journal with the novel to buttress her argument that I failed to meet my own challenge in writing it. Well, I shall leave it at that here.

Wednesday, October 20th

I FELT YESTERDAY as though I had held the whole of autumn in a few hours as I drove the familiar roads to Peterborough to see Laurie Armstrong. The leaves have not fallen; I drove along watching sunlight splashed through towering scarlet maples, through groves of saffron beeches, and sometimes a single tree as though on fire against dark pines. Once there was an exquisite elm standing alone in a field and I realized how many have been lost, for a healthy elm is now a rarity in New England.

Unfortunately, I got on the car radio the tale of unbelievable sadism—brown pelicans have been found dead on a beach in California, dead because some fiend had sawed off the upper bill, so they starved to death. Fishermen resent them because they eat fish, just as the fishermen here have decimated the harbor seals for the same reason. But this wilful, sadistic cruelty made me feel quite sick, and it was hard to get it out of my mind even when I turned to FM and got a lovely violin concerto. How does one deal with this kind of cruelty in human beings? How is man ever going to change? And what will change him? If there is a merciful God he must be in a towering rage. And because human beings are so unregenerate and beastly I begin to understand Huldah's wish to help only animals. They seem so innocent by comparison.

As I came over the mountain from Milford, I saw Mount Monadnock standing there, lavender against the pale-blue sky; such a solid comfort it was I had a wave of nostalgia for New Hampshire and my fifteen years of communion with the grand old mountain. Nothing will ever replace Nelson in my life, even the spacious world where I now watch sunrise over the ocean. Deep down inside me Nelson is home, and I am glad I shall be buried in the cemetery there under the maples, and next to Quig.

Thinking of death I wonder whether I shall ever see my mother again. I do not really believe in an afterlife, or at least not in a personal one, which would bring the beloved dead into its orbit. But one wonders.

Then I was in Peterborough and went, as I always do, to Woodman, the florist, to choose flowers for Laurie and always at this season to buy two cyclamens for the plant window here. It was fun to pick out seven sprays of different orange, bronze, yellow, and white chrysanthemums, to hold in my hands the colors I had been dazzled by all morning from the car window. I forgot to mention how beautiful the brooks were, the clear water, sometimes reflecting a group of flaming trees, sometimes rushing along over the rocks. I felt filled up with autumn color and autumn joy.

And there was Laurie, looking beautiful, so merry and warm as always, her light voice with so much tenderness in it welcoming me. No one says my name in quite the way she does. She says "May," and I feel blest. We had so much to talk about—I have not seen her for months—that the three hours flew away, and I could not believe at two that it was time for me to go. Chris was due here to put on the storm windows, and I had to get back to talk with him about putting up a wire that may make the bird feeders squirrel-proof this winter. So I tore myself away, and there Laurie was as she always is, standing in the doorway, waving as I made the turn around the driveway. A lovely healing day.

Thursday, October 21st

I GOT UP BEFORE FIVE, hoping to get a sense of time at my desk, but I did not make it up here till half past seven, after all. Now I have written two difficult letters, one to a friend who lost her father in the spring and has spent the summer recovering—living with nature and poetry. I have been thinking about her so much and wondering how she was, with, as she says, "a piece of my identity pulled away." The other letter was to a young woman confined to a wheelchair who, with the kindest intentions, has been trying for a year or so to make me into a militant lesbian, sending books, referring me to Audre Lorde and Adrienne Rich, as though I had never heard of them, and in general treating me like a very old party in need of help. I find this rather hard to bear. I know that she is brave and handling her terribly restricted life with great courage and reaching out wherever she can to life. But I'm afraid I am not a viable subject for her to take on and redeem. It has its humorous side. The phrase she uses about me is "a foremother," a foremother who has some- how not done what was expected of her and thus must be brought into the fold, chastised, and forgiven. I do not see myself in this light. It has been quite a burden to wrap up and send back books I already have and to have an un-

wanted burden of gratitude imposed on me, not her gratitude to me (she does not talk very much about anything
I have written) but my gratitude toward her. Unfortunately the result has been that I feel badgered and she has
become a source of irritation. I believe that our chief
responsibility is not to change others for the better but to
change ourselves.

The sky over the ocean was almost black early this
morning and I liked it. It suited my mood, which is not
rosy at the moment. Partly it is sheer fatigue. I have also
been wondering why it is that Americans must insist on
"equality," not on the political scene where it is valid but
in private relations where it is often not. I cannot imagine
thinking even, let alone saying to Basil de Selincourt, Jean
Dominique, Virginia Woolf, Elizabeth Bowen, or my
teachers Anne Thorp and Katharine Taylor when I was a
child, "We are equals"! I was too aware of all I had to learn
from and through them, and I gladly gave them love and
homage. If there are to be no distinctions between people, if achievement or simply a great wholeness of being,
as in the case of Basil, is meaningless, since "we are all
equal," then what is life all about? And for me, at least,
one of the most rewarding emotions is that of feeling in
the presence of someone whom I admire wholeheartedly
and from whom I know I can learn. It is a very pure
emotion. There is no envy in it, nothing but aspiration.
The reward is in the feeling itself.

On the other hand, although I am in many ways a
conflicted and difficult person, I have achieved something
and am worthy of being esteemed. False humility is just
as bad as arrogance—and what writer could ever be arro-
gant? There is just too much anxiety, too much self-doubt,
too great a sense of inadequacy for that to be possible.

And for that reason it is a little too easy for someone

who has not spent years and years trying to write well and has not achieved even a very little to say "We are equals, you and I," to a writer who has achieved something in a long life, and for someone of forty to say to someone of seventy "We are exactly alike" is ludicrous and an underestimation of what life itself does to force us to maturity.

Friday, November 5th

HOME AGAIN in a torrential rain, the whole walk plastered with the crimson leaves of the maple, all fallen, which gave an air of desolation to the house as though it had been abandoned. November indeed! It is always the saddest month here. But Edythe met the plane and we had dinner on the way, and in some ways it was just as well that my luggage had not turned up as we didn't have to lug it in. So instead of unpacking I lay down on the chaise longue with Tamas beside me and read through tons of mail. Then I fell into bed enclosed in the dear animals' warmth. They were very glad to have me there.

Today, dismal. It is half-past four, and I am still waiting for the luggage and look out on the sad brown field with tumultuous gray sea behind it, a sea that has a black line at the horizon and shoots up fountains of foam. This year I have been unusually aware of the entry into these changing days, especially All Souls, when the dead seem close to the living. In Victoria, before the film about me was shown, I read a series of poems on that theme, thinking so much of my mother. (The luggage came and I have just dashed down to get it at the florist, where I asked that it be dropped off.)

I had planned this trip months ago as a present to myself, a holiday, a glimpse of a part of the continent I have never seen, and a possible renewal—all this it proved to be—and I am very glad I went. But now I am home again, tugged forward into all sorts of decisions about readings ahead and human lives to be responded to. As always when I have been away, it is hard to sum up all that happened in the days between October 24th when I left here with the leaves still in full glory and November 4th when I got back to find them all fallen and the red berries on the cherries turned a translucent yellow. In that time I spent three days in Seattle with Kay Muller Stimson, three days in Victoria mostly to see Elizabeth Bristowe with whom I have been corresponding, and three days in Vancouver. In those nine days—only nine in all!—I read poems four times, the film was shown twice, and there were six book signings in bookstores. So the schedule was tight. But it was a tremendously rich time, quite apart from work and performance.

One of the great joys was getting to know Kay Muller again—we had hardly met since I directed her in a play at the Concord Academy more than forty years ago! And there she was at the airport, tall, handsome, with magnificent white hair that blows in a beautiful way in the wind and those clear blue eyes I remembered.

But before we landed I had already had a shock of joy, seeing Mount Rainier from the plane, standing high over the clouds in godlike splendor, all white. I did not see it again. But I fell in love with Seattle, magic city on its seven hills, lakes and harbors and ocean on every side. When we arrived at Kay's house high up on one of the hills, it was dusk and the city sparkled below us, through a screen of golden leaves, as there are big trees all around the property. Why is it that light through leaves is so magical? Another joy for me was to be welcomed by a *patapouf*, a shaggy dog, eminently huggable, and a very talkative cat that sat on top of the refrigerator like an owl while Kay and I ate grapes and cheese and began to discover each other and where we are after all those years.

Sunday, November 7th

THERE, two days ago I stopped writing the journal because I am writing poems again after months of silence, and for me writing poems means a muse and a muse means intense preoccupation, so it is hard to go back in time and record what happened years ago in inner time where a year sometimes is telescoped into an hour or an hour may be telescoped into an eternity. One of the problems of a journal written on the pulse is also that it must be concerned with the immediate, looking back only when the past suddenly becomes relevant in the light of the present moment. Not so with a travel journal.

The only way I can deal here with my journey to the northwest is to deal in essences, not try to describe the days in sequence. What stays with me is the staggering dimension of the landscapes of water and mountains—the Olympics, Mount Baker, the Cascades—so that when I looked out at the ocean here yesterday morning I expected to see a mountain range at the horizon! That and the great trees, the cedars and oaks, the firs, painted by Emily Carr, so I often felt myself seeing through her eyes —and the reason I knew her was that Liz Hazlette sent me her remarkable journal years ago when we first began to correspond.

In Victoria I was to meet two women who have been writing to me, both named Liz strangely enough. Young Liz Hazlette is a painter who uses batik in a most unusual way, not to make geometric designs but to create actual landscapes, which the use of the melted wax makes translucent. Middle-aged Liz Bristowe is a gerontologist with a big job that takes her all over the province. I had wanted to meet her for a long time, and she helped me get to Victoria by arranging book signings, a showing of the film, and a reading at the university. One takes so much for granted! When I got there I realized what a lot of time and energy managing Sarton must have required, but it was done with such grace that I did not quite take in all that had been involved until I was in the plane for Boston, thinking it all over.

Essences— By chance or with the guardian angel's help I had with me at various times three remarkable books of poems by three women. Constance Hunting's *Dream Cities* arrived the day before I left and I tucked it into my suitcase. Sheila Moon's *Whatever Time We Live* went with me also. Sheila Moon is a Jungian analyst in San Francisco. Once we had a marvelous walk together in the redwoods. In Victoria P. K. Page left for me her new book, *Evening Dance of the Grey Flies,* and I read it with a shock of admiration like laughter. It was exciting to be roused by three such haunting poets, and their poems ran like scarlet threads through all the days. Another thread was the Auden biography by Humphrey Carpenter, an exemplary biography, that manages to deal with all the

facts of a life and yet never fails to remind a reader of the
essence, Auden as poet. A holiday means time to read, no
letters, no typewriter. I reveled in it.

I want to keep here a sampler of the poems. They had
something to do, no doubt, with my writing poems again,
now I am home.

Burrs

The dog sheds burrs on my floor.
I gather them up. There is
a moral here: you can go out a door
through which you didn't enter.
From a burr's view, this twist
could mean a bright center
of next year's weeds, or death.
My dog cares only that burrs go.
For me, they're irritants. My breath
gets short at all disordered things!
This should not be. I know
it's peril! Whenever you cling
to a just order its twin revives
and chaos is throned. These burrs,
like my bunglings, if kept alive
could blossom in some other May
to star a field. It might occur,
Who knows. Dog, let us pray.

Sheila Moon

For Friends, On the Birth of Rebecca

Make all you can of beauty quickly.
The rush in the blood, the heightening
blush to the cheek of the lovely—
take measure of these, and advantage:
look at topography and time in this new face,

remark indent of valley, sweet dusky swell
of hills above milky lakes
(morning mist). Do not dwell
on vacancies of this landscape
but imagine a music for reeds, music toneless and
lunar
before it fades, recall the radiance of
other geographies in other spheres.
If you must turn away at last,
gaze deep here first at least.

Constance Hunting

Evening Dance of the Grey Flies

for Chris

Grey flies, fragile, slender-winged and slender-legged
scribble a pencilled script across the sunlit lawn,

As grass and leaves grow black
The grey flies gleam—
their cursive flight a gold calligraphy.

It is the light that gilds their frail
bodies, makes them fat and bright as bees—
reflected on refracted light—

as once my fist
burnished by some beam I could not see
glowed like gold mail and conjured Charlemagne

as once your face
grey with illness and with age—
a silverpoint against the pillow's white—

shone suddenly like the sun
before you died.

P. K. Page

So the essences were water, islands, mountains, a tremendous number of people, poetry, and, from the ferry from Victoria to Vancouver, a young eagle floating down among gulls, flashing his white. That was splendor.

Among the people, twice I met women who had just lost their jobs and sensed the animal fear, the smell of panic. They haunt me. Strong images of what unemployment means. In Vancouver, the historian Margaret Prang took me up to the twelfth floor of the university to show me the astounding view from her office. "A perfect study," I heard myself murmur, as I stood and looked out across the bay to the dark, high ranges with farther snow-covered ranges behind them and a brilliant blue sky reflected on the water. And she herself has something of the largeness of that view, a woman like my father in that she appears to be uncorrupted by the academic world, a nature full of light. Late in life she adopted two problem children in their teens and she told me a little about that as we walked over to take the elevator up.

In Vancouver also there was a marvelous dinner at a Chinese restaurant with ten women, all doing significant work. One works in a clinic dealing with incest and child abuse; one has a sheep farm on one of the islands; one, a former producer of plays; the two owners of Ariel, the bookstore where I had signed books that afternoon and had the joy of seeing Audrey Thomas again. Some years ago we had done a reading together in Toronto.

And in Victoria there was a long drive in the rain, with plumes of mist winding among the great trees like dragons in a Chinese painting, to a luncheon Liz Bristowe arranged, where I met eleven women, again all outside the academic world, thank goodness, all feminists and rich in a variety of experiences.

"yesterday I saw Raymond on his towering machine"

Monday, November 8th

IT HAS TAKEN me three days to get back to solitude and peace of mind, but this morning as orange light flooded my bedroom at six I felt happy. The routines have been established; I am no longer unpacking, washing clothes, getting in food, writing business letters; I have begun to live here again. The proof of that was that yesterday at last I rearranged the flowers, found some laurel to give a little body to the chrysanthemums in two jars, and started some paper-whites. The ones I set out six weeks ago are in full flower, and when I go by I get a whiff of that sharp spring scent. The wire Chris put up for me to hold the bird feeders is working and so far is not attacked by squirrels, so I have put another smaller feeder up this morning. Nancy Hartley came for oyster stew yesterday at lunch-time and will help me rake the tons of maple leaves all over the lawn. And yesterday I saw Raymond on his tow-ering machine starting to cut the areas of the field Mary-Leigh cannot do with hers because of rocks.

This morning I am fully aware that the presence of a muse literally opens the inner space, just as November light opens the outer space, and when the trees are leaf-less I am given a wide hemisphere of ocean. The clutter falls away. The nonessential things cease to trouble the mind. A miracle indeed.

On the other hand, for the first time since my birthday

the fact that I am seventy is with me as a warning. When I saw Dr. Chayka to check on my heart the other day and he said all was well, he asked me at what age my parents had died—each before seventy-five. And later in our talk he mentioned that as far as he could see longevity has a lot to do with heredity. I took that in when I got home. But the discipline this time must be, with this muse, to make every effort to live in eternity's light, not in time. If I begin to think of how little time we shall have at best, panic sets in, pressures build up. To live in eternity means to live in the moment, the moment unalloyed—to allow feeling to the limit of what can be felt, to hold nothing back, and at the same time to ask nothing and hope for nothing more than the amazing gift of poems. A love affair at this point is not in the cards, but poetry is here, and that is all that matters.

Today the deer hunting begins. I dread the heavy explosions of the guns at dawn and at dusk (there were none this morning, thank goodness) and must walk Tamas mostly down to the ocean and not in the woods for the next two weeks. That is the bad thing here in November. The good thing is the opening out of space, the austere yet brilliant scene, so much pure light that seems to say, "Clarify, clarify."

Wednesday, November 10th

WHEN I GOT HOME from the Northwest and saw the whole lawn covered with red maple leaves, I wondered how I could ever manage. Raymond is not well, although he has managed these last days to do his usual superb job of bringing order to the chaotic parts of the field. It has its serene form again now, a broad sweep down to the ocean, and rests the eye.

I decided three days ago that I must make a start on raking and found I could do quite a lot in an hour and a half. I took it as a lesson that, when a task seems impossible, the thing to do is to make a start at once, not wait for panic and fear of the effort to take over. And how fine it is to have some clear green lawn now around the big maple! Tomorrow Nancy Hartley will come and help me, and Janice says she will help this weekend. Raking leaves is my least favorite gardening job. I stuff the piles into big garbage bags and carry them behind the house and dump them over a wall steep enough so they will not blow back.

I am bogged down again in the mail. Yesterday or the day before I had news of a murder, a wedding, a poet friend in serious depression, a very old friend in a nursing home reaching out—and a thrilling report from Georgia on what she means to do with her thesis on *Lear*. It is exciting to feel her bringing it all into focus, after the months and years of minute analysis and comparing of the texts.

The sun rises these days in an orange clear sky, and this morning, lying in bed with my breakfast, I could see the ocean for the first time in months, for the leaves of an oak have fallen. Having a muse again has made me realize how badly I behaved this summer from sheer frustration. I felt pulled down, I suppose, buried under the tons of letters and all the people who came so eagerly to see me and were sometimes badly treated or not well enough treated. I feel ashamed of myself. Compared to many lives, especially to those with nine-to-five jobs, mine must seem like a perpetual holiday. And in some ways it is. The great luxury, of course, is to be able to sit for perhaps half an hour and do nothing, as I did yesterday afternoon when I came in from raking. The light becomes solemn at dusk, and I sat there watching it fade, and the coming and going of wings in the air at the bird feeders. It was peaceful.

Janice came for roast lamb and after what felt like years to each of us, we could talk about everything and renew the communion we share. It is a rare friendship, for there has been no tension in it, and we are able to give each other, in a very easy way, all that has been happening to us, inwardly and outwardly. It was so good to have someone to share some of my experiences in the Northwest.

Saturday, November 13th

I WOKE at half past four and lay in bed with Tamas fast asleep beside me and Bramble purring very loudly on the other side, listening to a gentle rain and feeling happy. I planned what I might do today, relieved that raking is out of the question. Nancy and I did a heroic job on Thursday, so that only some big piles on the driveway remain. The lawn is all green and smooth again. How satisfactory it is when I can get something done, finished, out of the way!

I am happy because there is someone to focus the world for me again and to hold time still. Everything falls into place; I have even managed to write a lot of letters since I got back nine days ago, as though floated, instead of struggling against intolerable pressures. How mysterious it is! And what is it that suddenly opens the door into poetry? A face, a voice, two hours of rich communion and the world has changed. I am back in my real life again.

So it all seems good. I can do what has to be done. I am alive. And seventy feels very young—but that is not new. What is new perhaps is to accept that this time it will not be a love affair. Circumstances preclude that consummation, and I sense that there the guardian angel has been wise. For I really do not feel up to either the excitement or the inevitable rousing of the daimon that, in my case at least, a sexual encounter brings out of its lair. So there are some changes at seventy that mean old age. I don't mind. All I ask is to write poems, and that I am doing these days, trying a new form, a series of prose poems, called "Letters from Maine."

Yesterday I drove down to Wellesley to see Eleanor Blair for the first time in ages, and how delightful it was to find her with a kitten! I saw the tiny black and white face in the window as I rang the bell, and for a while, all we did was watch the enchanting creature rush about pushing a white paper bag that had contained the sherry I brought, in the immemorial way of kittens. This one has double front paws and they are white, an added charm. Since Eleanor's dear old cat died last spring, I know how empty the house must have felt and also how she hesitated to have another cat because her sight is very poor now. Everyone who lives alone of whatever age should have a cat or a kitten. This one came from an endowed place with the beautiful name, Sheltering Home for Cats. Kittens are brought here so homes can be found for them; old cats are taken care of until they die or should be put to sleep. And there Eleanor found hers, a very good kitten who already uses her box. At the shelter there is a beautiful Himalayan who has come back from three homes because she apparently cannot be trained. I longed to have a try, but Bramble would be furious, so I must resist. Another problem cat at the shelter is called Bad Cat because he is so ferocious.

Altogether it was a very good day and I enjoyed the drive, although the sky was overcast with messy gray clouds without form, and the colors now are very somber. Only the willows stand out, golden, in the wintry landscape. Then, when I got home, after having a cup of tea with Edythe before she left, I read the mail, and in it were two remarkable letters about *Anger* from friends in New Haven and Dallas. The book, whatever its faults—and I begin to see them now—is reaching people. Writing it I learned a lot about myself and about Ned, one of the two chief characters, and it looks as though the readers, too, are being lead to self-realization.

Monday, November 15th

YESTERDAY I didn't see a soul all day. On such days time opens out, and after writing fourteen letters in the morning, I went out after my nap and just about finished the raking. I enjoyed stuffing piles and piles of leaves into a giant garbage bag and dumping them over the wall, enjoyed for the first time what had seemed an impossible task. The light goes so fast these days! By four the last rays of the sun are striking the end of the field, suddenly illuminating the Firths' house on the left. The November evenings are somber, but I love the smells, damp leaves and salt from the ocean.

Today it is raining, so the deer will get a break. I suppose it may be partly the fear of those deafening shots across the stillness of the woods that makes me have to think once more about violence, the psychological hair shirt we all wear these days when murder has become commonplace, and no one goes out in a city without wondering whether he or she will be mugged or leaves a house in the suburbs without wondering whether it will be vandalized. Writing these words down, it is hard to believe they do not exaggerate, but I know they do not. The rich are not immune, and perhaps that is a good thing, for we are all in this together. And the violence on the streets is matched by the violence we must deal with inside ourselves.

Last night I watched the start of a new TV drama called *The Blue and the Gray*. A free black man who had sheltered two runaway slaves was dragged out and hanged. Every black in the United States knows that his ancestors were slaves. I went to bed in misery thinking about this, the old, never-healed wounds, and about the Holocaust (which is never far from my mind). I was brought up believing that man was perfectible. I remember the tears in my father's eyes when the Senate voted down our joining the League of Nations, remember my mother flaming up when the first news of the camps in Germany came through and saying, "We must have martyrs." We know now that there were martyrs, but who has come to terms inside himself with the Holocaust? Most of us can no longer throw ourselves on God's mercy. We have to deal with the monster in man, the hatred, the anger, the latent sadism (think of the numbers of abused children!) without divine help. And compared to us, animals become almost saintly—few kill except for food. They do not indulge in mass murder.

How can we deal with it, the violence in ourselves? Somehow or other we have to find a way, religious or not, of sanctifying life again, for only if we can do that will it be possible to face the worst, and still bear with it in ourselves and heal it in ourselves, because we have again become part of the mystery, given up some primary need to terrorize and subdue, and quite literally fallen on our knees.

As I think of the violence in myself, what I see is a low threshold of frustration. My worst angers seize me—and it is over like a seizure—for one of two reasons. The first is being unjustly criticized or attacked. This rouses the devil at once. The other is being prevented from "leading my real life" as happened this summer when I had hardly a day of solitude here and had to respond to too many strangers.

It is because I now have a muse again and am writing poems that I am lifted above all this and can look at it and come to understand it. Forgiveness cannot be achieved without understanding, and understanding means painful honesty first of all, and then the ability to detach oneself and look hard, without self-pity, at the cause for violent behavior. This is never easy to do, and most people succeed in evading it, as many criminals do by some kind of self-justification or self-delusion. Self-protectiveness on a national scale can become very dangerous indeed, as we saw in the Israeli attitude to the horrible murders committed by Christians upon Palestinians in a refugee camp under the Israeli occupation. And it is there, of course, in the whole argument about a nuclear freeze. We cannot really preserve ourselves by attacking others, in the private world of the individual or in the world of nations. Quite the contrary.

Thursday, November 18th

UNDER THE HEADING "Three Lives," the Tuesday *New York Times* published this remarkable editorial:

To study the plight of Tina, Skandy and Caroline—three residents of the Central Park Zoo now facing eviction—is to recognize once again the parallels in human and animal lives. Tina, Skandy and Caroline need new homes because their old one, soon to be demolished, will have no place for them. But, neither, so far, have any other zoos. They are undesirable tenants, and for pitiful reasons.

Tina, who is an elephant, has a rotten temper. Dominated for fourteen years, since childhood, by her late cage mate, bereft at the death of the trainer she loved, she is angry, distrustful, incapable of social interaction. Her past is marked by arm-crushing and foot-stomping incidents and an occasional charge, involving zoo personnel.

Skandy, who is a polar bear, has a record. When a man broke into his enclosure recently, Skandy killed him. He behaved, we are told, like any threatened polar bear, but the publicity was bad. Common sense dictates an alias—Rosebud maybe. Common sense also says that sooner or later the petals would drop and Skandy would stand revealed.

Saddest of all perhaps is Caroline, who is a gorilla. Caroline's undesirability lies not in what she did but in what she is. Caroline is a post-menopausal simian, and therefore of no interest to any zoo that likes the prospect of a bonus in the form of little simians.

So Tina, Skandy and Caroline wait for homes that tolerate the paranoid, the guilty and the over-the-hill. And to those who wonder why the problems of this tragic trio are so unnervingly sad, one can but offer a paraphrase of a line by Gerard Manley Hopkins. It is ourselves we mourn for.

For obvious reasons my heart aches for bad-tempered Tina.

I woke yesterday morning wondering what was about to happen that meant joy and then remembered that Susan Garrett was coming for supper. I haven't seen her for months, and now in a week, because George has received a permanent appointment at the University of Michigan, she will have left the hospital where she has been director for five years. We met so rarely that it is absurd to feel as bereft as I do when I imagine York without Susan, and of course she and George will be back in the summers to live in their old house on the river, her father's house and her grandfather's where I have sat now and then on the wide porch and watched the sunset and the river turn bright gold.

But Susan is a timeless friend and we begin again where we left off. I lit a fire in the library for the first time this autumn and we had a good long talk, our lives so different, our sense of life so much the same. It is clear that the hospital job, grueling in its incessant demands, and which Susan has carried with such wisdom and grace, has in some ways not been rewarding. It is bad to come home at the end of the day too tired to save a few hours for oneself, too tired to be nourished by music or reading or friends. As we talked about it I realized that this past

summer was something like that for me. But I saw last
night that it is a universal dilemma. If there is not enough
space in a life or within a job for the soul to breathe, then
there is something wrong. Janice is going through much
the same sense of frustration and exhaustion in her job as
assistant director of the health services in Portsmouth.

Susan told me that the one nourishment these days is
to read Eliot's *Four Quartets* early in the morning before
the day starts. And that led us to talk of Eliot and of
religion. She buries herself in the *Quartets* but is afraid of
the depression they bring on, and she assented when I
suggested that Eliot's is a negative view, because (I dare
to think) he was not a believer. Never is the joy of religion
expressed, never is there transcendence. I remember seeing *Murder in the Cathedral* when it was first produced
in London in a tiny theater. I left in a kind of black rage,
because I had been put through a wringer but there had
been no catharsis. The choruses especially left nothing but
sand in my mouth. But that is partly why Eliot had such
an influence in the twenties when people did not want to
hear good news, at least not good religious news. The
zeitgeist was violently against such a view as George Herbert's, but now we go back to him who never denied the
desert in himself but pierces us still with the humanness
of his faith and his intimate relation with his God, often
complaining but never arid for long. He was a believer,
and that is the huge difference.

I have just called Susan at the hospital to get her to
reread Herbert. Oh, what a rare friend is she with whom
I can share poetry!

It was a wonderful evening.

I am giving myself this morning for my own work. I
have three poems buzzing around, not a good thing, for
how to choose among them? But I must have a try.

Friday, November 19th

WHAT LUXURY these days to wake up and know there is an entire day ahead for work and silence! I come up here to a wild disorder of Advent calendars to pack for various children, piles and piles of stuff to answer, but it is rather like a gold mine, full of surprises when I actually sit down and think about it all. And now there is less immediate pressure, let rejoicing and love well up. Rejoicing that Alfredo, my Italian friend who has been translating some of my poems into Italian, is getting married; rejoicing that there is a little girl called Sarton to whom I can send an Advent calendar; rejoicing in a letter that said, "You have given faces and names to forces which control and frighten so many people . . . myself included . . . . Instead of writing about anger you have made anger live"; rejoicing that I did write a poem yesterday, and most of all rejoicing because the last issue of *This Time,* a report from H.O.M.E., which Karen Saum edits, is the best ever and once again makes me realize that that experience down East has been the most nourishing thing that has come into my life for a long time.

This issue is rich in what has been accomplished and irresistible in its plea for what still needs to be done. I rejoice that I have earned well this year and can at once send a check. And what will it help do? "We have begun construction on a house for a family of six in Franklin,

Maine. We are able to work on it only up to $5,000, at which point we have to stop . . . no more funds. We cannot get that family in before winter unless some miracle occurs by way of more donations." (What if all the violence in the world could be absorbed into people building houses?)

Another item in *This Time* describes what goes on in Hospitality House:

The phone rang. It was a sultry July day. "Our summer day!" someone joked. It was late Friday afternoon, and a three-day weekend lay ahead. Most everyone had found a reason to go home early.

"I think you had better take this one," Doris called up to me in my office. "On line one."

The call was from a social worker in a nearby town. He had in his office a woman hardly in control of herself. She was frightened and desperate. With her was a child, a little girl of four who had been sexually abused by a neighbor. The special horror of the situation lay in the fact that the man had abused the mother when she herself was a child. The social worker wanted Cathy Tracy, our outreach worker, to come for them to bring them to Hospitality House.

Cathy was on call to an elderly woman dying with cancer who had no phone. It was two hours before she could be reached. She went and brought them home with her.

This situation and others like it occur weekly, sometimes daily. Local social workers, town managers, sheriffs and police call H.O.M.E. to provide emergency shelter for those in need. Sometimes there are as many as four families living together in the Hospitality House recovering with Cathy's help and starting to create new lives.

She helps them find rentals they can afford, obtain

medical care and counseling, locate jobs, and secure
state aid to get them started again. They leave Hospitality House, where, usually, they arrive with nothing, with the minimum requirements to set up
housekeeping on their own: mattresses, blankets, a
few utensils to cook and eat with, soap and linen.

The cost to run the Dorothy Hance Hospitality
House is $13,500 a year.

What if violence were given work to do? What if people could find fruitful ways to use their potential? It is
being done at H.O.M.E. every day of the year.

A day of rejoicing.

Wednesday, December 1st

I HAVE BEEN SILENT for two weeks or nearly because
Thanksgiving and my annual trip to Nashville, to celebrate it with Huldah and her friends, has intervened. We
are having exceptionally warm, gray days, strange
weather that feels too abnormal to be quite comfortable,
and a little sad as all the color seems drained out, a brown
and gray world this morning, with just a faint streak of
yellowish light at the horizon. While I was away they had
a small snowfall, and Edythe said it was beautiful.

This year the day after Thanksgiving Huldah took me
for my first view of the Great Smokies, piling two friends
of hers, Elizabeth and Marian, her two collies, and food for
picnics into the big station wagon for a three-day jaunt.
Down south the grass is still green, but I cannot deny that

even in those lovely woods, rich in rhododendrons and
azaleas, with brooks racing over stones and making small
waterfalls, November is somber. And we had no luck with
the weather, which remained most of the time simply a
prolonged drizzle. We had our picnics in the car, and the
tempting trails marked "quiet walkways" had to be
passed by. But we did explore one between downpours,
and at once the difference between gliding past in a car
and walking seemed immense. Every small detail, a bed
of brilliant moss; a single black gum sprout of a tree still
in leaf, a marvelous rose color; the lovely serrated ferns;
the tumbled-down stone walls where a cabin once stood
—all came into focus. Of course it made me long to go
back some spring when the birds sing and the wild flowers
are out. How glorious those banks of rhododendrons
hanging over brooks and streams must be!

We did have one supreme experience at a place called
Cade's Cove where the road makes a long loop around
open green pasture, a peaceful amplitude of gentle mountains on every side, a secret place once inhabited, now
very silent. And suddenly we saw a young buck standing
there a few yards away, in the misty air, looking like
something in a dream. He stared at us for a long moment
and then made a single slow bound over the fence and
disappeared. Later on we came upon two does, eating
tranquilly at the edge of the road, undisturbed by the
car.

That is the memory I keep, that and the dragon tails
of mist lying among the mountains.

After all this wandering, there and before that in the
Northwest, I cannot describe how good it was to come
home to Bramble and Tamas and to know that soon I can
hole in here and get to work again. There is just one more
"sortie" and then I'll be "home safe." "Ally ally in free"

as we used to shout as children as darkness crept in.

Now Christmas is upon me, and my lair up here is piled with wrappings and Christmas cards and red wool and lists, the kind of disorder that I love for it can be cleared away in a trice, and meanwhile I think of all my friends and the great gathering of them in my mind at this season, from Kyoko in Japan to Eldy in Geneva to Alfredo in Italy and all the others strewn over the States. So many dear faces!

Sunday, December 5th

IT IS AN EXQUISITE early morning here today. Even before the sun rose, the sea out there was luminous in the dawn, and now beyond the dark field it is shining, pale blue, so serene, so beyond human grief or confusion that I suddenly had tears in my eyes as I looked out at it. It feels like a blessing after some days of struggling against an undertow of depression. And it has brought me back to this journal, which I had almost decided to lay aside until after Christmas. Now I see that the inner life must be kept going under all the clutter, so I have put Janet Baker singing Chausson's *Poème de l'amour et de la mer* on the player and feel love coming up through the clouds, exactly as the sun did, and with the same absolute certainty of light given.

I am happy to be packing fifty copies of the tiny book of poems, *A Winter Garland,* that Bill Ewert has published for me to give to my friends this Christmas. None of my work has been published in a beautiful edition before. I am not a bibliophile, but I must confess that the elegant pages, designed by Michael McCurdy, and especially the title page, which has a shell engraved on it, does give me a special joy. Everyone at a certain point in the pre-Christmas shuffle must long to push it all aside and think quietly about friends and loves and ways toward renewal, now when the dark falls so very early and some part of the psyche longs for sleep and not to bother with packing up presents! But this book of fifteen poems is of a different order, so it makes me feel warm and awake as I think of each of my friends to whom it will carry a Christmas message. These are poems between muses, rather somber, but then who is not somber this year? It is such a hard year.

Yesterday I had an angry letter from a reader asking why I am such a snob and am not published in cheap editions that people can afford! Of course nothing would please me more, but one does not ask Avon; they ask the publisher and writer, and only if the books have shown in hard figures that they will sell. Norton is delighted that *Anger* has sold 14,000 copies, but what is that in the mass market? It is a disaster for a writer like me that prices are so high, but there is nothing I can do to change that. It is a boon that Norton is publishing in paperback editions almost all the journals and novels, but even the lesser price of a paperback is more than many people who read me can afford to pay.

Still nothing can change the happiness I felt when I went down this morning to get my breakfast at five and saw the marvelous light, as the sun, not yet risen, flooded the rooms with a kind of pale green, touching the paperwhite narcissus and every chair and table with its blessing. This house becomes then a great shell filled with the in-

"Even the stuffed animals have little messages to give"

cessant rumor of the past and I wander through its rooms, enchanted.

Even the stuffed animals have little messages to give; for each means a person, a moment, a sharing with someone I love, and I listened to their silent messages this morning and felt lucky to be alive, and to come upstairs to pack a little book of poems and send it off.

Thursday, December 9th

I GOT UP before five in the dark and saw a faint moon, waning now, high over the house, but when I came up here to my desk at seven, I felt a change in the light, looked up, and saw snow falling, big flakes blowing in the wind. That magic moment, the first snow! In a half-hour the field was white. It didn't last, of course. Now it is clear again and bitterly cold, around 20° with icy wind. But I remember the sensation when winter first makes itself felt (we have had abnormally warm weather lately), and there is a shiver of apprehension before the struggle ahead. Yet I love it, I love the challenge of it, and the white topsy-turvy world when there is a real snow and Tamas rolls in it and barks excited barks and Bramble races up trees. I love the sense of a huge change ahead and all that it will demand, the change, too, back into my solitude at last.

But now is the time for Christmas errands. Yesterday I went to Bedford, Massachusetts, to find Keats Whiting and Marguerite Hearsey in their new home at Carleton

Village, a retirement community where I have applied myself and may eventually go when my number comes up, perhaps in four years. I had an awful time finding the place, went round and round and got lost, until it became a nightmare. But at last I saw it, still in the process of being built, so it all looks rather raw. Marguerite and Keats have a double apartment; they had a door put in between the two, and it feels airy and spacious with a fine view out to the west so they see the sun set. It was awfully good to find them settled in and happy—apparently the transition was not hard—enjoying the ease of not cooking dinner (they have breakfast and lunch in their own quarters), of having maid service, and of no longer driving. When they need to do errands they take a taxi. We had sherry upstairs and a good talk, first about all this, and they laughed about how many people come because many of their friends are curious and perhaps contemplating the same sort of change, so they have hardly had time to unpack since the move. The best news for me is that animals are allowed. I had not dared to ask, but of course I would never move without Tamas and Bramble.

Keats and Marguerite are roughly twenty years older than I, full of concern about the state of the world as always, avid readers, so conversation is a feast for me when I am with them. Of course they have each other, and I wondered how it would feel for me alone. I did have a rather sinking feeling, especially in the dining room, which is quite beautiful, with fresh flowers at every table and kind, careful service. The sinking feeling was because it seemed strange to be surrounded by old people, and I wondered whether in the long run it would not be depressing. But Keats and Marguerite assured me that they had already found several congenial spirits and that they themselves have taken to this radical change in great form.

At lunch we talked more seriously. I wondered whether religion was not perhaps the only answer to the violence in the world, but Keats at once pointed out that the worst torture and war is going on in the Middle East in the name of religion, and so it has always been. Marguerite sees little improvement in man's state, but Keats reminded us that it is a great deal better to be a woman alive today, at least in the West, than it was in the Middle Ages. I was happy to recount my visit to H.O.M.E., the lodestar of this year for me, and before I left, Keats gave me a check to send along. What a blessing! In fact, the whole visit was a blessing and I came home revived rather than tired.

Monday, December 13th

LAST FRIDAY I flew to Cincinnati to help celebrate Heidi's seventy-fifth birthday at a dinner for eighty at the Losantiville Country Club and to do a book signing at the Crazy Ladies bookstore, a feminist cooperative. The contrast made for an invigorating two days that I shall be savoring as time goes on. But the Christmas frenzy is on, and I shall have to be brief here. It was beautiful to see Heidi and Harry in their magnificent apartment on the eleventh floor, spacious, filled with Harry's treasures, and animated by a secretive, elegant Himalayan cat called Mani and a Lhasa Apso, a ball-of-fluff-dog called Manu who is the most affectionate creature imaginable. I basked in all this beauty and luxury, had a nap, and then we all got dressed and drove off to the club. It was not quite the usual affair because Heidi had had the great adventure years ago of seeing India with Nehru's sister, Krishna, so the decorations and some of her own photographs spoke of India, as did the flower arrangements. The room was soon full of people, among whom I wandered in a daze, eating shrimp, drinking my Scotch, amused by the contrast it made with my life here where I almost never wear a long dress and where I am rarely among strangers. Soon the delightful grandchildren poured in, among them two little girls who had just been in a school performance of *Cinderella* and Chipper, my friend, looking extremely handsome and grown up in his first tuxedo. Altogether an occasion worthy of Heidi who, at seventy-five, still skippers her boat in Kennebunkport and still looks like a boy, partly because she is only five feet tall.

At three the next afternoon she drove me to a very different part of the city, a slum that is being rehabilitated, and there I found myself among "my people" at the Crazy Ladies—a subway crush of young and old but mostly young in blue jeans and sweaters, crowding around to get *Journal of a Solitude* signed (that is the one for the young) and of course *Anger*. Some had brought a great pile of my books from home. Many had things to say to me, but it was rather a rush as the line was long and the time short. At the end of two hours when I had not stopped making my mark, it looked as though the bookstore may have been saved (they are having a hard time), and everyone was happy. And on the way back to the Regency and Heidi, two women from the cooperative told me they thought they had sold $1,500 worth. Once more I felt lifted up on all the delightful caring of these people who read me.

It cannot be denied that it is these days a very good life for an old raccoon of seventy.

Today it is zero here, an inch of snow on the ground to light up the scene. The ocean streams against a background of black thunderous clouds at the horizon. And luckily the blizzard that hit Washington and Philadelphia went out to sea and never came here. I might have come home yesterday to eight inches of snow, and Edythe who met the plane might not have gotten to the airport at all!

Wednesday, December 22nd

I FEEL I have been climbing the Christmas mountain for weeks, so many things I longed to record here and didn't. But now I have come to a good pause I can lay down my knapsack and look at the view.

The tree is up and it is a dream. Last year I took a great dislike to the tree, which was enormous and rather ferocious looking. I felt it was so German! This one is beautifully proportioned and smaller, and Edythe and I had a lovely afternoon decking it, as we have done now twice, so it is becoming a ritual. Of course, almost every ornament brings memories of Judy and our trees at 14 Wright Street in Cambridge, and the little front parlor where it stood on a table, and where we invited our friends in, one by one or in small groups, for champagne and to sit by the Franklin stove. There Anne Thorp and Agnes Swift came bearing jars of wild cranberry jelly from Greenings Island; there we heard Dorothy Wallace with her daughter Anne and her husband, bearing Anne's tiny daughter in a basket, singing "Go Tell It on the Mountain," and there on one memorable occasion Barbara Hawthorne came with (of all singular and magical things) a bunch of violets, so forever after I have associated Christmas Eve with that scent. There Judy's cousin Nancy Carey came with her two small children and Ruth Harnden and so many other friends—and after the guests left we had restful lamb stew, which I always made for the holidays.

Later there were the Christmases of Nelson when the Warners came down from the farm on the Eve for chocolate ice cream with ginger ale poured over it and a cake Sally baked shaped like a tree with green frosting, and Mildred and Quig crossed the street, and Judy was with me. And now—it is hard to believe—it is the tenth Christmas here.

Why is it, I wonder, that Christmas brings so much depression with it, so many people struggle against an undertow? It is partly because this moment of light shines out of the darkest and shortest days of the year, the lowest ebb of the cycle when wise animals dig themselves in for a long sleep, while we, driven creatures, spend immense energy on wrapping presents, sending off packages, baking cookies (this I used to do but have stopped doing myself, so other people's cookies are specially welcome). Partly it is that memories well up and not all are happy ones. We are dealing with a host of faces and times and sorrows and joys, and there is no time to sort them out.

Every year Christmas becomes a real creation for each of us, and as it is created we are re-creating the moment when Love is born again, Love that will know pain as well as joy.

As I was writing that last sentence Tim Warren, Judy's nephew, called—it is 8 A.M.—to tell me that Judy died last night. I have prayed that she might be allowed to slip away, and now she has. But it is always so sudden, so unexpected—death—and so final. When I went to see her last September and held her ice-cold hand in mine, at the very end of the half-hour when she had made no sign of recognition, she reached over and patted my hand and held it over her other one for a moment. I must remember that and that she is free at last of the failing body and mind and is wherever spirits dwell.

Surely she dwells in me and will as long as I live, with my mother and Jean Dominique and Anne Thorp and Eugénie Dubois. But Judy was the precious only love with whom I lived for years, the only one. There have been other great loves in my life, but only Judy gave me a home and made me know what home can be. She was the dear companion for fifteen years, years when I was struggling as a writer. We were poor then, for a time had no car even. But strangely enough I look back on those days as the happiest ones. And that is because there was a "we."

We met in Santa Fe and it is to that austere flaming landscape, sunset on the Sangre de Cristos, that my heart goes now and to a poem I wrote for Judy that ends:

> For after love comes birth:
> All we have felt and said
> Is now of air, of earth,
> And love is harvested.

It is a comfort to think back to a few days ago when I made my annual pilgrimage to Nelson to the friends there who knew Judy and knew us together. For once there was no blizzard. I stopped first at Laurie Armstrong's in Peterborough, bringing her the little book of poems, which is dedicated to her—what a joy that was, and to find her looking radiant with a big white silk bow at her throat, taking me out to lunch, and the good talk, which always comes back to Ben, her husband dead for many years, and to Judy. For we have shared many griefs, but they are translated into pure love and rejoicing when we meet, and Laurie says, "What would I do without you?" and what would I do without her? She is ninety-one so the question becomes poignant.

From there, all warmed, I set out for Nelson fifteen miles away up hill and down dale, with Mount Monadnock appearing and disappearing. Parker Huber tells me he will be climbing it on Christmas Day, as he always does, to pay his respects to the sacred eminence. At Dublin where the road to Nelson turns off, I always remember the first time I took it when I was looking for a house to buy, how interminable and lonely it seemed, miles and miles through woods with hardly a house to be seen after the glimpse of beautiful red-brick Harrisville by the lake. I passed the round excavated rock that is filled by a spring and has "I will lift up mine eyes to the hills" graven into it. I passed the banks where trailing arbutus grows. It seemed a long journey this time, a journey made through thickets of memories, until at last I came out on the village green, austere and silent as always, and knocked on Mildred Quigley's door. And there she was, just as always, sitting in her armchair with a cat playing at her feet, the old dog eager to be caressed, and Quig's paintings on the walls, and his violins, those he had made himself, hanging in the kitchen. For the first time Mildred talked about how she missed him, for it has become a lonely house now that Tami, her daughter, is gone from 2 until 11 P.M. every day, and she who was such a great reader resorts to television because of her failing eyes.

From there, grateful for a non-icy road, I went to the Warners, happy to see the meadow by the Frenchs' with sheep in it once more, for Buddy has come home, and the little boy, a bearded man now, has decided to raise sheep and continue his sister's absorbing love of them. Once when I asked Cathy, then about twelve, why she loved sheep, her answer amazed me, "Because," she said, "they are so grateful." It was a sad visit to the Warners this year because Grace, the matriarch of the family—though that word hardly fits the tiny fragile person she is—was in the hospital seriously ill with pneumonia. We sat around the table in the tiny kitchen where everything happens at the old farm—Sally, Helen, Gracie, Doris, and Bud, with two infants playing around us while their mother worked— and talked about Grace and how lucky it was that she had finally allowed them to take her to the hospital. I gather it was a close thing. Gracie always makes me a wreath and this year had also made a little panel of dried flowers, a milkweed pod and one of the feathers from her pheasants. She showed me the new boots she had bought with my check, but we did not have time to go out to the many small barns where she keeps her family of animals and birds. Esmeralda, the donkey, is dead, but the pony, the old sheep, and the goat are still there, and the Muscovy ducks, and now more and more ornamental pheasants. These are her passion and I can see why. Their colors (one is a brilliant gold) seem magical in the somber landscape, like visitations from paradise. These are hard times for Gracie because the price of grain and feed has gone up. She works hard cleaning for people and gardening in sum- mer and this time looked awfully tired, I thought. I hated to leave, but I wanted to be sure to get to the hospital in Keene in time for a visit with Grace, so off I went, marvel-

ing once more at the courage and sweetness of this remarkable family. They seem to live in perfect harmony,
and this in very close quarters. Each has a special talent.
Sally is the cook. Helen and Bud, the eldest, take care of
the cows and workhorses, Doris drives the school bus, and
Gracie, of course, tends to her "peaceable kingdom."

I had not seen the new hospital in Keene, and it is quite
splendid, so I found Grace, surrounded by flowers, in a
large and beautiful room with only one other patient in
it. When she saw me, her eyes filled with tears, and she
said, "This is my best Christmas present," and so it was for
me, as I pulled up a chair so I could hold her hand. Such
a frail, tiny body now, as though all the life were gathered
into her shining blue eyes. I realized after I left her that
it is the first time we have ever had a real talk alone. I have
always seen her surrounded by the family. So it was precious to listen to her speak of her anxieties about Gracie
who has terrible migraine headaches, and of Sally who
looks awfully tired, partly because she is now nursemaid
to little children, a bit too much perhaps, as I had sensed
when I was there, but this is how the Warners live, doing
for each other and never complaining. It was good to hear
last night that Grace is home again and they will all be
together for Christmas.

It was well after dark when I got to Chesham to sink
into the peace of the old Chamberlain house and have a
drink by the fire with Beverly and her mother. An especially rejoicing visit, as I had not seen Beverly since she
had courageously resigned from the bank where she had
worked for twenty years to work instead at a job she loves
as an accountant at *Yankee* magazine.

What I think as I write is that all these people who
were my neighbors ten years ago could be summed up
with the words "true grit." They all have it.

Wednesday, December 29th

THE DAYS have gone by too fast this strange warm Christmas, which has broken all records. It is 50° outside today with a gray sky and the sun looking wanly through the clouds. One of my best presents was a review of *Anger* signed L.M. in the *West Coast Review of Books*. (Who is L.M., I wonder, he or she?) The last paragraph reads:

> One of the amazing things about May Sarton is her variety. None of her books is anything like the others. Each focuses narrowly on a single vital experience typical of human life, and each contains such depths, such concentration of wisdom, that reading it is like plunging into a frigid but healing mountain lake. This book moved me not only to tears but also to a heightened understanding of myself. Surely even the finest literature can offer no greater experience.

I have complained so much about bad reviews, here is one I can be proud to set down here.

I want to go back to the last of the visits within the New Hampshire days. That was to see Lotte Jacobi in her studio deep in the woods in Deering. There she was, glowing with life. As usual we sat in the warm kitchen drinking tea and eating bread, cheese, and smoked salmon, and we talked and teased each other about our mutual propensity to become violently attached to someone, she at eighty-seven and I at seventy, the living proof that love is always possible, that special kind of love that always brings poetry with it. With a rather mischievous gleam in her eye, she admitted that disillusion sometimes follows, but why not? Anything at all is possible, even falling out of love, she seemed to tell me, and everything is good that brings more life, that makes life sparkle if only for a month or two. I gave her the little book of poems and read her one or two. I love this little book and begin to think that all books of poems should contain only a few! But of course that is extravagant. For even a tiny book is expensive these days. We talked also about our hope to be together next June on Star Island for Art Week. I do hope I can manage it. My dream is to take a drawing pad and simply forget about words for a week.

I had looked forward to Anne and Barbara's coming to share Christmas Eve dinner in the middle of the day with Lee Blair, but Barbara had the flu so they had to cancel and will perhaps be with me tomorrow instead. But Anne did a wonderful thing. She asked Janice to get me one red rose and to place it under the tree "for Judy." So "joy and woe were woven fine" in the tree this year. I missed them, though, on the Eve, as Anne knew Judy well and I long to speak of her with those who did.

In a way, however, it was good to have a quiet Christmas Eve here with Lee alone. We lit low candles in front of the exquisite crèche she had made for me, a copy of an eighteenth-century one, each figure carved with infinite skill and delicacy and painted. It has given the library a soul this whole Christmas, a Christmas when it was most needed, a Christmas full of absence.

Ever since then there have been a few people in every day—Janice and Maryann for Christmas dinner at night. Then all the candles could be lit and we opened presents in that lovely gentle light. And the next day, and the next, and yesterday a few friends for champagne in the late afternoon. This is a time for real talk, but this year I am starved for solitude and silence, for January first when I shall at long last have it.

So many things have been happening here these days and one or two especially have given me something to think about. The first was an unexpected call from Pat Carroll in Los Angeles where she is about to open for six weeks of Gertrude Stein. She called to thank me for the little book of poems. I told her about Judy and after we had talked for a while she said "Happy grieving!" just before she hung up. It startled me at first and then I saw how much truth there is in it, for as long as Judy was still alive but in limbo I was in limbo too and could not mourn. Now, little by little, the good memories begin to flow back, and the Judy I loved begins to live again.

The other event has been reading Lewis Hyde's extraordinary book, *The Gift: Imagination and the Erotic Life of Property,* which was sent to me in proof. I find I have turned down page after page to go back and read again. Here is one passage among many others that stays with me:

> In the world of gift, as in the Scottish tale, you not only can have your cake and eat it too, you can't have your cake *unless* you eat it. Gift exchange and erotic life are connected in this regard. The gift is an emanation of Eros, and therefore to speak of gifts that survive their use is to speak of a natural fact: libido is not lost when it is given away. Eros never wastes his lovers. When we give ourselves in the spirit of that god, he does not leave off his attentions; it is only when we fall into calculation that he remains hidden and no body will satisfy. Satisfaction derives not merely from being filled but from being filled with a current that will not cease.

Saturday, January 1, 1983

IT'S A PERFECT MORNING on which to start fresh. During
the night about an inch of snow fell, just enough to change
the world, lay ermine on the pine trees, and change the
sodden field to white, so beautiful against pale-blue ocean,
as calm as a pond, and the sun rising bright orange in
transparent sky. I went out without a coat on to brush a
path to the road and to the bird feeders; it is still just under
freezing.

   The edge of my mind is not as sharp as it should be
because I had quite a New Year's Eve yesterday, and an
amusing and enlivening one, the best I can remember for
many a year. I got off a flotilla of notes in the morning,
thanking for presents, then at noon met Dr. Annella
Brown, formerly head surgeon at New England Hospital,
who had invited me out for lunch at The Whistling Oyster
and told me she would come in a "magnificent car." So I
was watching for something special but hardly for what I
saw turning in to the parking lot at Foster's. After a few
minutes, a low-slung, immensely long, custom-built gray
car drove in, and there she was. It resembled in its atmosphere of *grand luxe* a scene in *Brideshead Revisited*,
slightly incongruous in York, Maine, but that only added
to the charm. I knew from her letter that Annella and I
had many friends in common and a mutual love of the
Dordogne in France where she has a house, it seems, and

where Judy and I spent two marvelous holidays in the late forties. Annella, like all women surgeons, I imagine, is rather a general, used to having her way, but I was happy to give her her way since it was so kind. She had lost her friend of many years in April and I have lost Judy, so that too we had in common. What fun it was to dazzle the personnel at The Whistling Oyster as we drove up. In fact, it was all very amusing, with a half bottle of Montrachet to enhance a delicious meal, in my case oysters boiled in an incredibly delicate sauce and laid on fresh raw spinach, and then we splurged on a chocolate chestnut cake for dessert. I got home just in time to fill the bird feeders and let Tamas out, and then Nancy Hartley picked me up to meet two friends of hers from the library where she works to go to see *Tootsie,* that admirably funny and tender movie in which Dustin Hoffman plays a woman. Waiting in line to get in, we shared a huge Coke with four straws and got into fits of laughter. Afterward we were lucky enough to get into a restaurant in Portsmouth called Codfish Aristocracy, my first experience there. It is in an old house and our table was in a small room and quiet enough so we could talk in peace, and I was home before ten. Altogether a remarkably busy day for me, and a happy one. But "going out" does take the edge off and I look forward now to not getting myself ready for anything at all except work. Work, of course, is my real holiday always, so this is a day of joy and relief. Three months for myself at last! Little unhurried walks with Tamas, lunch or supper occasionally with dear friends, but no visiting firemen, no public appearances, time to think, time perhaps to tidy up some of the disorder in this house.

And that reminds me of what Anne and Barbara did for me. We had our delayed Christmas dinner and opened presents on December 30th, and luckily it was a fine day and easy driving, but after lunch we heard scrabbling in the closet where I keep birdseed and, sure enough, a terrified red squirrel darted out and into the library, then finally down the cellar stairs. Anne went down and opened the door (too heavy and stiff for me) and off he went. Then in about an hour of very hard work, she and Barbara cleaned out the cupboard and filled a big metal garbage can with all the seed and put it outside the doorsill of the porch. I have suffered from the disorder in that cupboard for more than a year, so what a superb Christmas present they gave me, those best of friends! I can now, one of these days, get at the shelves and make things shipshape again. That's the way to start a new year! After they left, inspired by Barbara's gift of small leeks from her garden, I used up the remains of the Christmas chicken and made soup. What rich, full days these last ten have been!

Sunday, January 2nd

FOR A FEW DAYS anyway I want to note here what has been accomplished, partly to pace myself, partly to see that something is accomplished each day, though what pursues me after supper is what has not been! All day yesterday I felt the relief of no immediate pressure, so for once I took Tamas and Bramble the long way round through the woods, the road just dusted with snow, so their footmarks made charming patterns behind us. That was fun.

Before that I had written two pages of the journal and

a poem about Judy in the "Letters from Maine" series. And for the first time in weeks I played some music— Ferrier singing Pergolesi's *Stabat Mater,* which I have not listened to for several years. It felt good not needing to go to town even for mail, and after lunch Tamas and I had a long rest. That was when the day began to disintegrate, for, after having a cup of tea and filling the feeders, I had planned a huge tidying up here in my study, but all I succeeded in doing was to empty the couch of a disorderly pile of Christmas cards, sorted out and put away for next year. At least there are a few feet of clear space before my eyes this morning. Then I wrote one longish letter to Kay Martin, and then it was time to put the Greek spinach pie Sofia and Char brought me for Christmas in the oven. At nine I was in bed, exhausted.

Of course, yesterday was not typical, as I had made or received several long-distance calls for the New Year, so it was an interrupted morning after all. This morning I'll dive into letters and hope to get at least some of the thank-yous off the immense list. Here is Bramble asking to go out! So down I go the three flights of stairs.

If all goes well I hope to read over the two hundred pages I have down on "The Magnificent Spinster," so that tomorrow I can begin to work. I have not looked at it for a year. What shall I find? A spur to some good work or a disaster? We shall see.

But life is so much more complex at any given moment than any list can suggest, how is one to gather it all in? I have been up since five, and it is now a quarter past nine. Where have four hours gone? Of course there was break-fast to get and after it I lay in bed and read the last issue of the *Times Literary Supplement* and a piece of George Garrett's new novel in *Sewanee Review,* such a lively, rich work. Then I put fresh sheets on the bed, put last week's in the washer, did the dishes, watered the plants, and

came up here determined to clear out the open movable
file where I keep ongoing work and letters to file. The top
basket has in it a chaos of things to do with this journal,
the four folders that contain it, photographs I may want
to use, clippings, and so on. All this was buried under a
cruel accumulation of manuscripts people want me to
read, cruel because I resent being plagued at Christmastime. And when shall I get to *them,* I wonder? They now
lie on the couch and at least the journal tray looks "ration-
alized," a word Cora DuBois often used. That is a real
help.

When I took Bramble down, I picked up the Virginia
Woolf calendar Heidi gave me and brought it up here.
How enlivening to read "I sometimes think only autobiography is literature—novels are what we peel off and come
at last to the core, which is only you and me." It is enlivening because I don't agree. There is always some sleight of
hand going on in writing autobiography. So much has to
be left out, especially things that might hurt or dismay
people. But in a novel one can say everything. The novel
is often autobiography distilled and/or transcended.
Anger is a case in point. And, on a much higher level,
Virginia Woolf's own *The Waves.*

Tuesday, January 4th

FOR THE LAST TWO MORNINGS I have been reading from
half-past five to half-past six the manuscript of "The Magnificent Spinster." Yesterday I was relieved to find that
the first part, childhood on the island, really feels alive.

But this morning the hundred pages that take Jane Reid (in reality, Anne Thorp) into her fortieth year seem rather labored. I have chosen to call it fiction so that the imagination can to some extent run free and so I shall not be tied down to minute particulars. I shall enjoy having this whole imaginary world going on in my subconscious under everything else, under my walk with Tamas, under any reading I do, with me as I fall asleep and as I wake.

Yesterday I also copied out two-thirds of the poems I have been writing since the intervention of a new muse. The problem is how to keep something alive that is so tenuous, based on a single meeting of a few hours early in November. The muse herself is withdrawing—and why not? The chances that we shall meet again are rather slight. It may be that I shall have to take this as a gift from the gods, but not a lasting one. But, oh, it has been wonderful to be able to write these poems, such a sense of liberation, of using my best gifts again, and especially of being fertilized after the sterile and exhausting summer.

At the moment, between the reemerging novel, poems, this journal, and the piles of letters still to be answered, as well as several manuscripts to read and comment on, I feel a little too pressured, but it is a good pressure. The morning races by, this one interrupted in a maddening way because the refrigerator stopped running in the night and I had to go down to talk with the gentle man who came to fix it. It is running again now, God knows why, but he thinks I had better have a new thermostat.

Thursday, January 6th

IT LOOKS as though the time has come for a pause. It is raining. I have a bad cold, which exploded yesterday after lunch, when Edythe and I were taking down the tree. When she left, the library seemed suddenly empty and desolate. That is the magic of the Christmas tree, that it comes and goes, that it cannot be kept forever and is therefore a kind of angel. This year it was a tree of memory because of Judy—I thought of her small, deft hands when I detached two walnut half shells that had been made into tiny bird nests, each with a bird in it, which Judy bought years ago. She did not do this sort of thing often, so they are precious.

It was comforting to undo the tree with Edythe who had helped me deck it, but my streaming nose made it a little awkward, and I was relieved when I could lie down with Tamas and sleep for an hour. My chest is rather congested this morning; the refrigerator is again behaving erratically, so the man is coming again today, as the new thermostat won't be here for a week. And I know there is not much point in trying to work this morning. Yesterday I broke the ice and wrote three pages of "The Magnificent Spinster," so I am picking up my knapsack and am on my way. Every new book is like a pilgrimage, a long long walk where faith in the eventual destination has to be renewed again and again. I am happy to have set out once more.

Tuesday night Eva Le Gallienne called—she has Tuesday nights off as the White Queen in *Alice in Wonderland* —and it was wonderful to hear the vigor and warmth in her voice. "How young you sound," I said, and she said she could not believe that she is nearing eighty-four. I had somehow imagined that her mother had lived to be ninety. Not so, I was told. She died before she was eighty. We talked, of course, about *Alice* and the bitter fact that a long cruel review in the *Times* had wrecked its chances in spite of a very good one in *The New Yorker* by Brendan Gill and lots of others. But Frank Rich delivered the poison, and Le Gallienne thinks they may have to close at the end of this week. It costs $160,000 a week to keep the play going and the theater is only forty-five percent full, as I read in the *Times* the other day in a piece about the bad year it is on Broadway. Only musicals are withstanding the recession. Tickets are wildly expensive and the reason is not profit but the huge expenses involved. When I saw Le Gallienne last summer, she told me, as I remember, that the costumes for the cards would cost $1,500 each! So people cannot afford to go to the theater and the prices cannot be lowered because of costs. It is a vicious circle.

Le Gallienne said she did not mind for herself but for the company. They opened December 23rd, so it will have been a very short run. I see Broadway as a dragon that devours the innocent and the truly sophisticated, devours the pure in heart, and no knight to ride up at the eleventh hour to make a rescue!

What makes Eva Le Gallienne exceptional is the intensity with which she lives and the richness of her world whether she is acting in a play or not. There she is lucky, or it would be closer to the truth to say, gifted. Now she will have her garden in the spring and be able to watch a pair of bluebirds nesting perhaps and, of course, enter-

tain her usual dinner party of raccoons and skunks every
evening at half-past eight when she provides a meal for
them at the back door. Perhaps she will translate a book
she likes from the Danish or Norwegian. Perhaps she will
get back to an autobiographical book titled "The Blue
Room," after the library in Weston—who knows what she
will do? But the ring in her voice makes it very clear that
she will not be downed.

Monday, January 10th

THE INCREDIBLY MILD WINTER goes on with its attendant
flu and colds. Mine is better, but these past three days
have been a struggle, whether because I am rather de-
pleted or simply because the sheer bulk of what has to be
faced every day on my desk is staggering. I cannot imagine what it might be like to wake with a truly clear day
before me, a day for my work alone. But that will never
happen—now there is a book about homosexuals and suicide to be read in proof, so once more I am unable to *read*
even what I choose to read, let alone to write what I
choose to write. The Dinesen biography is by my bed, but
when shall I get to it?

Still, something has been accomplished in this first
week of solitude. Yesterday and Saturday I wrote twenty-
five letters and one poem, a sonnet, "Requiem" for Judy.
I am now afraid the form was too tight and the result
elliptical, too much had to be condensed. But while I was
writing it I played the Fauré Requiem and for a few hours

yesterday felt happy, with that happiness that comes from total concentration on creation. I know no other like it. During the week I see I have written two poems, six pages of this journal, and made a start at getting back into "The Magnificent Spinster," but that is still nebulous. The good thing is that it is alive in my mind, so when I walk Tamas or am lying in bed after breakfast for a little think, it stirs. Ideas, hopes, doubts, and new ways to handle this really tough subject are there just under the surface and accompany me through every day. That is the sign that I must not despair. But there are very real technical problems. Simply writing this much here shows me that what I have to do is not worry about pages written now but let the imagination go where it wills and make copious notes. One of my faults as a writer is a compulsion to finish, to get on with things fast. This is why the work of Sisyphus that the letters demand is such a challenge to me as soul-making. I have to learn not to despair when something can never be finished. True, I wrote twenty-five this weekend, but there is still a boxful at my feet! Everyone tells me "Just don't answer. Shove it all aside." But no one, I think, can imagine how next to impossible that is. You cannot bury ghosts. They come back and haunt. There is no night when I do not wake at some point, saying, "Oh, tomorrow I must write to so and so."

But of course lovely things come in the mail. A woman potter who wrote to me the other day said that her husband introduced her to my work and always gives her a new May Sarton book "as an act of love and our friendship" on Mother's Day. Last year he gave her *A World of Light* and inscribed it with this passage from Montaigne: "To storm a beach, conduct an embassy, govern a people; these are brilliant actions; to scold, laugh . . . and deal gently and justly with one's family and oneself . . . that is

something rarer, more difficult, and less noticed in the
world."

Tuesday, January 11th

WE ARE HAVING A WILD, warm nor'easter, hurling down
two inches of rain last night, it seems. Now it is going out
to sea, and I can watch the huge surf showering fountains
of white at the end of the field and hear that wonderful
roar in the distance! Tamas is in his bed, refusing to go out,
although it is so warm, over 50°, breaking all records, a
crazy winter. I went out to retrieve the big feeder, which
had apparently been blown down and then dragged off,
perhaps by a raccoon. All things considered I am glad it
was not a blizzard, although the dirt road out of here will
be pretty soggy and slippery when I go to fetch the mail.
    Yesterday with the help of a half Ritalin I had a mag-
nificent morning of work, first the journal, then four pages
of the novel, as well as making voluminous notes about
what is to come, so perhaps the momentum is there at last.
I say "at last," but it has only been ten days since I began
to think about it at all. Then in about ten minutes I wrote
a sonnet for Judy and sent that and the first sonnet, "Requiem," about the tree, off to her family. I still mind that
there will be no memorial service.
    The evening was a full one, too, as I watched the first
hour of *Nicholas Nickleby,* the great British production,
for which tickets sold for $100 last year on Broadway.
Occasionally television is a real gift, for there I was in a

front-row seat. The first part at Dotheboys Hall is horrendous, of course, and after an hour I could not stomach
more. I then went to bed at nine and read to the end of
the biography of Maximilian Kolbe, *A Man for Others.*
That was to go from one hell to another, for Dotheboys
Hall was very much like a concentration camp. Only with
Kolbe we are witnessing, through this book, a light that no
suffering, not even death by starvation, could extinguish,
a compassion so active and constant that even in that hell
he never ceased to minister to others, and a faith so constant that he could keep his serenity and live in the light
even at Auschwitz. No one could doubt after reading this
book that he was a saint and will now work miracles if only
by his example.

Every authentic word we get about the Holocaust
brings new insights. For me this one dramatized the
Nazis' hatred of priests, ministers, and any person who
professed his Christian faith or his Jewish faith in a merciful God. They were out not only to destroy and murder
human beings (almost all European gypsies died in the
camps) but to degrade them first. In this the Nazi ethos
was different from any I have ever heard of. There have
been mass murders before, but never before, I think, such
a power of evil. To turn a man into an animal through
torture, starvation, and at the same time work him to
death, and then jeer because he has become an animal—
this is evil that cannot be eradicated. And that is one of
the things this book makes me wonder about. Kolbe was
unique in his belief that even the SS, who tortured and
beat him, were to be forgiven and to be regarded as sav-
able souls. I have always felt that only one who had endured the camps could forgive, that I who had not suffered in them could not, because it was too easy. Christ on
the cross said, "Forgive them for they know not what they

do." Christ could say it. But can we forgive things done to others? Forgiveness is the spiritual link between the torturer and the tortured, the I and Thou is *there*. It is also necessary that we forgive ourselves for wrongs we have committed. Have the Germans ever really faced what they did? Only then can the poison be absorbed. When they forgive themselves, perhaps we can forgive them, and I cannot separate Germans from Nazis. It is also to be considered that the Nazis wanted not only to murder the Jews; they wanted to eradicate God from the German world. That is one thing this book makes clear, and it is terrifying.

The hardest thing we are asked to do in this world is to remain aware of suffering, suffering about which we can do nothing. Every human instinct is to turn away. Not see. It is, I'm afraid, exemplified by Reagan who refuses to imagine the suffering of twelve million unemployed and the degradation of men and women who are deprived of work and treated in this country like pariahs.

Wednesday, January 12th

I FORGOT to say something about Maximilian Kolbe that touched me several times as I read the book, and that is the way he brought together in himself the male and female. So many of the people who recorded their impressions spoke of it. So many spoke of his motherliness. He

was not afraid to show it because of his devotion to the
Immaculata, as he called Mary.

Yesterday was a hard day, although I did get something done on the novel. I felt blown about by various
kinds of distress, for the mail brought a request from the
IRS that I appear on the 28th with all the figures for 1980!
Of course a letter like that throws one into a panic at once,
but when I called the office in Sanford to ask a few questions, I spoke to such a gentle person, she who will go over
it with me, that it seemed less of an ordeal. I'll hunt out
the papers this weekend. Amazing how a kind voice on
the telephone can bring comfort.

The second blow was a cold and angry letter from the
muse. It has been weeks since I have heard anything at all,
and I think that in the silence I had come to see that the
distance is too great and the hazards of misunderstandings so immense, the chance of our meeting again so
slight, that a withdrawal was inevitable. Still, that letter
was hard to lay aside and I boiled like a kettle on the stove.
Not with anger, just with being so stirred up. This morning I opened the Woolf calendar to this: "It is true that I
only want to show off to women. Women alone stir my
imagination." I recognized that at once. And it made me
feel better, less crazy and impossible.

Also in the mail was a letter from an English nurse who
had been writing me for several years but had been silent
for the past two. She has emigrated to Canada, apparently
been maltreated in a hospital job, hoped to get down here
to see me and gave me a phone number. Her letter, so
distressed, had taken two weeks to reach me, eighteen
days in fact. So after eight I called her at once. She was not
at the number given, they told me, and I was given the
number of another hospital where she might be reached.

There they said she could be found, but I had better have her call me back—"collect," I said. In a half hour or so I heard her gentle voice, and it was worth the hassle to be in touch and to be able to reassure her that I am here and will keep in touch now. This morning I packed up three books to send to her in Winnipeg where she is going to try to find work and has found a place to live. She had told me in her letter that she had not been able to bring my books with her and, on the telephone, that the poems especially had kept her alive.

Then at nine Christiane Hepp called me from Houston to say that Vincent had had a hemorrhage of the brain and was now blind in one eye and recovering slowly. I also heard yesterday that a friend in New York has been hospitalized for possible heart trouble. How fragile we all are! How lucky to be alive at all!

Now I must write letters about all this and God knows when I shall get back to work. I did get up at five and have been watching the sun rise, brilliant orange from a purple haze at the horizon and a slightly ruffled, pale-blue ocean. What a calming sight! For whatever troubles and anxieties pour in here, the sun still rises.

Friday, January 14th

VINCENT HEPP called last night. How happy I was to hear his vibrant voice with good news about the brain scan! He has been told to do absolutely nothing; his recovery depends on that, so he watches the cats, he told me, and the flowers I sent yesterday, as much for Christiane who bears the brunt of all this shock and confusion as for him, but I am happy to think he can look at iris, heather, and daffodils as well as cats, and so live in an impressionist painting for a while. He told me that he feels compelled to write and gets up sometimes at 2 A.M. to scribble, and that sounds like a very good sign of returning powers.

But I am again feeling harassed. That is because I have had for various reasons to leave the house before ten for the last three days. That cuts the morning in two and increases the pressure so much that I end by doing nothing except letters. Today I have to go to Portland for the semiannual checkup on cancer. Yesterday to Portsmouth to be weighed in at Diet Center and start my yearly six-week diet to lose twenty pounds. So I came home with apples, oranges, grapefruit, lettuce, green peppers, skinned chicken breasts, and began the thing hardest for me to do, to drink eight glasses of water a day. I feel very well on the diet once I get used to a certain amount of deprivation. It precludes any meals "out" for six weeks and adds to the good enclosure of winter.

Last week the galleys of a book called *"I Thought People Like That Killed Themselves"—Lesbians, Gay Men and Suicide* by Eric E. Rofes arrived, asking me for comment that could be used. It came when I had about decided to free myself for a while from such responsibilities, but after forty-eight hours, I felt I had to look at it and I am very glad I did. Rofes, a Harvard graduate, is twenty-eight years old. In his accompanying letter he said, "I became interested in the connection between gay people and suicide shortly after reading *Faithful Are the Wounds.*" I am glad that that novel is being read at Harvard.

Rofes's is a very good book, a very sad one, sad because

in so many of the instances of suicide he relates, the reason is fear of exposure, either to parents, to the job milieu, or to society in general. The anxiety, self-doubt, and trauma almost every homosexual carries is hard to imagine, even now when things are so much more open than they were when I was young. I realize more and more that my own position has been privileged because I have no immediate family and because no "job" is at risk. That gives me a great responsibility to be open and to talk about this matter, and I begin to understand, also, why I have been of use, have, perhaps, made some harassed and depressed people feel a little safer, more able to accept and honor their own lives. The more the homosexual is isolated and driven into ghettos, the less whole and at ease he must feel. I want to make bridges between the two worlds and that, I suppose, is why I have been loath to associate myself with "gay" society. When minorities are forced to be defensive and to live apart, the whole society suffers and is deprived. I see this clearly with blacks. There are so many walls still between black and white. Will they ever come down?

Eric Rofes is brave. He is also compassionate enough to put himself at risk to defend his friends. I gather that he has known more than one contemporary who committed suicide. I admire his courage and salute this book.

It would be interesting at this juncture if someone would write a book about homosexual marriages, making clear that there are a great many happy and viable ones all around us. The general public unfortunately usually hears only about gay bars, drugs, the corruption of children, suicides, and disaster. It is as if all we knew about heterosexual society was wife beating, plural divorces, molestation of children by their parents, incest, alcoholism, and *nothing* else!

Saturday, January 15th

THERE IS EXCITEMENT in the air as the first real blizzard of the season is on the way. The supermarket was jammed with people stocking up; and Thelma, the postmistress, spoke of the way everyone is a little tense. But it is still amazingly warm, just above 30° with a high wind and some snow. The real stuff is to arrive late tonight and through Sunday, but then it may stay south of here. Who knows?

It has been a good day. Nancy Hartley, my staunch friend, came over at eleven, and we walked Tamas down to the ocean in the high wind. Then we tackled a job I have been putting off for two years, cleaning out a cupboard here in my study that had become what my mother used to call "a glory hole," where everything I didn't know what to do with had been stuffed. Nancy laughed when we opened the door into a wall of paper bags, unwanted Christmas junk, old typewriters, and even a whole box of pens and desk things that goes back to Nelson! We piled what we could into giant plastic bags, made a box of objects to give to a church sale, and piled up a mass of old catalogs. Then down four flights of stairs to the cellar with it all for Raymond to pick up! Now I keep going to the cupboard and opening it with astonishment. So tidy, so bare, so ready (I fear) to be used as a dump again, but I shall try to keep order there for a change. It does compose the mind!

I heard rumbling around downstairs while I was rest-
ing with Tamas and Bramble, and it turned out to be
Raymond, bless his heart, coming to take the rubbish before we get snowed in. Poor man, I felt so sorry for him
as he had not expected the gargantuan piles he found in
the cellar, but he got it all out, and that is splendid.

I love the big storms, the snow and the high seas,
except for a slight anxiety that the lights may go out. Then
the heat goes off, there is no television and no light to read
by except candles and a rather dim battery-run lamp I
keep by my bed.

I am hoping that next week I shall feel less pressured
or that I can make myself calm down and not be so driven.
The novel can well go on through this year, as this journal
will be finished in late April, at the end of the circle of my
own year, and with that (presumably) in the works at
Norton I shall have some money to live on. But the pressure is partly that if I fail to keep the momentum, I lose
ground with the novel. It has been a big heave to get back
into it, but it is now alive in my mind, so even when I am
driving to Portsmouth to the Diet Center I am thinking
about it. It is there under everything else.

Sunday, January 16th

I WOKE to a totally transformed world, and we are enclosed for the next twenty-four hours in the wild white
snow. When I went down at half-past five, the first thing
I did was to see if I could push open the porch door, but

the drifts against it make that impossible. Fortunately, the front door, which I rarely use, is sheltered and I was able to open it about a foot, so after breakfast I went out and managed to shovel through a four-foot drift to a cleared space the wind had made on the terrace, and good Tamas ran out and did his business, so all is well. Especially as the lights and phone are still working.

The birds are frantically trying to eat against the high wind and I wonder what I can do to refill the feeders, thirty yards or more to the right of the front door. But maybe I can push my way through without actually shoveling. We shall see. It's just 60° up here, but I am comfortable in two layers of sweaters.

I want to celebrate our first real snow, maybe write a poem. Maybe file a whole tray of letters. But something singularly rare and good must be accomplished. The trouble is that even a small physical effort before I come up here drains energy and I feel rather sleepy at the moment, simply from ten minutes of shoveling.

Tuesday, January 18th

ALAS, no great deed was accomplished to celebrate the snow. And yesterday was a rather bitter day because first I got into a sterile struggle with the novel, finally settling for some note making and a list of the characters. What it needs now is more thinking and less attempt to write for a few days. Then an overwhelming lot of mail threw

"I woke to a totally transformed world"

me into despair. I spent all morning answering and did no work.

Just for my own edification I am going to list yesterday's letters, if only to persuade myself that I am not crazy to find it hard to sort them out and respond!

1. A very long letter from Doris Beatty about her ninety-eight-year-old mother's death, the funeral, and a brief note about the family and this remarkable woman. I was too tired after the morning's work to read it all but did so in bed before I went to sleep.

2. A very long handwritten letter from Vincent Hepp, who finds himself wanting to write down all sorts of memories, intuitions about himself and his wife, and asked me to type it out for him. The stroke has affected one eye, so it is difficult for him to read. When I read what I had been asked to do, I felt dizzy for about thirty seconds. I did that copying yesterday afternoon and early this morning, about two hours to finish it and write to him.

3. A letter from Marjorie Bitker in Milwaukee. She is an old friend and an excellent critic and reviewer, who is now having to take care of her husband as he slips away and is less and less able to cope with his formerly rich and active life in international affairs. Marjorie and I correspond fairly regularly.

4. A fan letter from an Italian woman living in Rome who picked up *The House by the Sea* in the house of English friends in Spain. It is amazing to see how my books land here and there, so far away!

5. A charming letter from a young man in southern California who two years ago did graduate work in oral interpretation of literature and in the course of it spent a semester reading my poems and finally doing a performance using a few of them. He lives in the country in the house where he was born (so rare in America). About his work on the poems he says, "I spent weeks and

months entering your poetry. The experience was one of the most meaningful of my education. . . . The poems walked through my day with me, around the house, watering the plants, feeding the cows, seeing my life." That letter I answered with real pleasure this morning.

6. A letter from Margaret English, an apprentice with me at the Civic Repertory in the thirties and later a member of my company, whose friend, Kappo Phelan, was one of the directors of it. We all three spent a wonderful spring in Conrad Aiken's Jeakes House in Rye, Sussex. It brought me the sad news that Kappo died some years ago.

7. A letter from a young woman in San Francisco whom I helped out a little when she had no job. She is now happy and settled, I was glad to hear.

8. A letter from Keith Warren, Judy's brother-in-law, about possibly printing a memorial folder with photographs and my poem in it. He is the most wonderful old man I ever knew, the dearest, and has always said that the Matlack sisters, one of whom was his wife, were his special charge. (Answered today.)

9. A letter from an eleven-year-old girl in Brunswick, Maine, who has found my poems useful in making a notebook for her reading class. (This I answered this morning too.)

10. A letter from Maire Hillman, who wrote a piece about me for a Finnish journal. It was quite a thrill to see my face there and some writing about my work in a foreign language. She sent me a copy of the good review of *Anger* in *West Coast Book Review* and said she thought the novel was very good. Also, she pointed out that it got five stars beside it, the only five-star among sixty novels, except one by Ngaio Marsh.

All these letters went to my heart. All are precious, each in a different way. But all distract the mind and make it hard to shut them out and concentrate, hard to create. All of this made me forget to call Georgia as I had promised to do yesterday evening! But maybe tomorrow I can take Tamas on a real walk—he has had only small ones since the snow—and get back to the novel, if only to think about it for two hours.

It is very cold, wind chill below zero, certainly. Ten above when I came upstairs at three.

I have lost four pounds in five days so far. But now and then these days I have so wished I could make some brownies or have a drink! Never mind, in six weeks I shall fly up the stairs as light as air, so it is worth the deprivations.

Wednesday, January 19th

FIVE BELOW this morning, but the sun is out and I hope I can get the car started by eleven. Tamas did not want to go out; he and Bramble are snoozing in their beds.

I am now reading with the pleasure of a cat with a saucer of cream Charles Ritchie's third volume of diaries, *Diplomatic Passport*. He was high up in the Canadian Foreign Office, stationed in Paris, Bonn, was later the Canadian ambassador to the United Nations, and he was an intimate friend of Elizabeth Bowen, so she makes an occasional appearance in these pages. Mostly Ritchie gives the reader the great pleasure of seeing the non-professional side of a distinguished professional man. I smiled when I read this passage last night: "I should like to be living alone, or almost alone, by the sea somewhere, allowed three visitors a week chosen by me, lots of books (and perfect eyesight to read indefinitely), solitary walks, and short sprees to places of my choice with people of my choice." That is my life here at the moment, except for the letters, except for the work, and no time for "sprees." But it is fun to imagine other lives. I should like to be for a month in some old-fashioned foreign resort such as Madeira, in an old Grand Hotel with good service and a large room with a balcony, and to be there with a good friend, not a lover, with whom I could go for walks and picnics, something of the happy-go-lucky atmosphere Janice and I experienced on the QE2 when we crossed over together two summers ago.

This morning I feel more cheerful. Partly I went over what I have done since January 1st in the way of work— twenty pages each of journal and novel is not too bad, after all. Plus more than a hundred letters. I know because I had to buy another roll of stamps yesterday.

I finally got through to Eleanor Blair at 6 P.M. yesterday. I had been anxious because there had been no answer since I began calling during the storm on Sunday. Yesterday she finally answered in a very excited and happy state because she had survived four days without heat or light! She has a small open fireplace in her parlor and managed to get wood up from the cellar and keep that room at 50°. Candles her only light, and a flashlight. Elsewhere the house was 40° or even colder. No hot food (I must remember to get her a Sterno). She managed by wearing three or four sweaters and going to bed fully dressed, but when I called she had had her first hot bath —lights and phone came on yesterday morning—and was going out for dinner. She said she remembered her pioneer grandmother in upstate New York and thought "If she could do it, I can." At one point she and her tenant managed to fry some bacon on the open fire. That was the only hot food except hot breast of chicken a kind neighbor brought over during the weekend. The kitten helped and provided a little warmth at night. She sounded euphoric last evening. It must be wonderful to do the impossible, as she has done, to surmount the ordeal and, as she said, "to feel very well."

Friday, January 21st

THE COURAGE OF PEOPLE! It happened that after complaining about my state of siege by the mail, three letters gave me such great rewards and brought me such a renewed sense of how remarkable human beings can be and are that I felt overwhelmed to be the receptacle of so much love and to be allowed into so many lives.

The first was from an old lady to whom I write now and then—we have never met—who lives in Albany, New York. I sent her the new paperback of *Plant Dreaming Deep* for Christmas. She says she has trouble sleeping but does not want to take pills, so

this is my routine. Once awake I get right up, go into my little kitchenette with *Plant Dreaming Deep*. Arrange chair for good light. This is about 1 A.M. to 3 A.M. and time between. Little kettle pushed over electric area on range. Hot tea soon. Maybe some cookies or fruit. *Read*, often three-quarters of an hour. I feel this way, May Sarton is *talking* to me about all these things here. It has been an excellent treatment, dear. No pills. I really don't think much of pills, when I can find comfort and relax as

I read your account of things and people. I do feel very close to you, May Sarton.

The second letter brought me an extraordinary tale of overcoming the impossible. The writer, a young woman, suffers from a disease related to narcolepsy, so rare that there are only forty recorded cases in U.S. medical history. She writes:

My body slipped into a coma, totally destroying my reading, writing or normal functioning of life.

Immediately after hospitalization in Boston, I was told I had a syndrome, similar to narcolepsy but differing only in that there was no known successful treatment or cure. The physicians, the best in the field of neurology, proceeded to place me on experimental medications which almost totally destroyed my peace of mind as an individual and as a member of society.

I received a form of "speed" that is lethal to most humans. My thoughts were unfocused; my words were altered, sentences were too numerously and speedily delivered.

I realized that I would have to control the manner in which I reacted physiologically to the drugs. Alone, I would have to learn how to harness their minimum benefit to keep me awake, while acquiring the ability to subtract their negative side effects.

May, I nearly went nuts. I lived alone in Boston, working, doing cardiovascular surgical research at Harvard Medical School. At night I would return to my studio after lonely walking Harvard Square or the basement of Filene's (walking kept me minimally awake). I could no longer look to other people to add meaning to my life—I had to find happiness within myself first, to make peace with this treacherous beast inside me.

Slowly and painstakingly I began to teach myself to read again—to the dismay of my doctors who said I would never be able to resume my studies at Brown University. My first book was in French, *Le Petit Prince,* the second book and others following that were authored by you.

Journal of a Solitude obviously can be read by anyone who needs to find peace and order within themselves but it had and has a slightly different meaning for me . . . . I needed to learn the difference between loneliness and solitude.

That summer, and following winter and spring, I not only continued to read, but taught myself to write. To the pleasure of my doctors and employers at the research facility I have now co-authored four separate articles in medical journals.

She ends her letter, "I am forever indebted to the great gift you hold—that ability to communicate in a straightforward manner, tools that one may use in his own unique life, to become."

She is expecting to go back to Brown University as a student this fall!

The third letter was from a woman in the Midwest in a transition period in her life. "A Dominican sister counseling me last spring recommended *Journal of a Solitude* as I was trying to encounter my loneliness and enter into a more authentic solitude, the kind Nouwen describes.

"Reading your works for the first time was like going out into the morning garden in spring after too many days indoors, exulting in the sunlit roses and fresh air. I felt resurrected!"

She goes on to say, "More than anything I think that you have put your finger on the pulse of what is essentially real about relationships between women.

"For years I had struggled with an inner conflict that arose from my special attraction to certain women. . . . I have come to accept my own androgynous nature and regard my love for a woman as beautiful and mysterious. Your novels are affirming as I no longer think I am an extraterrestrial creature roaming the earth!"

Well, that's enough for today. My cup is full to the brim.

Sunday, January 23rd

I HAVE BEEN PUZZLED about something these cold nights. When Bramble is out, Tamas senses her presence at the door and barks loudly to alert me, but the other day at around five, I went upstairs to put on the outside lights (the button is beside my bed) and looked out to be sure they were on just as two does bounded away from the euonymus bush right beside the porch door. Tamas made no sound at all and seemed unaware of their presence! So he must have some psychic connection with Bramble. It is odd.

Susan Kerestes, my first guest since I began my diet, came for lunch yesterday. It is she who has brought me sheep manure for the garden, as she works on a sheep farm on weekends. Such kindness! So I knew she deserved a lobster, especially as, curiously enough, lobster is on my diet—without butter, of course. Susan is rightly proud of working at L. L. Bean in one of the few true craft jobs still left, the hand-sewing of moccasins and boots, and in her spare time she is writing poems. That means very early in the morning before she goes to work. She and her friend, Cynthia, own their own house, and Susan is just twenty-six! We had a splendid two hours, talking about many things, the Holocaust and then on to how one handles a traumatic memory (she had a bad experience of violence

in New York City when she was fifteen and can't get rid
of her anger, she says); about how one learns to use form
in writing poems. I think one learns by absorbing poems
by a poet one loves and getting the beat and the form into
the unconscious. When need arises, it is there and pops
out. One does not learn by imitating form consciously, as
is often taught in schools and colleges.

Both Bramble and Tamas attached themselves to
Susan at once, and after I had gone up to rest, she took
Tamas for a walk. I knew I had to rest as I had written
twelve letters in the morning before ten and began to feel
exhausted. I had to get my 1980 tax papers in order for the
ordeal ahead with the IRS on Friday. That turned into a
nerve-wracking search as a whole batch had been mis-
placed and I finally unearthed them in the folder for 1979!
Disorder is costly. Making order is cheap by comparison.
So I am determined this winter to clear up various pockets
of disorder in this house. Nancy comes today to help me
in the file room, a black hole of paper and Christmas
wrappings and unfiled stuff that goes back for years.

Something of great moment in my life happened this
week, which I have not mentioned yet. On Thursday, Tim
and Phyllis Warren—Tim is Judy's nephew—brought me
a fat book that Judy had asked be given to me after her
death. It contains about sixty pages of handwritten poems
by her. I haven't a clue as to when she began this or when
it ended. Reading it has created a complex of thoughts
and feelings for me, among them great admiration for her
powers as a writer. She had an amazing gift for evoking
sights, smells, tastes that bring back whole areas of childhood, and especially the summers at their house, Hidden
Hearth, in Matunuck, Rhode Island, and also of the house
in West Newton where she grew up. But there are con-

stant references to pain, to mental anguish, to the silent
acceptance of pain. All of this appears to relate to times
before we met.

   She was intensely aware of nature in all its forms.
There is a long poem about grasses, how they change
through a summer, for instance.

Tuesday, January 25th

SUNDAY was a fine productive day, chiefly because Nancy
and I did a heroic job, getting the file room cleared of
hundreds of boxes and the cupboard all in order. So at last
I can look in there without shuddering, and next time she
comes we can begin to sort out my papers. We had shrimp
for lunch and a salad and I reveled in her telling of the
years in Spain (her husband was in the Air Force and
stationed there; they are now divorced). They loved Ma-
drid, so she knows that city well, but what delighted me
was to hear that every Friday after work they took off for
the weekend to explore one region or another within
driving distance, just roved around without reservations.
That is what Judy and I did in England, in the Dordogne,
and in the south of France—such happy memories.

   Before Nancy arrived Janice brought Fonzi for a run
with Tamas. It is sheer joy to watch that dachshund fly off,
ears flapping in the wind, intoxicated by freedom as he is
usually on a leash. Tamas is a bit bewildered by such
violent action and tries to nip Fonzi when he feels encir-
cled by this piece of lightning. But on the whole each goes

his own way, each more interested in people than in dogs.

I wrote twelve letters, morning and afternoon, but yesterday I felt horribly tired and dull. I had used up too much energy on Sunday, I fear. I am now starting a new section of the novel, full of problems. But I did manage four pages in the morning, so perhaps at last it is gathering momentum. The agonizing self-doubt is always there, of course, and I have to remember that this novel is like all others, a continual effort to surmount it and spur myself on like a rider through a frustrating thicket. I found this today in my Virginia Woolf calendar: "This insatiable desire to write something before I die, this ravaging sense of the shortness and feverishness of life, make me cling, like a limpet to a rock, to my one anchor."

But when she wrote that she was young, and I am old. So the pressure is even greater. I keep trying to put together, in harness, the fact that I feel so young but am not. Because I foresee having to leave this house in a few years, I savor its beauty more than ever. Waking in that wide room, watching the light come through the lovely small-paned windows, three in a row, never fails to rouse an atavistic memory of well-being that must go back to Wondelgem when I was a baby, for in that farmhouse the windows were very like these, casement windows. When I go down after breakfast to tidy up, the sun is flooding the plant window, and the azaleas, pink, red, and white, become translucent under its rays. The silence here is amazing. This morning I became aware suddenly—I was still in bed—of a gentle, persistent murmuring of waves against the shore. That is the only sound all day long, except for a very occasional truck or car, which I hear coming from far away, and the planes from Pease Air Force Base that roar over now and then and sound rather threatening.

This deep silence—at this moment I hear crows cawing but they only punctuate it briefly—is nourishing. I suffer for lack of it in any city now.

And in these weeks of work and silence, when I see only two or three people in seven days, I am never lonely. I feel well, so full of ideas and "things to do," so fully conscious, so centered in work, that this is as close to happiness as I can imagine. "For what is happiness, but work in peace?" I wrote long ago in Santa Fe.

Saturday, January 29th

IT WAS QUITE an adventure yesterday to set out at 7:45 to drive to Sanford for my 8:45 appointment with the IRS. A fine clear day and the car started all right (I had a nightmare in the night that it wouldn't). After all the anxiety and the hassle of finding and arranging the papers and checks involved, I felt quite calm, so I enjoyed the drive and seeing a town near here that I had not seen before, rather sad, the center gutted because of shopping plazas outside. My interviewer, as I had divined from our brief phone call some weeks ago, was kind, sensitive, and very efficient. It took three hours of concentrated effort on all the figures—I sometimes felt like an animal lost in a maze—but at the end I was found to be in the clear, except for one mistake of $900, a mistake in my favor, made by the firm who did my tax that year. What a relief to pack up my briefcase and get away in the car, free! From the start I kept thinking of what the same sort of interview might have been like in a communist or fascist country, the bullying, the browbeating of people by officials not trained to be human and kind. And I was grateful for this country! Of course, the bureaucracy can be maddening even here. Lately I have received two completely mutilated letters from Europe, one of them black with machine oil, enclosed in official apologies for "the new machines at work now." And my correspondance with Social Security computers would make a hilarious short piece if I had time to bother with it. That, too, is now settled after months. So the New Year begins in the clear as far as finances go at least.

This morning I wrote a letter to a young woman who had asked me to read a four-hundred-page novel. The Christian in me agreed to do it because I feel so sorry for anyone trying to get published these days, but the pagan in me (as Kot used to say) resented the effort and the hours and hours of reading involved. Unfortunately, the novel is not good *enough*, but I wanted to give some encouragement. One can recognize "a writer" as opposed to someone who "wants to write" after reading about twenty pages. Integrity forces one to go all the way through.

Now tonight I can read for pleasure again and dive back into the rich and fascinating new biography of Isak Dinesen.

Monday, January 31st

I CAN'T BELIEVE that one of my precious three months of solitude has gone, and only forty pages of the novel have been composed in all those days, but this middle section is by far the hardest, and if I can pull it out by Easter, then the final section will be pure pleasure as it takes place on the island where the novel starts when Anne was a child in paradise.

Nancy Hartley came for me at quarter past twelve, and we set off to see *Gandhi* in Portsmouth. Three very intense hours that not only give one an unforgettable portrait of the man himself but put in a fierce light the kind of courage that nonviolence demands when pitted against physical assault. All the way through I kept thinking of Martin Luther King at Selma, in this violent country, and his ability to get thousands of blacks to use nonviolence and bear what it cost (Montgomery where the blacks walked to work for two years to protest discrimination in buses, for instance). How proud we should be of them! But it is still remembered by most Americans, I fear, with the troubled mind with which we contemplate the Vietnam war. And discrimination still goes on, for the war against that has to be fought and won over and over again. The tragedy of India was of course that once that incredible victory, freedom for India, had been won, the religious and racial wars began. The film does not shy away from this, but the fact remains embedded in my consciousness that one man can change the world, one single man with a vision.

If his vision is evil like Hitler's, it is far easier to accomplish. On television there were acknowlegments of the fiftieth anniversary of his rise to power. Hatred and violence are so close to the surface in all human beings, it would seem, that it is very easy to give them free rein. How infinitely harder to bring tolerance and love to the surface! And why is this so?

I think it is because hatred and intolerance spring primarily from fear of what is different in any way from ourselves—they are self-protective. (Hitler persuaded the

German Aryans that the Jews were a menace.) Love and tolerance are vulnerable, always. And the miracle of the spiritual genius of a Gandhi or a Martin Luther King is that they are able to persuade us that love *can* be strong and tolerance *can* be strong, stronger than hate. The Gandhi film makes tangible the dignity of nonviolent men and women and the loss of it in their attackers. A man beating another man has no dignity, has lost his *virtù*. Luckily for the Indians, the British had a tradition of justice that finally made it impossible to continue massacre and oppression of the nonviolent. There they were different from the Nazis, who gloried in the massacre of nonviolent, innocent Jews, gypsies, and Christians.

The tragedy is also that war, even nonviolent war, rouses the heroic in men and women, but the day-to-day struggle after victory to maintain human rights, to make peace among factions within the free, to go forward from there, is infinitely harder.

Reagan's greatest failure is that he never appeals to the best in us, never asks sacrifice that would be meaningful to the common man, never lifts the spirit. What a mean-spirited, dreadful time this is in our country!

Thursday, February 3rd

A WILD SOUTHEASTER has blown up from Florida to batter us, rain instead of snow, and in a way I wish it were snow as rain at this season makes one long for spring. There are spring flowers in the house, a blue hyacinth that

drenches the porch with its scent and the third lot of
paper-white narcissus just in bloom. The azaleas are still
a glory of pink, deep rose, and white in the plant window.
They make up for the miserable cyclamens, which did
badly this year, I cannot imagine why. And, best of all, I
have two cinerarias, one brilliant blue with a white circle
on each flower and one the most ravishing pale blue, a
tight bunch of rosettes in its crown of healthy green
leaves. I love seasonal flowers, cannot bring myself to buy
chrysanthemums now and cannot resist the tulips in the
florist's window. But cinerarias are most precious because
they are only available now. In California they plant hundreds in flower beds, a whole spectrum of blues, lavenders, whites, purples, pinks. Here, in winter New England,
we treasure one or two.

I have lost eleven pounds as I reach the halfway mark
of my six-week diet, but I am bored with the same food
over and over and have a cold suddenly. I woke yesterday
sneezing wildly and feel rather miserable today. I had
hoped it would be a twenty-four-hour blow like the storm,
which is on its way out to sea.

It often happens to me that a book lies around for a
year and I have no wish to read it and then, suddenly, it
is the food I need and I devour it happily. This has happened with Matthew Fox's *A Spirituality Named Compassion* (Winston Press, 1979), which was given me by
Linda Jacquot more than a year ago. Perhaps I have come
to it these days because of the section on Creativity and
Compassion. I feel bereft now that the muse has with-
drawn and no poem comes to interrupt my hours at my
desk, as it did often all through the halcyon days of November.

What originally put me off Fox was the absence of an
authentic *style*. The actual telling is done in a rather pe-

destrian language, which never lights up the material for me.

Now I am coming to see with Fox about many things and the most important his plea that less emphasis be laid on the Cross and more on the Empty Tomb, which has everything to do with life resurrected and engendering more life—"Behold, I make all things new."

Sunday, February 6th

FIVE ABOVE ZERO this morning and a dazzling winter day. I feel revived, my battery revved up by my holiday yesterday, the first in four weeks. I drove over to see Anne and Barbara at Deer Run Farm. Two miles from their house in the valley at the top of the hill I was stopped short by Mount Washington blazing white above the sharp blue peaks of the Presidential range. At this point in the road, beside a little cemetery, it is often shrouded in mist, but it was there yesterday, a magnificent glimpse, as I have rarely come upon it covered in snow, mantling the whole broad expanse as though it were set apart from all lower mountains, a dazzling god.

The farm always takes me by surprise, nestled in the valley, its lovely dark red and the enormous barn with Muscovy ducks and prize cocks pecking in the foreground and then Anne and Barbara running out for warm hugs of welcome. There is always so much to see and hear, always as on every farm some deaths to report. The oldest Muscovy duck died last week, and now his widow, mourning, stays on the porch rail by the front door, and Anne thinks she is waiting for him to come out as they had brought him into the house near the end. That morning one of the ornamental cocks had died. The cold takes its toll. I had to hear the hard news that the hens are recovering from bronchitis and did not lay for two weeks. Two weeks' eggs represent twenty-seven dollars and that money was badly needed. But they are all well now after being given antibiotics in their feed and have become good providers again.

So much has happened since I was last there! Barbara has been working on a sculptured design of sea horses cut out in a flat slab of soapstone, and there it was, a remarkable design of eelgrass and floating sea horses interwoven, lying on the wide pine boards of the trestle table Anne had worked on this autumn and brought in from the barn for Thanksgiving. It had been the family table in Lynnfield but was too long for the kitchen, so it was quite a job to shorten it and refinish it as well as the benches on either side, which Tommy, Anne's son, had made. Now they can seat eight comfortably close to the warmth of the wood stove in the kitchen.

Then I had to see what Anne had done in her studio, what was originally the front parlor of the house, all painted and tidied up, bookcases built, and her grandfather's clock set on a stand against one wall. On the easel, a large canvas just begun, which will be a stone wall with wild flowers growing against it. She is developing a much freer style in her painting and I shall be interested to see what happens to this one.

Then we sat down with a drink (my first in a month!) to exchange all the news. I asked Anne whether she had learned to be such a good carpenter from her father. And the astonishing answer was that she had taught herself, and when she opened up a wall for a door from the studio to the bathroom she had never done such a thing in her life! Since then she has become a mason as well as a carpenter. The new stove in the studio, which heats the whole house, now has a fine brick back. It is hard to take in that they moved to North Parsonsfield only six years ago. The things accomplished in the garden, the barn, and the house, not to mention the wood, which they are thinning out as they cut their firewood, are simply astounding. I could never do any of it. For one thing, I haven't Anne's patience and slow careful tempo. She never hurries. Each job, whether it be enclosing the hens' apartments in the barn or building a stone wall or painting a painting, is done with the greatest patience and exactitude.

One of the things I heard about was that the bluebird they had saved as a baby fallen from the nest and brought up, who had flown off finally at the end of summer two years ago, came back last year and nested on the place. I knew that but I did not know that at migrating time he was leading a flock of twenty-four bluebirds. What a sight!

This extravagance of bluebirds seems like a good image of what Anne and Barbara have achieved at the farm. On sheer nerve and energy, they have created a life there that stands like a signal to us all that it is quite possible to make a rich life on no money at all. Everyone who passes by and stops to inquire about the herbs Anne sells or to buy eggs or to see Barbara's sculpture goes away, I feel sure, with a new sense of what the good life is.

It was lovely to come home to Edythe, who had looked after Tamas and Bramble all day, and tell her all this as we

drank a cup of tea. The hardest thing about living alone
is not having anyone to recount such a day to. And beautiful as Mount Washington was, I drank a deep breath of the
marvelously alive blue ocean as I drove up to the house,
·   and was happy to be living here.

Tuesday, February 8th

YESTERDAY, limbo, while we had a real nor'easter that
piled up two feet of snow on the terrace. It is the first time
I have ever seen snow top the wall. Usually I am excited
and happy when we are enclosed in the whiteness. For
hours I could see nothing but that from my windows, only
now and then a shadowy bush floating into sight. Mary-
Leigh's house was simply not there. The problem is the
animals who are used to going out to do their business.
When it had not stopped by five, I managed to push open
the front door and shovel a small space for Tamas, but he
would have none of it and came right in, so he had contained himself for twenty-four hours by this morning, and
I slept badly worrying about him. At 3 A.M. Bramble
meowed loudly and I took her down and let her out.
Luckily the snow had a frozen surface, so she ran off and
came back in ten minutes, clearly relieved. After that I lay
awake listening for the snowplow and got into an anxiety
panic, very stupid of me. I woke in tears, once more tried
to get Tamas out into that small cleared space. I was anxious about him and the birds, impossible to get anywhere

near the feeders. What made it worse was that I discovered that the plow had come but they had not shoveled the path. I felt old and foolish to be so upset. After all, this is New England and we are supposed to be hardy souls. Finally at half-past six I called Janice, and that angel promised to come over with Maryann and shovel me out. With that hope in sight I got into my boots and shoveled from the front door all down the terrace, a narrow path, and then released the piles of snow in front of the porch door and finally out to the feeders. This is more shoveling than I have done in years, heavy snow, more than two feet deep. It was satisfying to see that I could do it. But what a relief when my saviors came and set to the huge job of clearing the mountain the plow had pushed against the garage doors! *That* I had not been able to see from the house and it was a shock. Clyde really let me down this time. For if he was not going to shovel, he might have managed to do better to ease my way out.

I feel a lot better now, thanks to Janice and Maryann. Janice had already done her own shoveling before they came and Maryann had been snowblowing since 3 A.M., so it was heroic of them to come and rescue me. We had a cup of coffee and then off they went to the Public Health Association in Portsmouth where they work. And I guess I'll get out now, pick up the mail, and get in food.

Yesterday I did a little work on the novel and wrote an uninspired poem. I wanted to describe what it is like alone in the house in a blizzard. At times the wind was horizontal, an amazing sight. And in the afternoon I finished the income tax. So it was not a wholly wasted day, but a strangely depressing one, I don't know quite why. Usually I am exhilarated by a big storm like this. This time it threw me.

Wednesday, February 9th

SOMETIMES a small thing can change the color of a whole day. I was drinking a cup of tea downstairs on the porch when I heard a lot of scrabbling outside on the wall and thought "it must be a giant squirrel," but when I went out, it was Chris fixing the wire for the bird feeders, which had fallen before the blizzard. When he hadn't come over the weekend, I figured I wouldn't see him till spring as the wire was buried in three feet of snow. But there he was, got it up in a trice, hung up all the feeders and suet for me (I had had to hang them in the cherry tree again where the squirrels would have destroyed them eventually.) It gave me a real lift that he bothered to come, a merry and wise young man. "See you in the spring!" he called as he left. Then he will come to take off the storm windows.

Altogether it has been a good day. After a gray day yesterday the sun has been out, and as it set I watched the long February shadows of the trees. It is five now and still light, and what a difference that half-hour more of light makes! It is wonderfully silent and beautiful all around, so silent I have not wanted music even. I have been writing letters and lifting my head now and then to watch the light fade over the immense dark-blue perimeter of ocean, quiet today after the turbulence of yesterday.

In today's mail several interesting letters, among them

one from a woman who has written me before as she tells
me,

This, the third letter, is in recognition of the part you have
unknowingly played in launching me into a new phase of my
life.
    Your description of how throughout your life you have
created environments for yourself and how these environments
have influenced your work caused me to look at my world and
the role physical setting has had in my life. I saw that I had no
place to call my own in this big house. I saw that I had never
dared ask for either time or space that was inviolate. This fall
I cleaned out a spare room that had been used to store toys and
my son's outgrown clothes and set out to create a private place
for myself. I culled photos from closed drawers, books from
scattered shelves. From the corners of the house I gathered
together the parts of me that I had hidden away. I hung the
pictures, shelved the books, unpacked my cello, and sat and
waited for the fusing to begin. It did. . . .
    Had I not had this private space and had I not begun to
demand private time for myself, I never would have dared to
do something as "selfish" as going to school and taking impracti-
cal classes in English and the classics. But I did have that space
and I had made those demands so I was able to take the next
step.

    I found this letter extremely interesting. There must
be so many women who have not dared to demand "a
room of their own," who have not realized how closely
bound up one's identity can be with the frame in which
one lives.
    Of course I now live in a big house in a very beautiful
place, but what came to my mind as I read the letter was
how I tamed very bleak rented rooms in London in the
thirties when I was young. The walls were brown. Nothing had any charm except when I could afford a shilling

CREDIT: MAY SARTON

"I managed to shovel a path to the feeders"

to light the gas fire. But somehow, by arranging books on the desk, buying a few daffodils from a cart in the street, putting up postcard reproductions of paintings I loved and a photograph or two, by leaving a brilliant scarf on the bureau, the room became my room and I began to live in it, to live my real life there, to know who May Sarton was and hoped to become.

It is dark now. The snow is deep blue and the ocean nearly black. It is time for some music.

Saturday, February 12th

THE WHOLE EAST COAST to below Washington has been hit by a huge blizzard, but last night the weathermen thought it would go out to sea south of Boston, so I went to bed without anxiety, and even when at midnight the house was buffeted by high winds I turned over and went to sleep again, saying to myself that it was just a big blow. But when I went down in the dark at five and turned on the light over the front door I could see thick veils of snow falling and such a drift in front of that door that it could not possibly be pushed open.

This time I have not been in the bad state I was in on Monday when I felt quite desperate. I wrote letters all morning and by noon the snow had stopped and I went out and managed to shovel a path to the feeders from the porch door. The snow on the terrace is at least three feet high now and the wall is buried!

All day there has been huge surf plunging into foam

below the field and now at five, as the dusk comes, there are long white lines of foam almost at the horizon and the ocean is a wonderful dark slate color. The setting sun touches the breaking waves with rose.

But I wish Clyde Dixon would come now and plow us out, though just where he will be able to put the new eighteen inches of snow is a question—and will he shovel this time? So all is in suspense again.

Anyway, Tamas did go out late this morning and function in the small space I had shoveled myself. Bramble took one look and fled back indoors.

This morning I had some lines running through my head and roughed out a poem, maybe a little more of a poem than the one I tried to capture in the last storm.

It is hard to believe that in three months the field, so absolutely white, will be its ragged spring self again with a host of daffodils poking up through it. But that is why I love New England, the violent changes of weather. They are exhilarating.

Monday, February 14th, Valentine's Day

NOW I HAVE FINISHED the Isak Dinesen biography I miss it and wish I still had it before me. When the huge book of her letters came out last year, I devoured it, and when I ordered the Judith Thurman biography, I wondered whether it might not seem redundant. Not at all. This is partly because the letters give us the woman as she saw herself, and she was of course a great mythmaker, not only as a writer but in that other creation at which she worked as hard and imagined as deeply as in her stories, the creation of a mythical personage, not made into a myth after her death by others but made into a myth while she was alive, by herself. So part of the fascination of this biography lies in the discrepancies between art and life, or the fabrications that went into her life as well as her art. The Karen Blixen who became Isak Dinesen is an astounding creation, and it is this that Thurman's biography makes clear. Thurman succeeds in fusing the life (the myth) and the work and making Dinesen herself understandable.

Far from diminishing her greatness it brings it into sharp focus and made me see again what a masterpiece *Out of Africa* is, the perfect example of what makes a work of art, experience distilled, sometimes even distorted, so that truth transcends fact. This is of a quite different order from Anaïs Nin's narcissistic evasions and distortions in her journals, she who also succeeded in making a myth of herself.

When I read the letters last year I was shocked by Karen Blixen's snobbism, the outrageous statement, for instance, that it was worth getting syphilis (she got it from her husband Bror Blixen-Finecke) to become a baroness! But after reading the biography I began to understand that her snobbism was rather like the snobbism of W. B. Yeats, an ability to connect with the aristocrat and the peasant but never with the materialistic middle class. The Irish peasantry provided Yeats with a folklore that went deep into the past, as the aristocracy provided him with an ethos he could value because it too was steeped in the past. For both Yeats and Dinesen the aristocracy was com-

posed of landed gentry, dependent on a peasantry, as the
Dinesen coffee farm depended on the Kikuyu and the
Somali. Dinesen might have written, as Yeats did in "The
Gyres":

> Conduct and work grow coarse, and coarse the soul
> What matter? Those that Rocky Face holds dear,
> Lovers of horses and of women, shall,
> From marble of a broken sepulchre,
> Or dark betwixt the polecat and the owl,
> Or any rich dark nothing disinter
> The workman, noble and saint, and all things run
> On that unfashionable gyre again.

Dinesen's stories were laid for good reason either in
eighteenth-century Denmark or in Kenya. The African
farm was a failure and her whole great work as a writer
began as a phoenix rising from the ashes. But without the
experience of Africa it's clear that she would never have
found the material she had in hand, so whatever the tragedy (and it included the death of her lover, Finch-Hatton),
her final triumph had its roots in the African farm.
There she was literally a legend, "Lioness" her people
on the farm called her because she shot the lions that
marauded and preyed on their animals. There she could
exercise her genius for understanding primitive people
and her courage and sense of honor. As one of her
Danish admirers said, "She knows everything about the
sublimation of loss, about suffering as the nourishment
of genius, about pain's resonance as harmony in a work
of art."

But when she lost the farm and had to go back to
Denmark, she had lost herself for a time as *legend*. The
last years brought her triumph and fame as a writer of

genius, but as she re-created herself as legend and succeeded grandly in that creation, she did it partly by less
noble means. She seems to have needed to seduce (not
sexually so much as by her dominance as an entrancing
wise old woman) one young man of genius after another.
She had to see herself *reflected*. And when she looked for
her own likeness in someone else and so saw herself mir-
rored, she failed as a human being and did only harm,
whereas in her relation to her servants and friends among
the Kikuyu and the Somali, she could not see herself mir-
rored but had to exercise imagination and generosity to
a high degree and take in a world utterly different from
her own. Being one kind of legend enlarged her as a
human being; the other diminished her because it was
fundamentally self-serving. So the same admirer I quoted
above goes on to say about Dinesen in old age, "and all the
same she yielded to the most banal human moods and
impulses, pettiness, impatience, caprice, stinginess. She
suffered from a craving for power in spite of her generosity; she toyed with human fates in spite of her contempt
for such toying; yes, she suffered from self-contempt in
spite of her mighty legitimate self-confidence and pride.
She was a paradox, outside of any moral category."

Yet downstairs I have a photograph taken at Rungsted-
lund by Cecil Beaton three days before she died. She sits
with sunlight streaming in, an old-fashioned posy in her
emaciated hands, one of her famous turtleneck sweaters
high on her throat, and the extraordinary face, the eyes
closed, suffused in an ineffable smile, the smile of one who
has suffered everything and accepted everything. It is
that image I keep, and perhaps now I shall be able to write
the poem about it that I have had in the back of my mind
and in my heart to write for years.

Thursday, February 17th

I DID MAKE A TRY at the poem and read what I had
sketched out to Char to see how it sounded. Char
Heidema is a new friend I met a year or so ago. She has
moved to Maine from Denver and teaches psychiatric
social work at the University of Southern Maine. I invited
her to lunch, the first guest to come here since I holed in
January 1st except for Nancy and Janice, my "regulars,"
and Susan Kerestes one day. I enjoyed talking with her,
but it is clear that having someone to lunch doesn't really
work. Getting ready even such a simple diet meal as I had
to offer—shrimp salad, a half grapefruit—distracts my
mind, and an hour or so of intense talk uses up the psychic
energy I need to call on when I write letters in the afternoon. It is quite ridiculous to have to hoard energy like a
miser, but these precious "free" months have already
been half used up. The sense I had of a peaceful large
amount of time has changed, and I begin to count the days
I still have for unimpeded work.

It has been a good and fruitful time in spite of the
constant doubts about the novel, but the poem about
Dinesen needs a lot more thinking about, as I realized
when I read it aloud. I lent *Out of Africa* to Char as she
has not encountered Isak Dinesen. What joy to give her
this great adventure ahead!

In the early morning after my breakfast, I read for a

half-hour or so a book sent me in proof, Linda Huf's *A Portrait of the Artist as a Young Woman.* How much resistance there still is to a woman who dedicates herself to an art! Huf is interesting about the very few such novels published on this theme in the nineteenth century and how universally condemned they were as unworthy of their sex and its taken-for-granted responsibilities as wives and mothers. Even now, what young woman writer would dare assert herself, demand the time, space, and freedom from domestic responsibility that every young male writer takes for granted? Of course it is partly that the *Bildungsroman* is written at the start of a career, and what young woman writer is sufficiently self-confident to hold as premise the right of genius to make extreme human demands at the expense of what is known as "normal life"? The violent egotism of Thomas Wolfe, Joyce, Dreiser, or Farrell would be difficult for a young woman to justify, because a young woman is far more split between life and art than a young man is who expects a wife to "take care of him" and make his work possible. Curiously enough, Willa Cather, in her heroine Thea in *The Song of the Lark,* did create such a determined, ruthless woman artist, an opera singer. The men in Thea's life were her supporters and she used them, though not sexually, in much the way that such men use women. Only in that novel men are not the enemy because they are there to serve genius. I expect this has been noted before, but for me it came as a fresh insight through Huf's excellent analysis.

And all this, I suppose, is vivid in my mind this morning, because I met again in a small way what the cost of creation is and will always be. I ask a young friend to lunch and the edge has gone for the next morning's work! I no longer face the conflict I faced when I was young between

what I saw as my first obligation, to write well, and my
other obligation to be as good a human being as possible.
How often I questioned by what right I could justify such
selfish work! For when one starts out to write, who can be
sure that it will prove useful? I know now that my work,
whether it lasts or not, has been useful, so that particular
conflict—especially now I am old—is far less intense than
it was when every day as I sat down at my desk to write
I battled out whether I should not be somewhere in a slum
teaching deprived children and give up the hubris of pre-
tending to be a writer of value.

It is quite incredible that I am seventy and that I feel
so young, much younger than I felt when I wrote *The
House by the Sea*, but isn't it true that one often fears what
is ahead, and then when one gets there it is not at all what
one feared? These days seventy is not old, especially if
good health is in the cards. I have been lucky in inheriting
my father's constitution and not my mother's, for she battled various illnesses all her life, in spite of her incredible
vitality and courage.

The phone just rang, and it was Tami in Nelson, Mildred Quigley's daughter. Mildred fell and broke her pel-
vis two days ago and now has pneumonia, and it is touch
and go. When I saw her last at Christmastime we had a
good talk, but I sensed her extreme frailty. She weighed
under a hundred pounds, she told me, and I sensed that
she dreaded the winter months ahead. Tami told me that
her mother had talked with her doctor in the autumn and,
evidently believing this might be her last winter, made
him promise, if it came to that, not to use support systems
but to let her go. I am relieved to hear that he agreed,
after talking it over with the children, to follow this wish.
I am more and more convinced that people die when they
are ready, except in the case of violent accidents—and

Mildred is ready. What an unquenchable flame she was!

It is good to know that Barney and his wife are coming from New York, so her three children, Tami, Barney, and Terry, the eldest, will all be at her side for this final passage. I can only pray that she goes now in peace, that she does not have to make the huge effort to recover.

The other day I had such a vivid remembrance of something she did years ago when Judy was staying with me in Nelson. Mildred was not demonstrative, but she was very perspicacious and sensitive about people and their value. That day in spring she came over with a bunch of white violets from her garden for Judy, "because," she said to me, "they are so like her." That was not something Mildred would do any day, or for anyone. It was meant as a tribute.

Monday, February 21st

MILDRED'S FUNERAL was yesterday in Keene and I decided to go, in spite of the long drive there and back. I have been anxious about Laurie, who is having a hard winter, and thought it a good idea to make the trip partly to see her for a half-hour and take her the Dinesen biography and some German Speculatius cookies that I discovered the other day, which have the taste of childhood in Belgium for me. I really hated to part with them, so greedy have I become on the diet!

It turned out to be a beautiful pure blue and white day, and it was a great pleasure to make the familiar drive across hill and down dale under snow. Every hill had children scrambling up it carrying Flexible Flyers or red trays; on many small houses the Christmas wreaths were still up, and because of the warm weather several herds of cows were out behind barns. But the best sight of all was, over and over again, to see the long blue shadows of trees on snow, so characteristic of February. So it turned out to be a pilgrimage back to all I loved when I lived in Nelson, the New Hampshire of the dream. That was vivid as I reached the top of the mountain and sped down into Peterborough and there was Monadnock, all in white, then where trees began, a wonderful dark blue. It stands there dominating the whole region and I was happy to salute it.

I found Laurie in her wrapper, sitting by the fire in her bedroom, that delightful small room that looks out to the mountain, with a shelf of loved books on the mantel, including John Donne and Shakespeare whom she rereads these days. I pulled up a chair, and she held my hands in her warm ones and, as always, we talked about friends, about books, and laughed at our own foibles. She ended by telling me wonderful stories about Mrs. MacDowell whom she knew well and who, she said, had a marvelous sense of humor. Laurie has a pile of her letters, and we talked about where they should go after her death. And from there to the Dinesen biography and my own fears about a biographer. Several people unknown to me have written lately to ask whether they could do mine, and my answer is always the same. "Not till I'm dead." But what hazards there are! Of course Carol Heilbrun will presumably be there to make the decision.

And then it was time to wrench myself away, feeling again what a rich friendship this is.

It is not good to go on a long all-day trip when on a diet.

I felt ravenous when I got to Keene with a half-hour before the funeral and finally remembered a diner in the center of town. There I ate a small Greek salad, feeling guilty because it had olives in it and cheese! That and a glass of water proved not exactly filling but had to do, for, in these last days on the diet, it is a point of honor not to succumb to a hamburger or a hot turkey sandwich and the glass of milk I longed for.

I got to the funeral home with minutes to spare and joined friends at the back of the room. It was here at Foley's that I attended Quig's funeral. I remembered that there is a real connection between the Foleys and the Quigleys because one of the last commissions Quig was able to carry out was to paint their three boys, and he carried it through although he was already very ill. It was moving to find myself among my old Nelson neighbors— two of the Warners, Helen and Doris, sat in front of me, and I recognized several people whose names escape me. The family sat beyond a large passage that separates the two rooms and were not visible. But the small, plain coffin was and, set above it, one of Quig's paintings, of the village green with his house in the foreground. There was a huge arrangement of red and white carnations above the casket, not many flowers. Who can afford them these days? All this was accompanied by rather soupy recorded music, including "The Impossible Dream." I guess I was the only person in the room who had come alone, and I felt self-conscious and lonely, trying not to cry. But at the sounds of "The Impossible Dream" I couldn't help it because in a curious way it fitted Mildred. Her dreams were almost all "impossible," but she never lost that fiery core of conviction and hope that kept her alive through all the disasters and the never ceasing anxieties about money. She had until the very end an unquenchable interest in life, never stopped giving and caring, and I have an idea that every person in the room had at one time or another been restored by her sense of humor (it never failed) and her wisdom. When the bookmobile came to Nelson, as it does every three months, Mildred would borrow twenty or more books and read them all. One of her impossible dreams was to study archeology. One of her impossible dreams was to rescue the dear dilapidated house and that, thank goodness, was at least partially realized after Quig's death when I undertook to have it reroofed, reclapboarded, and a flush toilet put in. I can still see tiny Mildred on a scaffolding painting it the dark brown she had chosen, determined to do that herself, as she did.

These reveries were interrupted finally by a minister's voice. We in the back could not see him, so at first I thought the eulogy had been recorded. It was a rather strange creation, as the reverend spent at least ten minutes on a very long tale about himself and a friend hunting in the bog below Nelson for pieces of detritus—rather like driftwood, pieces of rotting trees that could be made into works of art. The point was slow in coming, that they ended up in the Quigleys' kitchen with their feet in the stove, getting warmed by good conversation and hot coffee. He quoted a short passage from my chapter on the Quigleys in *Plant Dreaming Deep* and read the 101st and 23rd Psalms. He also addressed us gathered there as "folk" several times, and I detected a rather patronizing attitude, perhaps not meant. But it was not appropriate in relation to Mildred, herself one of the most literate people I have known and with a very sensitive and precise sense of language. People who live in the boondocks and have never been anything except poor are not necessarily "folk"!

So I minded that Mildred's distinction was left uncelebrated.

Of course the hardest part was filing out by the coffin and then hugging Barney, the younger son, and Terry and Tami, all of us unashamedly weeping.

Strange to come out into brilliant sunlight and to join the knot of old friends standing there to talk about the Mildred we had known. I shall never again be part of a community as I was in Nelson. It was balm to be among them and to feel welcomed after all these years.

But it was time I left for the long drive home. At the turn-off for Nelson my heart beat fast, and it was hard to know that never again would that house be the same. Never again would I push open the door and find Mildred with a cat sitting on the arm of her chair, her eyes bright, an open book in her lap. In two days all that had become history.

Oh, how glad I am that a little of it at least I have recorded and celebrated, and that at this very moment someone somewhere is reading about Quig and Mildred in *Plant Dreaming Deep* and so these two are still alive to befriend and restore the stranger at the door.

Thursday, February 24th

YESTERDAY, browsing around in an old journal for something else, I came upon this marvelous passage by De Quincey about Dorothy Wordsworth:

The pulses of light are not more quick or more inevitable in their flow and undulation, than were the answering and echoing movements of her sympathizing attention. I may sum up her character as a companion by saying that she was the very wildest (in the sense of most natural) person I have ever known and also the truest, most inevitable, and at the same time the quickest and readiest in her sympathy with either joy or sorrow, with laughter or with tears, with the realities of life, or the larger realities of the poets.

This paragraph brought Mildred vividly to my mind. These are gloomy days because I am stuck on the novel, and to extricate myself, am reading a series of letters Anne Thorp wrote to her best friend during the two years she was working for the Unitarian Service Committee after World War II in Germany. The letters bring her back vividly as a person, her immense "goodwill toward men" and women, her love of fun, picnics, the visible world especially in spring, and her selflessness because for months while she learned the language (she was fifty-five) she was mostly an observer and perhaps also a receptacle for all the stresses of the staff at the Nachbarhaus in Bremen. There is very little of the inwardness of all this but of course that is what I must get at when I can begin to write about it and re-create it all. On my desk I have a beautiful photograph of Anne that Agnes Swift took. I look at it often and sometimes feel accused for not doing a better job, for not being more thorough and patient. The problem is that the material is so rich and various and she was deeply connected to so many people over her long life. The book teems with characters whose names, the invented ones, I forget. The responsibility I have undertaken is awesome, and these past days I have wondered whether I could ever succeed. It will not be good *enough* in any case. No novel can project all the complexities of one human being, or do justice. What it can do is what the

impressionist painters sometimes achieved, evoke a landscape (the landscape of a mind and soul, in this case) with
small notations that add up and finally communicate a
radiant whole. Can I do it for Anne and her life? It is worth
a try.

Friday, February 25th

YESTERDAY was the last day on the diet. I went to the Diet
Center in Portsmouth to get weighed and I have lost
eighteen pounds. I had hoped for twenty, but when I
lugged in twenty-five pounds of sunflower seeds yesterday and thought "well, I am carrying eighteen pounds less
around all day," it felt good. It is wonderful to be off the
diet and I celebrated by going out for dinner with Janice
and Priscilla to our favorite restaurant here in York called
Spice of Life. Especially at night, when the Victorian
lamps that hang from the ceiling are lit and the dark wood
paneling lights up, it feels very much like a restaurant in
France. It was great fun to be there. Janice and Priscilla
bought us a liter of the house Burgundy, which added to
the festive atmosphere. I had veal in a mushroom sauce
and my first real dessert in six weeks, cherry cheesecake.

Before dinner I lit the fire in the library for the first
time since Christmas and we had our drinks there with
Tamas waiting patiently for tidbits of cheese, and I, taking
my first swallow of Scotch since mid-January. With these
two, who feel like old friends now, I can relax and enjoy,
enjoy not being May Sarton, the writer, and talk about all

the things that really matter such as our dogs, dreams of the garden this spring, politics, and life in general. It was a charming lighthearted evening, and I went to bed in a peaceful state of mind for a change.

Maybe I'll have the courage to clean out the cellar, the corner of it where I grow plants under lights. That is the next to last chore I had planned for this winter. The last one is to clean out the garage. Once the garden is available and all the spring work to be done, there is never time for indoor clearing out. What a triumph if I can get it done! Soon I shall be starting the tuberous begonias down there and it would be so fine to be able to do that in an orderly fashion.

Monday, February 28th

I DID CLEAR OUT the corner of the cellar where I keep plants. What a satisfaction it was! It took only an hour and a half. It just shows once more that half the battle in these matters is getting started, pulling oneself together for the effort involved. I find that harder and harder to do alone, but this time I managed without Nancy's help, so I was quite proud of myself.

Compared to writing even one decent page of a book, clearing out the cellar or a cupboard is nothing, of course, and one reason I have found it hard to "get started" is that by the end of the morning at my desk I have spent my primary energy and am tired, lately a little too tired. That is because what I am doing now—reading Anne's letters and making notes—requires immense patience with little to show for the concentrated hours. This morning I have copied out five single-spaced pages of parts of letters that I may be able to translate into a series of vignettes of those German years. For it seems to me now that that will be the way to make it all vivid, not try to tell the whole story but by evoking some precise images bring it all to life.

As I typed this morning I became more and more aware that what we need here in the United States today is just such wise and patient leadership and hard work as the Unitarian Service Committee and the Arbeiter Wolfart did in Bremen (where Anne was stationed) after the war. For years it seems we have simply turned our back on places as much in ruins (parts of the Bronx, for instance) as a bombed city. We have turned our backs on the deprived children who live there, and everywhere the cry seems to be "crack down on the criminals," never on building centers of life where children could grow up into human beings. We consider ourselves a civilized country, but forty percent of Americans, it seems, are illiterate, can neither read nor write! The figures are so staggering I find them hard to believe. For thousands of American children what Katharine Taylor called "the basic needs" are not met—food, clothing, protection, first of all, and then, as Anne jotted down, the spiritual needs:

1. the longing for respect and love
2. the sense of belonging, of being included and of being able to contribute. "The quality of the relationship with others is of great importance."
3. the need to feel, as one grows, that one can develop one's powers and take one's part in society. One seeks skills, more understanding, some form of creative expression, good human relations.

In large areas of this country, none of these needs, even as simple as food and clothing, are being met. The wonder is not that there are so many criminals but that there are so few.

I wake these days in a state of malaise. I wake to great anxiety about our future here. And I wonder why no concerted effort is being made, even by the churches, to attack and at least make a beginning at "waging peace" at home, as we did to such good effect both in Germany and in Japan after the war.

Tuesday, March 1st

I TREMBLE to see that the third month of work time is starting today, and I have accomplished so little in the first two. But a lot goes on here besides creation these days. Nancy Hartley has done a splendid job of arranging all my letters to Camille Mayran and hers to me since 1955. I have just wrapped them up to send to the Berg Collection for safekeeping. Each time I separate myself from a correspondence, it is like dying a little and also burying the dead. Camille Mayran is in her nineties now—the last letter is dated 1982, and I must write her once more now to tell her that our friendship has gone to the archives. Oh dear, that does sound so final. But in this age when the writing of letters is becoming rare, when the telephone too often takes the place of reflection, and when the voice dies, there is nothing left. I rejoice in this correspondence of nearly thirty years and like to believe that the friendship it communicates will one day become, for someone who finds it, as fresh and alive as it was for us who met almost entirely by letter and became intimate by letter and grew to understand each other, little by little. When I met her at a tea at the Julian Huxleys in 1938 (it must have been in that year or in 1939 for her novel *Dame en Noir* had just received the Femina-Vie Heureuse Prix and she was in London because of it), she was elated and on the brink of fame. Then came the war—first her house in Beauvais was totally destroyed with her library and all her papers in it. She and her husband, her daughter and son took refuge then in her parents' house in Tarascon, and that was destroyed by American bombers during the liberation. Her husband died—partly as a result of the too hard labor expended in trying to rescue part of his library from the rubble. After the war she lived in Strasbourg, where her daughter is professor of literature at the university, and summered in an old farmhouse in Provence where I was twice able to visit her, the last time with Judy. During those years she wrote little and felt forgotten. How happy I was then that in 1980 Julliard brought out a remarkable book, *Portrait de Ma Mère en Son Grand Âge,* a book that contained portraits also of her uncle, André Chévrillon, that adorable man and that rarity, a French Anglophile, and of Charles Du Bos whom I had read and so greatly admired in the thirties.

Hers has been a life of one loss after another, and not least the loss that is inevitable if one lives beyond ninety, the loss of her world, of her friends, and her sisters. In this context I see that our friendship has had a real value for her, as it did of course even more for me. For me she has been a shining link with France itself, and with the part of me that was born with the French language, that uttered its first words in French. The marvelous language she wrote in was civilization itself and taught me more by the way she expressed herself in it than I can possibly say. Because she had time, and because she cared, and because she was ultrasensitive to English literature and its qualities, her letters about my poems and novels came to me like manna from heaven. No one else has read my poems with such attention and such generous appreciation.

Letters! The other day my letters to Judy came to me. So I am pulled hither and thither these days, rich days, where the past floods into the present.

It happened yesterday that just after I had written a sentence or two about how we are not waging peace at home, I read a galvanizing piece by Richard Cohen in the February 27th *Manchester Guardian Weekly,* about the most nourishing journal that I see. It is titled "The War on the Poor." I feel I must jot down here a few paragraphs, if only not to forget.

> Now, into the third year, the war continues. The attack has been relentless and it is clear that casualties are mounting. The evidence is all around us—the dazed, the dispirited, the refugees hitting the road in a vain hope for a better life elsewhere. Occasionally there is a fatality, but no one has made a body count. Nevertheless, the toll is mounting. The War on the Poor continues.

Cohen then itemizes the cuts the Reagan plan demands in social services.

> All this has taken its toll. Alcoholism, depression and the inevitable consequences of that, suicide, are up. So is wife-beating. Children, the raw materials of any country, are undernourished and undereducated. This is the true infrastructure of the society and it is rotting at a very young age. Suffer the little children.
>
> In many cities, people are eating at soup kitchens. In Detroit there are eight of them, some of them reporting that for the first time in any memory, the

people being served are not just bums and hoboes with shopping bags full of newspapers, but families— mothers and fathers with children. Kansas City has these kitchens—and Houston and Trenton and Tucson, too.

All this is remarkable testimony to the success of the war. The poor are in full retreat. In some places they are cold and homeless. In other places they are merely out of work and discouraged. In all places they are miserable. This must be no one's fault but their own, otherwise we would do something about it. The commander in chief knows this. He pursues them vigorously. These things are never easy, and anyway the plan says there are no other choices.

Thursday, March 3rd

YESTERDAY I got the transcript of the interview for the *Paris Review* from Karen Saum. What a task! I wonder how she ever found the time with all she has to do at H.O.M.E., juggling twenty things every day. I had dreaded the interview last autumn because, although I trusted her absolutely as interviewer, I knew I had talked too much about myself and my work in too many interviews last spring and summer. And I approached it without enthusiasm. At present it is thirty-six pages long, so maybe it can be improved by large cuts. I spent three hours yesterday afternoon and this morning vetting it and making small stylistic changes, but it is quite impossible for me to judge whether it works or not. I have said all that is in it so many times before, and, I'm afraid, said it all better, especially in *Writings on Writing*, which was published in 1980 by Connie Hunting at Puckerbrush Press. Anyway it is packed now to go off to Deborah Pease. One thing accomplished!

I too have been juggling rather a lot these past days when the past invades the present, not only the Mayran letters but my letters to Judy that Timmy Warren sent me. I have just glanced at them, but already they tell me how rich those springs in England and France were in the forties—and how much I had forgotten. But I would like to disentangle myself from letters soon.

Karen asked the question "How is seventy different from sixty-five?" I don't see much difference, except that time accelerates. The days go past with frightful rapidity, and so do the years. It is plain that I am not ready for old age! But then time does not stand still in old age I fear. On the contrary, from all reports it simply flies away, and that is what I am beginning to notice.

These last nights in bed I have been reading a very moving book sent to me by an English friend, *A Message from the Falklands, the Life and Gallant Death of David Tinker, Lieut. R.N.* Tinker was killed by a bomb that hit H.M.S. *Glamorgan* in the Falkland war. The book is composed of his letters to his parents and to his girl (whom he married the year before the war) when he was abroad on various ships, and they begin with his schooldays, then his training as a midshipman and a year at the university where the navy sent him before he was commissioned. I found the book fascinating, to watch his growth as a human being from the first excitement and exhilaration at the thought of seeing action to the bitter realization of how ill prepared the British fleet was to defend itself (no proper air support for the ships) against the Argentine missiles, especially Exocet, and, in the end, his certainty that it was an unjustified war, fought and temporarily won at too high a price. Do men have to go to war over and over again and in every generation to find out that war is hell and should be avoided at all costs? Tinker quotes Wilfred Owen more than once in his letters home and is bitter about Margaret Thatcher "trying to be Churchill."

Tinker himself comes through as what we admire most about the British—the saving sense of humor, an ability to be detached and think through even at highly emotional moments, the capacity to feel deeply without becoming sentimental, and a beautiful serenity under great tension. It is hard to bear his death.

Three weeks before he died he was writing to his father, "Certainly the trivia of life and the important things are all brought to mind by this. And how much the trivia are at the forefront of normal life, and the important things put away, or not done, or left to do later and then forgotten. Here, certainly, the material things are unimportant and human 'things,' values, and ways of life are thought about by everybody."

Sunday, March 6th

SPRING is in the air these days but not yet on the ground where there are large patches of snow everywhere, and the road in is deeply rutted in mud. When I wake at five there is already faint light, and I eat my breakfast watching the sky turn rose or orange just before the sun leaps out like a jack-in-the-box, it happens so fast. One window is open up here in my study for the first time since November. The chickadees are singing their spring songs; the purple finches are coming back to feed, and at this

moment a flock of starlings in the big oak are carrying on
an extended conversation, making what sounds like prolonged wheezes in counterpoint to abrupt jo-cular songs.
It is so silent up here this morning that the houseflies
buzzing against the screen sound quite violent.

Last night after supper I did something I rarely do,
turned on the television to a police drama and was caught
in it for a half-hour until I felt sick of the violence and
went to bed. Much has been written about the effect of
violence on children. I felt it keenly last night where there
was such an atmosphere of sadism, sexual as well as everything else, a positive glorying by the police in shooting
down the criminals, and sensed in myself, much to my
amazement, a below-the-level-of-reason-or-charity wish
to have a gun in my hand and shoot it! When I was safely
in bed with Tamas and Bramble, I shivered with the im-
pact and the absolute realization, on my own pulse, that
watching violence on television must help create violence
in the streets. The illiterate, the desperate, the unsound
of mind are presented with an exhilarating kind of *action,*
and because the actors on the screen are actors, not real
people, and the multiple deaths are only "fiction," the
imagination is short-circuited and the real death of real
people, the real torture of real people, becomes simply
taken for granted. Death itself, violent death, becomes a
fiction.

It's rather a joke that with all the letters I am immersed in these days I am now reading Sylvia Townsend
Warner's letters, edited by Bill Maxwell. For the second
time—the first was when I read a selection of Colette's
letters—I am bothered by the editor's cutting radically,
so, instead of taking part in a relationship, the reader is
given simply literary excerpts, descriptions, brief com-
ments on politics, and so on and I find it unsatisfactory. I

miss the salutations, for instance, and the closures that frame a letter and often define the relationship, at least give the reader the sense of a whole moment in time and place. Excerpts lack continuity and appear to take place in some literary limbo.

Sylvia Townsend Warner is one of those rare writers who cannot be "placed," a delightful, warm, original whose every book became an event for her admirers, partly because each was sui generis. I remember very well when I read *Lolly Willowes* and *Mr. Fortune's Maggot* how astonished and delighted I was, and then how surprising to find a re-creation of 1848 in Paris and a remarkable delineation of a lesbian relationship in *Summer Will Show.* I have never heard anyone speak of this book, but I consider it a treasure.

Here are a couple of passages I marked last night. The first is to a friend who was of two minds about remaining married:

21:vii: 1946

Stop, take thought. Consider the lilies. Whatever [   ] fell in love with it wasn't a Mother's Help. You say that you have been too much together. What you mean is that you have not been together enough, that you have been incessantly chaperoned by a fatal spirit of helpfulness and unselfishness. . . . I say it with my true heart, the worst injury one can do to the person who loves one is to cover oneself from head to foot in a shining impermeable condom of irreproachable behavior.

The second is to Paul Nordhoff:

4:ii: 1949

We were so very glad to get your cable with the news of your daughter. I hope she will be very, very happy;

and I hope she will be without fear. I am quite sure
that to be fearless is the first requisite for a woman;
everything else that is good will grow naturally out
of that, as a tree has leaves and fruit and grows tall
and full provided its roots have a good hold of the
ground. Bring her up to be fearless and unin-
timidated by frowns, hints, and conventions, and
then she will be full of mercy and grace and generosity. It is fear that turns women sour, sly and harsh to
their neighbors. It was Shakespeare's Constance who
said she was "a woman, naturally born to fears." Not
naturally, I think; but hereditarily; and so to be
guarded against fear before all else.

Now it is nine and I must get to letters, not to be read
with delight but to be written reluctantly, and what I
want to do is order dwarf gladioli, Abyssinian lilies, and
Mignon dahlias for the summer garden. Maybe this afternoon. I love it, though, that life is so full these days. Three
months of bliss, time to read for pleasure, time to think,
time to struggle along on the novel, uninterrupted.

Tuesday, March 8th

THERE has been so much bad news lately, so many friends
ill or dying, that I want to set down two pieces of very
good news. I called Vincent Hepp in Houston the other
day and he answered the phone himself and told me that,
after two months of doing absolutely nothing except get
up at night to write childhood memories, he has a clean
bill of health and will be able to go back to work very soon,
at first for an hour at a time, then gradually longer each

day. Two months ago he was facing possible permanent injury to his brain from the stroke, so this is a remarkable recovery. I felt tears of relief running down my cheeks as we talked. Christiane has borne the brunt of the anxiety of course, and now she has nearly collapsed, but at least the worst, D.V., is over for her, too.

Then I saw a moving sight on television the other night. Poor Tina, the disagreeable elephant that nobody would take when the Central Park Zoo was closed, has been taken in by a private zoo where there are several elephants and has responded beautifully to a kind keeper there. Her ugly temper, like that of a neglected, lonely child, was the result of her much-loved former keeper's death. And now she also has companionship with her own kind. It made me remember a poem that haunted me for years, which I have never seen quoted, "The Tranquilizing Influence of Other Whales" by Marian Storm. It is about a terrified whale that is fatally wounded by hunters. On managing to reach a pod of whales, "the tranquilizing influence of other whales was soon apparent," and she died in peace.

Tina is now under the tranquilizing influence of other elephants and all is well.

Friday, March 11th

IT IS THE FIFTH STRAIGHT DAY of rain; the snow is almost gone and the field a dull brown again, and as the heavy downpour has relented this morning to Scotch mist, I think I can take Tamas out. Yesterday it was a real deluge,

with high wind as well. I just long for some salt air and a
vision of big surf and can hardly wait to get out and away
from this once more letter-strewn desk. From here the
ocean looks almost calm, but I can see the long waves
rolling in through the mist, curling over in a beautiful
way, then cresting into white foam.

This morning I hope to finish notes on the last of
Anne's three years in Germany. It may well be that this
enforced pause was necessary, for I find that I begin again
to carry the novel around just under the surface of my
mind, so it has not died on me. I am reading a lot of things
that enliven me these evenings. One is Sylvia Townsend
Warner's *Scenes of Childhood,* which I bought when it
came out last year but never got around to reading. It is
rather rare to laugh aloud in one's bed at night, and that
I have done several times—a lovely book. And I am coming to the end of the letters. Poignant at the end when she
lost her friend, Valentine Ackland, and at eighty or more
found herself alone. In a letter to Bill Maxwell (11:xi: 1969)
written the day the coffin was carried out of the house, she
says:

> I am passionately thankful that she is out and away,
> and that in a fashion we are back where we were,
> able to love freely and uncompromised by anxiety
> and doubtful hopes and miseries of frustration. One
> thinks one has foreseen every detail of heart-break.
> I hadn't. I had not allowed for the anguished compas-
> sion and shock of hearing her viola voice changed to
> a pretty, childish treble, the voice of a sick child.
>
> Death transfigured her. In a matter of minutes I
> saw the beauty of her young days reassert itself on
> her blurred careworn face. It was like something in
> music, the re-establishment of the original key, the
> return of the theme.

Don't think I am unhappy and alone, dear William. I am not. I am in a new country and she is the compass I travel by.

And in a letter two weeks later to Marchette and Joy Chute, she says:

Your kind hearts will want to know how I am getting on.

Well, not too badly for a one-winged partridge (did you know the partridge is the emblem of fidelity?). There is a great deal to do, which I am thankful for, but as I slog on doing it I am revived by coming on fragments by her, letters, passages copied from everyone you can think of, feathers (she loved all small feathers), deposits in pockets, always including a pencil and a pocket comb, but also including lumps of sugar in case of a deserving horse, chocolate drops for dogs, interesting pebbles, small notes from me on the lines of "Remember to have coffee" "Keep warm" "Come back soon."

Her love is everywhere. It follows me as I go about the house, meets me in the garden, sends swans into my dreams. In a strange, underwater or above-earth way I am very nearly happy.

Early in the following year S.T.W. found piles of hers and Valentine's letters to each other and set herself to arrange them, write a preface and connecting material, and made them into a book. This, I take it, will be published. And that is something marvelous to look forward to!

In another letter S.T.W. quotes a friend as saying to her, "Even desolation is a world to be explored."

Even if I don't get much work done, what rich days of reading and reflection these are! The more precious as they are ebbing away. I often think of Emily Dickinson's phrase "to make routine a stimulus, remember it can cease." And having time to work and think is surely a great blessing, even when it rains for four days in succession and one feels rather limp and stodgy.

Monday, March 14th

UNBELIEVABLE, the sun is out! It had been promised for yesterday, and I must say that when I went to the window at five and opened it to sniff the air I was very discouraged to feel fine rain on my face. But this morning I could tell even before I got up that the sun would rise in clear air at last. And so it has, making a dazzle of ocean now, shining so brightly it hurts the eyes.

Yesterday was not all gloom. As I was walking Tamas along the Firths' road I saw pussy willows shining overhead, bright silver catkins out on the high branches. And on the terrace the snowdrops that last year managed to push through hard ice have come up through that still-snowed-in corner. Pure magic. There is a fat clump of them along the fence and a rather frail group under the maple tree where last year the men piled such mountains of leaves that it looks as though the violets have been smothered and won't come back. But even in the drizzle yesterday the pond to the left of the field, very full because of the rain, shone with a soft brilliance. Light on water—how moving it is! And how different it is on a pond from the dazzle on ocean, for the ocean is never altogether still, whereas the pond can be a soft mirror, and so it was.

Tamas and Bramble have spring fever and go dashing about, Tamas's nose to the ground. Every now and then he gives an excited bark as some scent, frozen till now, is being released again. Bramble suddenly makes a dash to nowhere or scoots up a tree.

Now that I have pussy willows and branches of forsythia (not in flower yet, but they will be soon in the warmth) in the house, I know that spring is on the way.

It's the season when my nostalgia for Europe and especially for England becomes acute. The worst thing about New England is that spring comes all at once and after such an interminable limbo, instead of as in England in a slow sequence, which starts in January with snowdrops and crocuses and moves on to daffodils and fruit trees in April so one has time to taste each resurrection.

I think of Connie Hunting who is over there at this minute. Shall I ever go back? I sometimes think not. England is full of ghosts, and besides I feel my traveling days as far as "abroad" goes are over.

On Friday an interruption at 10:30 A.M. appears to have short-circuited the novel for the time being. It was a very kind woman at Social Security who is trying to straighten out the ridiculous contretemps I have been in about a small amount paid to me two years ago, too long a tale to go into. It resulted in a series of crazy letters hurled at me by their computer, one telling me that since my income was to be $100,000 (!) something or other would happen. I wrote back that the computer had had a nervous breakdown and suggested they look at my figures again. This was months, maybe a year, ago. I have shuddered every time a letter from the Health Services arrived. Now perhaps it will, at long last, all be laid to rest.

But that call took my morning as I had to hunt down royalty figures for 1981 (royalties on books published before I was sixty-five do not count as income for Social Security). And when it was done I felt gutted of any impulse to work. Perhaps I can finish copying out passages from Anne's letters from Germany, but I see clearly that I have reached a dead end.

And so it is time I went out into the world. And I really look forward to reading poems at Phillips Exeter Academy tomorrow.

Thursday, March 17th

IMAGINE a city of boys and girls between the ages of fourteen and eighteen, a city with many rosy brick buildings built around green squares, a city of white towers, churches, a magnificent modern library, an art museum, playing fields, tennis courts, everything a civilized person could want—and you have Phillips Exeter Academy. I was stunned and a little dismayed by it, so rich, such immense opportunities for an elite—and that is what is troubling of course. Here in the United States we appear to be becoming more and more a country devoted to amenities for the rich, more and more neglectful of the poor. Of course there is no such thing as absolute equality, even in heaven, but what one dreams of is opportunity for all, so that the elite can come up from the bottom as in France. Here with many of our people unable to read or write, we appear to be making two nations, the poor and the rich, with almost no connection with each other. Of course Phillips Exeter, like all prep schools, does provide many scholarships. An effort is made to even things out, but the atmosphere remains extremely "privileged."

Of course it rained, a deluge, as usual when I read! But I had fun and felt at ease and happy to be reading my poems for the first time since early November. It was a rest to be dealing with something achieved, instead of struggling with the unachieved and perhaps unachievable novel.

Yesterday morning I answered questions from two creative writing classes for nearly two hours. I found it tiring because there did not seem to be much spark to try to ignite. The questions were not very keen. Of course shyness enters in. It is not easy always to ask the pertinent question. The person who did ask good questions was Rod Kessler, who is at Exeter this year on a writing fellowship.

The talk took place in the Elting room (I may have got the name wrong), a high-ceilinged Victorian room where the faculty meetings take place. The walls are covered with trophies, stuffed heads of water buffalo (who could shoot one of those gentle, tame, useful beasts in cold blood?), tiny deer, lions, a rhinoceros, a baboon, a giraffe. It is such a cemetery, really. And the effect is both somber and, in some strange way, hilarious, hilarious because it seems so preposterous a reflection of the man who gave the money for this building and demanded that the results of his bloody adventures be exhibited inside it! The students must have a high old time matching the stuffed animal heads to the heads of their professors—and I can imagine many a farce based on this mortuary monument.

It was awfully good to come home, bearing croissants for Edythe, who had stayed overnight and walked Tamas, and to relate my adventures to her over lunch.

Friday, March 18th

JANICE came for supper last night. That weekly exchange of our lives has become a precious part of this winter, a kind of anchoring for each of us. In telling her about Exeter I remembered something I had forgotten yesterday, that the mother of someone I stayed with is dying in her own house, beautifully cared for by round-the-clock nurses, unable now to speak (she has Parkinson's). On her bed table is *A Reckoning*, and from it the nurses read aloud to her. It is what she wants most to hear. I set this moving item beside something Janice told me last night as she related a traumatic day at the Health Center. It seems that for several years the nurses there have been very concerned about an old lady whose son has managed to strip her of a fortune, sometimes locks the house so that the nurse who comes to give her injections and make her comfortable cannot get in. Total neglect. The old lady herself does not criticize her son, and it is illegal for the police to break in so she can have help. Yesterday she was found soaking in her bed, nearly unconscious and clearly near death. The nurse wanted to get an ambulance at once and get her to the hospital, but the son would not allow it. Finally Janice herself got to the woman's doctor, who has not seen her for months, and insisted that he go there himself to see what was what and to give necessary orders. Janice has been through the wringer over this, of course, and looked exhausted. At last it was arranged that two nurses would go during the night with police escort to do what they could to ease her death. An appalling story.

A great deal is known now about abused children, but apparently very little about the abused *old*. But anyone in a public health service comes upon it all the time, so Janice tells me. And this case is not one of extreme poverty, not at all. It is simply a case of hardness of heart and innate brutality and self-seeking by a son toward the mother he has robbed, who is clearly dying and whom he will not help die in dignity and surrounded by love. I do not want to believe that it is possible!

It has also been hard to believe that five men raped a young woman in a bar in New Bedford last week to the egging on and applause of the other customers, not one of whom tried to help the woman or called the police. Have things always been as bad as this? Or are we paying now for the neglect of *souls?*

It's a cold gray day and I feel cold and gray inside.

Sunday, March 20th

NOTHING BUT RAIN and more rain. Poor Tamas got no walk yesterday as it was a real deluge all day, but the new Fox Run Mall where I had to go to sign books at Lauriat's was jammed with people. It was not any fun. The store is hidden away among a lot of junk shops, hard to find, and my impression of the crowd was deadening, the faces full

of dull curiosity, no light in any of them, trundling small
children in strollers, hardly ever smiling or laughing, just
wandering and staring at things they could not afford in
a kind of avid daze. The store is open, no doors, and we
five authors sat in front being looked over like prize steers
at a fair. Hardly any books were sold. I did talk some with
a young woman who is assistant manager and was happy
to discover that we like the same authors. She reminded
me of Shirley Hazzard's *The Transit of Venus,* which is
about the best modern novel I have read in years, so all
was not lost.

I was so glad to get home, Tamas asleep in his bed,
Bramble who had demanded to go out just as I was leaving
meowing loudly to explain that she was furious at getting
so wet and being abandoned for two hours. I had a half-
hour or so to get ready for Jill Felman, lay the fire, light
it, and snatch a cup of tea. I haven't seen Jill for ages, since
September, she said, and as always we had a happy fiery
discussion about our lives and the world in general. She
is graduating from law school this year and is determined
to find a way to work in the defense of women. But I was
happy to sense that she is ready now after two years of
hard studying to get back to writing. Her talent will force
her back one of these days whatever else she does. But she
had reached a dead end two years ago and I was all for her
change of profession (from teaching creative writing to
the law). Teaching writing may sometimes dissipate the
creative energy of a writer, and the academic world is not
in the long run "the real world," I'm afraid.

Of course we talked a lot about violence and especially
about the rape in New Bedford. I had seen on Channel 5's
"Chronicle" the night before a very good discussion about
it. They brought out what had not occurred to me—that
if the woman had been beaten rather than raped, the

chances are someone would have come to her aid. The final remark on "Chronicle" made the point that even worse than the devastating scene itself was the attitude of men who were questioned on the street the next day, several of whom said, "Well, I'm waiting to see what the woman's reputation is." The inference is nearly always that a woman who is raped "asked for it." It seems almost incredible and is such a macho view that it arouses rage in any woman. Rape is brutally painful, more physically painful probably than being punched in the face, and it is infinitely more degrading and humiliating than a beating, so what woman would "ask for it"? Much to my amazement and horror, Jill told me that more than one of her friends has been gang-raped. It happened to someone recently in Durham, for instance, someone she knows. Jill is convinced that no woman ever gets over it.

"Why," she said vehemently, "have men not reacted to it themselves? Why are there not organizations of men against rape, men who would automatically, and out of conviction, go to the aid of a woman threatened?" Why not indeed? For most men, even men who would not do it themselves, rape remains a kind of *droit de seigneur,* I suppose. I have often thought that in cases of rape the penis becomes a gun. And I was not surprised when Jill told me that one of her friends had actually been raped first in the usual way and then by the man using a gun as the means of penetration!

It is not really a sexual act at all (which is also why no woman "wants it"); it is an act of aggression and hatred, the desire to dominate by force, to humiliate and punish, exactly as the Nazis did in the camps, to turn a human being into dirt, to crush a human being with the heel of a boot. No one would dare suggest that the Jews in the camps "wanted it."

I looked at the faces of the four men on the screen. They were sullen in court of course. Only one looked intelligent or aware or had the slightest delicacy in his features. And what are they thinking now?

Another thing "Chronicle" brought out was that if the woman had been beaten nearly to death, they would have fled the scene. They stayed in the bar. They apparently felt no guilt at all, not even fear of the police.

I'd like to wash this out of my mind as children used to be told to wash their mouths out with soap after using a "dirty" word. It colors these gloomy days.

I'm off to Wellesley to see Eleanor Blair, at long last, and that should do it.

Tuesday, March 22nd

THUNDER AND LIGHTNING and torrents of rain last night. For a time while I was getting my supper I didn't dare have the television on. Today it is mild and wet, although when I came up here the sun was showing faintly through the mist and there was a silvery path on the ocean. Two gulls were silhouetted on the point, standing there like two people looking out.

However, I did have a dazzling sight of spring at Eleanor's where, along the house, two huge clumps of lavender crocuses, the biggest crocuses I have ever seen, had opened in the sun. I could hardly believe my eyes. And then there was a tiny bunch on the round table where we ate, lavender crocus and snowdrops. Those I could look at closely, the thrust of the orange stamen standing up so straight, cupped in the lavender petals. When I left, Eleanor gave me that bunch to take home. Bliss.

She was brimming with the good news that she now gets talking books on cassettes, and the library to draw on is immense. She has been reading Conrad, but there are also lots of new books and I highly recommended Anne Tyler's *Dinner at the Homesick Restaurant* as one she might like to try. I could sense the exhilaration this new adventure has opened up for Eleanor. And of course the kitten is a perpetual adventure, too, as she is a dandy acrobat and ballet dancer whom Eleanor loves to watch and can see because the kitten is black and white. We had an elegant lunch, a fruit and avocado salad all arranged "like a Matisse," Eleanor said, and ice cream and the brownies I had made for dessert. We had such a good talk that I flew home feeling revived and happy. My wonderful old friend. Eleanor is one of the few people I now see who knew Judy and loved her and remembered that Judy did not like her coffee too hot! Little traits like this bring a person back so vividly, I was thinking about Judy all the way home. By the time I had persuaded Edythe to have a cup of tea (she was here as usual to walk Tamas and take care of things while I was gone), it had clouded over. But I was determined to get out and find moss and a tiny pine tree and to make the Japanese dish garden I have had in mind, because, due to the rain, the mosses are so brilliant in the wood this year. I did accomplish that. So now there is a miniature world beside the chaise longue, a small pool, several temples and a fisherman standing on the bridge, and several different mosses turned into a garden of small fields and (one moss is in flower) a patch of long grass. So altogether Sunday was a very good day.

Yesterday disappeared as some days do. I did manage

to write a long letter to a young woman who had sent me
a five-hundred-page novel in manuscript, which I have
been reading this past week. I wanted to get the letter off
while it was fresh in my mind, the story of an obsession,
and troubling because it forced me to think about my own
obsessions in the past. I have been both of the protago-
nists, the older woman who is involved with a younger
woman but irritated by the excess of emotion and the too
lavish giving that pours over her, and so becomes cruel.
And the young woman herself who has not yet learned
that "giving" is very often "asking." However, I have
never been in love with someone much younger than I.
I have simply pushed the young away. None has ever
become a muse; I suppose that is why.

Lately I have been waking up happy. And that is
strange because I am bogged down on the impossible
novel. Perhaps simply giving it up for the present has
brought into the foreground what a good life I lead these
days, what a happy and fulfilled life. I say this in fear and
trembling—do not tempt the gods. But these days there
are no furies at the window—that I do know for sure.

It made me happy that Deborah Pease (who is now the
publisher of the *Paris Review* and was my student at
Wellesley) really loved the "Letters from Maine," and it
is possible that they will be published when the interview
with me comes out. That gave me a lift. It also made me
realize freshly how far from writing poems I am now, and
ever since late December when the door was closed in my
face and the poems stopped. No lines run through my
head these days. More than one person has said "Why
can't you be your own muse?"

It would be fine if I could. But this is a matter of what
happens, not what can be willed. "Dear hearts and gentle
people," I can only answer you, "poetry does not happen

for me without a muse." That truth is frustrating often, but it is the truth and has been the truth for the past sixty years at least. It may be that you who ask me that question must accept the fact. What for you may seem like failure (surely if I was grown up enough I could be my own muse is what is implied), for me is mystery, and I am very glad that there is still a real and not-to-be-analyzed mystery in my life. *Je ne regrette rien.*

Ah, that is the reason I am happy these days. I do not regret anything, not even a moment's encounter that set poetry running through my head and was then cut off. The poems are there and they cannot be taken from me by the muse herself or by anyone else for that matter.

I am happy because I feel alive and well and in a constant state of expectation before each day. What surprise may be hidden in today? What marvelous moment of shining on the ocean through the mist? Yesterday while I was waiting to get into Filene's to find a linen jacket for my trips in April, a woman said she had seen a robin. Shall I see the first one around here today? Who knows what may happen? I am ready to be connected with whatever does.

Friday, March 25th

SO FAR nothing has happened outdoors but cold and more cold, so my hopes that I could get some gardening done are shattered. It was 16° this morning—the poor crocuses! The daffodils are up about four inches and some are in bud. Indoors the forsythia I picked last week has blossomed, so spring is around, but when shall we feel safe? Yesterday it snowed in North Carolina (where I shall be bound in a few days). Unbelievable.

I like to think this is a peaceable kingdom here, and most of the time it is—fat gray squirrels upside down eating the dry corncobs I got from Audubon so they would not suffer too much because the new feeders keep them off, lots of goldfinches still in their olive winter suits, chickadees, and downy and hairy woodpeckers come and go all day. But when I came home from Portsmouth the other day there was a dead red squirrel under the feeders, a bloody and awful sight. Bramble? She is a fierce hunter, but it was strange that only the head had been eaten. And now I wonder. Twice lately I have seen a silent shadow of great wings fly off. It is either a hawk or an owl, and that may be who performed the savage act. I rather hope it was not Bramble.

These mornings when I brush my hair before going down to get breakfast I have to face wrinkles, the first sign of old age. It's not easy to accept, but I remind myself that they do not really diminish the beauty of an old face. Lotte Jacobi, for instance, has never been as beautiful as she is now, and one simply does not *see* the wrinkles. What one does see is the aliveness inside, the twinkling humor and the wisdom in her eyes. "We love the things we love for what they are." And an old face that looked too young would be troubling. Still, I do mind. If old age can be an ascension, it is at the same time a letting go, yet maybe it is only a true ascension when one does let go. Much harder than for me, of course, must be the wrinkles of a woman who has been a real beauty, her identity bound up in that beauty and the homage it elicited.

I remember Jean Dominique telling me, when she had become too blind to see her own face in a mirror, that it was a strange alienation, as though she did not exist because she could no long meet *herself* as others saw her.

Yesterday was a festival of a day because Morgan Mead, who has not been here for more than a year, came bringing our lunch, a rich mushroom soup, an elegant salad with Belgian endive, and a loaf of French bread. At once we were back in our open, laughing, probing, loving friendship as though we had met the day before, as though no time at all had elapsed. I lit a fire in the library and there we sat, as usual, with our Scotch and talked for an hour, unhurriedly. It was so good to see Morgan looking as young as ever, and as handsome.

We figured out that we have known each other for nine years, and in that time we have both endured some hard times and come through stronger and more sure of what we really want of our lives. Morgan is a house-owner now, a teacher, and director of admissions at Browne and Nichols School in Cambridge. He still wants to write and knows, in the summer holidays, that he is fulfilling a need when he gets down to facing an empty page again. It may not be a bad thing for a writer at his age, still not thirty, to be in the midst of life, taking on responsibilities, learning what it is all about before he writes a great deal. Starting too young, one may get written out. There is just not that much substance to work with. True for a short-story writer or a novelist like Morgan maybe, though not for a poet.

After he left I felt cross that it was so bitterly cold outdoors. I wanted to garden, to feel earth in my hands, not pour out words on a typewriter. But, cross or not, I did get a few letters ready to mail.

"the whole tiny bay boiling with white water"

Monday, March 28th

THIS MORNING when I walked Tamas down to the sea we went into a great roar of surf, and as we came near the edge we saw the whole tiny bay boiling with white water and immense combers charging up the pebbled beach, a glorious sight. Neither Tamas nor Bramble pays the slightest attention except that Tamas stands and smells the sea, his nose lifted high, as though in such stormy weather some rare smell were floating toward him. Bramble climbs down the cliffs and terrifies me I am so afraid she will get washed away. All this excitement came after a wild rainstorm last night. The windows rattled. The surf thundered, but we three slept soundly nevertheless.

On Saturday I dashed over to Deer Run Farm to see Anne and Barbara for a last visit before I take off next week on nearly a month of poetry readings. I like to touch base with them before an adventure. And there all was flourishing, including fifty chicks Anne had had to bring in from the barn because of these last very cold nights. They were burbling away in a pen by the fire in her studio, much to the delight of Peter, the pet cock, who is often indoors and who examined this event closely, going all round the pen to see what was what.

But the landscape is gloomy at this season in Maine, brown and dank, just a slight thickening of some branches of trees to suggest that they are waking up. At least the maple syrup harvest has been good this spring because of the very warm weather we had earlier on. I bought two small jars to take as presents for friends I shall see en route.

Yesterday I drove to Concord for Sunday dinner with Judy's family, Keith Warren, her brother-in-law, and Tim and Phyllis Warren, her nephew and his wife. Unfortunately, Judy's sister has flu. I had so hoped she might be with us. But we had a lovely talk. Tim has been immersed in Judy's papers, letters, journals, and writings, and has been bowled over by this aunt's inner life about which he had known little.

I was moved to see him, for he has the dark Matlack eyes and eyebrows and now that he has gray hair I was struck by the resemblance to Judy. And even more so when he chose one of her poems to read aloud, savoring each word just as she would have done.

Keith, Tim's father, is now over ninety, quite deaf and "legally blind," but he still transmits such a tender and joyful sense of life, his face pink, his eyes twinkling, that one forgets that he is now a very old person. He told me that he goes to sleep remembering nursery rhymes, and we had quite a discussion about whether Mother Goose was American or English. Apparently she did have an American incarnation, though I had felt sure she was English, for how could my English mother have taught me those rhymes if not?

I very rarely have a "family day," and in spite of nursing a cold and feeling rather low in consequence, I basked in it and was grateful for Phyllis's apricot soufflé dessert.

Before lunch Keith showed me a batch of letters he has received from Judy's friends to whom he had sent the charming folder he put together to memorialize her,

which Tim had printed by his own printing firm. Keith
has a genius for family celebrations, writes delightful
birthday verses, and makes every single person in his circle feel cherished in a most remarkable way. What a
honey of a man he is and always has been!

Friday, April 1st

IT'S A FOOL'S DAY all right for anyone who hoped for a
little spring weather for Easter, and I dread taking Tamas
for a quick walk in the grim cold air before I go to the
airport to meet Georgia. But maybe it will wake me up as
I feel like a hibernating bear who sticks his nose out to see
what is what and decides to go back to sleep for another
month.

There is cheerful news, however. The *Paris Review*
will publish the "Letters from Maine" with the interview
in their autumn issue. I am delighted that they like them.
I never have the slightest sense of security about the
poems. It is odd. These poems, written for the autumn
muse, ended in December when she withdrew, but the
other day I heard that she will come in June for a few days,
and that is a great spur to get the garden in order and in
general lifts my spirits, for if the door opens even a crack,
poems will surely slip in through it. I can hardly believe
she is coming as I had disciplined myself not to hope.

As always when I am about to take off on a series of
public appearances, everything piles up. Yesterday a let-

ter from Ursula Nicholls Heathcote stirred me up. She has
been one of the Greenham Common women in England
who, on New Year's Day this year, climbed over the fence
of the USAF/RAF base where silos are being built to contain ninety-six cruise missiles. It was not a one-shot protest. Women have surrounded the site for nearly a year,
in bitter cold and rainy weather. Ursula and some of her
friends were arrested and she spent two weeks in jail. In
her letter she told me that while in solitary she found
comfort from some lines of my poem "Innumerable
Friend." That stirred me. But in a different way I was
even more stirred up by her report on the prison and the
very harsh treatment they all received. There appears to
have been an effort to demoralize and humiliate, although
the three women were *nonviolent* protesters, of course.
I sometimes think nonviolence arouses rage in the police
and law officers in general. It implies moral superiority. Is
that why?

Ursula was so outraged by the whole experience that
she intends to devote the rest of her life to fighting for
prison reform. She is sixty-two. After reading her description of what she went through, it occurred to me that
every middle-class "safe" person should have to go to
prison at some point to find out what that locked world is
like. It is hard to imagine what one has not experienced,
and this goes for life in the slums, for unemployment, for
illness. Rare is the person who has the imagination to
share in the suffering of others. And once more I come
back in my mind to the words of Christ, "What ye have
done unto the least of these, ye have done unto Me." If
we could believe that, feel it on the pulse itself, the world
would be radically changed, of course. For about what we
have not experienced on the pulse, we are dreadfully
smug.

I want to bear witness to what Ursula experienced. She writes:

During the two weeks I was in two prisons, I was in six different cells with twelve different companions. Most women and girls in Holloway and East Sutton Park come from poor, deprived families and they are inadequately equipped to cope with the petty cruelties in-built into the System, let alone the more serious punitive discipline invoked and used against them. I have seen in prison so many women crying and have heard so many crashing window shutters for hours on end during the night. So much pain and so little compassion—so much niggling "correction,"—so much dull routine boring work for outrageously low pay—between 44p to 12. 10p (the latter is pay with overtime) per week! This money is spent in the prison canteens.

Just after exercise of twenty minutes on Monday February 28th, the day before release, feeling very joyous because I had been with other Greenham Common women—I was put on report for what "they" call a disciplinary matter and taken to solitary confinement. Given the charge sheet and another printed paper about "THE PROCEDURE," I was able to refute the charge in writing on the other side of the charge sheet *if* I chose to do so.

When I was taken from my cell, I was told by the officers not to bring anything with me as I would be seeing the Governor very soon and be back in my cell within half an hour. By then I had learned not to believe anything "they" said to me. I took a book and letters—well chosen *Burger's Daughter* by Nadine Gordimer about the treason trials in South Africa—this helped me later on to put my own situation in proper perspective. Remembering and thinking of women like Winnie Mandela, I knew I was enduring mere pinpricks.

I was left for five hours "stewing." When taken eventually into a room nearby, to my surprise the Governor was a large man sitting behind a large desk. I was standing in front of the desk with two officers one on each side of me, I was told by "him" to face the wall. This I refused to do, saying "I face my accusers," and then I requested a chair to sit down, but this I was refused although I pointed out I was old enough to be his mother. At this point he reminded me that I was a convicted prisoner. I then asked him if he was the Governor of Holloway —he did not reply. I continued, "I take it then that you are her representative."

A senior woman officer who had been standing beside him then moved beyond my eye contact to a position behind my left shoulder. . . . He said, "Do you understand the procedure?" I replied, "Yes."

"Do you plead guilty or not guilty?"

"I cannot plead guilty or not guilty. It is not a black and white case. There is a great deal of grey matter in between," I replied.

"Do you understand the procedure?" he said, once again.

"Yes, I understand your procedure but your procedure is not my procedure, and therefore I will not proceed with your procedure, until you proceed with my procedure—which is—you have three witnesses in this room. I have none. Since February 21st—one week ago—I have requested to see my solicitor—now may I sit down?"

"No, you may not."

"All right. I will sit on the floor or perhaps faint across your desk."

I was facing a very angry man.

He said, "Take her out of here."

All the time I was in prison I felt I was in Jabberwocky land —it is a Catch 22 situation and the truth does not operate in there. It is a series of what "they" call white lies and procedures aimed to raise and lower morale. I spent my last night in Holloway in a cell which had a sliding door built into the wall. It would cut the prisoner off from light, fresh air and heating as it would slide into position across the only shuttered window below which was the one radiator in the cell. This discovery did not help to reassure me!

When Ursula was finally released, she discovered that in the final search of her belongings three letters had been removed from her suitcase, plus the petition she had written to Mr. Whitelaw, Home Secretary of State. Other letters she had written while in prison and posted through their censorship box were never received. She says that her belief in British justice has been shattered. "For the remaining years of my life I intend to devote some of my energy towards changing and reforming the Prison System, hopefully leading eventually to the de-prisoning of society."

Saturday, April 2nd

YESTERDAY I fetched Georgia at Logan Airport, and now she is working away at *Lear* downstairs. It is good to have her with me, and for us to be working together and alone in the silent house.

Before supper and after we each had a nap, the sun came out and, from low in the western sky, illuminated the combers as they broke into foam, an extraordinary sight, so we walked down and watched the scene from close by at the foot of the field. Tamas and Bramble, who had been shut up indoors for five hours while I was gone, were very happy to join us.

This morning I heard a robin and the sun is out in a clear blue sky, the first for weeks.

Easter Day, April 3rd

AT FIVE I woke to glorious light—the whole sky, I realized when I got to the window, was a brilliant gold, just before the sun rose. That was Easter in itself, although it has clouded over now and rain is due.

I feel rather silent this morning, in a pleasant lull, when the domestic self takes over and I have Georgia to look out for. She brought not only croissants and elegant French pastries but a huge meat bone for Tamas, so huge I decided to use it for soup for us, as for Tamas it might have seemed like being given an elephant! There isn't much in the house because I am leaving so soon, but I found some navy beans, celery, onions, and, for lack of salt pork, cut up three sausages—and in a minute I must go down and see how it is doing. We'll have it for supper after our elegant Easter feast this noon at the York Harbor Inn.

This is the earliest Easter I can remember and that explains why it does not feel like Easter, no green grass, nothing in flower as I look out over the brown field to a silent gray ocean. Not an exhilarating sight. But indoors there are flowers and three Easter baskets, one that Georgia's daughter made for me with a baby panda in it and lots of eggs and a charming book, and Betsy Swart sent a musical Paddington bear who tinkles away when he is wound up. I feel spoiled and delighted to be. Why not?

Georgia is beginning to let down and be able to rest. The load she carries at home is very heavy these days, so what I hope I can do for her is make a warm nest where

she can sleep, feel free to be herself, and do what she feels
like doing. Very rarely can the mother of two children
afford to let down in this way.

Wednesday, April 6th

IT'S HARD TO BELIEVE that I'll be reading spring poems
in Charlotte, North Carolina, this evening and that there
everything is in flower. But yesterday at last I had a
glimpse of spring here. When I walked Tamas, the peepers were peeping ecstatically and the large frogs in the
swamp were carrying on like businessmen at a Rotary
luncheon. And when I got back from town with the mail,
Raymond was busily taking the salt hay off the borders, so
now they are cleared and I can see the green shoots coming through, a few tiny puschkinias in flower, and a group
of species tulips. Crocuses are turning up all over. But,
alas, only one of four Imperial fritillarias I planted among
the tulips has come up. I read somewhere that their
strong skunky smell keeps rodents away, but I'm afraid
my mice and chipmunks loved it, as they have eaten three
of them and nearly all the tulips.

Never mind, so much else is now in view I know there
will be a spring. I hate to leave at this moment of rebirth
in my garden. But last year we had a blizzard on this very
day, so who knows?

This morning I saw two goldfinches, nearly gold again
after their winter in olive suits.

I'm starting off in the clear in more ways than one, as
I went to the bank and drew vast sums from savings and

paid my taxes. I can remember that the first year I ever paid a tax (it must have been 1933 when I was drawing a tiny salary as director of the apprentices at the Civic Repertory in New York) I felt proud to be an American citizen and helping to keep the country solvent. It seemed a great event, proving I was a grown-up person earning my living, at twenty-one. Now I am proud because at seventy I am able to support myself in comfort and have enough to help other people. But I am less proud of being an American now and less happy when I think how much of this treasure will go into missiles, many of which will be obsolete by next year. The appalling waste! For war matériel does not move back into the economy as automobiles and hundreds of other things needed by consumers do. It just sits around and rots.

Unlike poetry. It will be lovely to read poems again tonight. I never hear them unless I am asked to read, and it is like hearing music, hearing it come alive from the black and white pages of a score. Most of the young poets I read appear to have little sense of the sound words make, and I wonder whether they read their own poems aloud.

What a fine day to be off on a journey!

Monday, April 11th

"WILDNESS AND WET! Wildness and wet" is the order of these days. I got back yesterday under heavy gray sky, with a bitterly cold wind blowing rain in soon after I arrived, and it was a stormy night, but this morning I heard the happy squawks of the pheasant, and there he was on the wall, fat and splendid after the winter. I was sure he had been shot last autumn, so what joy to see him again in all his glory!

As I had hoped, I found the spring bursting out all over in Charlotte, the white dogwood in full flight (it does look like a flight of birds), the azaleas in splashes of crimson and white around the houses, and the grass emerald green.

At the foot of the field, I just saw a fountain of spray about twenty feet high leaping up from behind the dark grass, and I can hardly wait to take Tamas and Bramble down to see it. It may still be wintry here, but the ocean, turbulent and wild, gives the scene a powerful vitality and élan.

The two readings went well, in spite of bad acoustics in a low-ceilinged dining hall for the first and a baby who cried and screamed rather a lot during the second, which took place in the chapel at Queens College with a packed house and wonderful acoustics. I did feel happy hearing the poems *land* and felt the audience with me to the end. What both readings did was lift me up over the scary threshold of this month of public appearances and give me confidence. I felt extremely nervous before the first one and somewhat dampened by the rain and thick humidity. But I was able to rest in the comfort of Diane Wilkerson's house and listened to a chorus of birds as I rested.

What a leap it was from the dull browns and grays here to the heart of spring! I felt slightly drunk on that opulence of flowers and green and wished I could burst into song like a cardinal. There were two rewards for the readings. One was to go over to Marion Cannon's Witch Hill on Thursday evening after signing books for an hour. The other was seeing Ellen Hildebrand who had driven up from Rembert, South Carolina, looking amazingly well although she had just had major surgery a week ago. It was tantalizing not to be able to have a real talk with her and her friend, Eleanor, but I had to stick to my knitting and sign my illegible name so many times and meet so many people, some who had come over from Knoxville, that it could not be more than a glimpse.

Then at last we were off, Susan Durham, who had arranged the readings at Queens, Diane Wilkerson, and Marion. I had heard so much about Witch Hill, imagined it so often, and looked forward so much to seeing it at last, but I did not expect to feel that I had been suddenly transported to Belgium to one of those great houses seen from a train window when I was a child, houses I longed to explore.

First impression, Marion herself looking tiny at the top of a wide flight of steps, pushing open the immensely high white front door. Diane and Susan helped with the luggage, so we all found ourselves for a moment in my bedroom—the four-poster bed, the ravishing sunken bath next door like a small swimming pool, the long windows opening out into mossy grass and tall trees. Then we went back into the salon, with its high gray-green walls, a great sense of space and timeless peace. There we had a nightcap and Marion put on lights so we could see the courtyard at the back of the house and the swimming pool where the neighbors come with their children all summer for swims and picnics. Marion had described all this when I visited her in her house on Captiva, but it felt like a wholly new and unexpected experience, dreamlike in the intense pleasure it gave me. For this is the house of a poet, and it is full of soul, and like all poems, full of surprises too. Off the salon, for instance, there is an immensely high, long wall of books with a ladder that slides along so one can stand on it and propel oneself from shelf to shelf.

There I had two days of real rest, breakfast in bed and two hours or more each day of just lying there and thinking, watching birds come and go, and ruminating without pressure on what I may be able to do with the novel. It is so rare that I ever have open time like that, it felt like several Christmas presents rolled into one. One afternoon we managed to get an hour without real rain—just a Scotch mist—and went to call on Mrs. Clarkson and see her secret garden, called Wing Haven.

When she moved there with her husband many years ago it was simply rough red clay without a tree or bush to grace it. Now it has become a series of what seem like garden rooms, separated by box and ilex hedges, each one designed to lead the eye down a perspective to a small statue or fountain or small corner with a pond such as one might discover on a walk through a wild wood, this one, that day, a bluebell wood. Camellias were in flower and some lovely azaleas, not the thick massed blaze of color I had seen all over town but less severely pruned to show single branches and single flowers. Mrs. Clarkson is so gentle and self-effacing it is hard to believe that she created all this almost single-handedly. In the past few years, she has opened it to the public and she now has help, but what work and thought and genius went into its creation! I was entranced. Not only by the flowers but by the inscriptions on marble that bid you stop and think before you step over the threshold of another secret flowery room.

It was a real holiday for me, and I brought back a great many haunting memories in my knapsack, to be explored and rested in as time goes on. It does go on, alas, and I have come back to a welter of mail that must be answered today and tomorrow before I go to Boston College on Wednesday to read poems celebrating women.

Sunday, April 17th

IT IS QUITE THRILLING to end this seventieth year with reading poems to such loving and responsive audiences, and I am happy as a lark in spite of foul weather all along the way, so cold one cannot smell the earth and only a very few daffodils have managed to flower under the heavy blows of rain and high wind. The outer scene is still dismal.

It was exciting Wednesday evening at Boston College to step up to the podium in the theater and see the whole audience rise to their feet and applaud. Lately this has happened sometimes after a reading but never until then to greet me at the start. Perhaps the gesture was elicited by the two beautiful brief introductions from Sister Anne Morgan and Margaret Dever. They each said something cogent and fresh about how they see my work. That kind of introduction is rare, and it makes a real difference to the atmosphere, of course. And then I was happy to be doing a wholly new arrangement of poems, as this reading was intended to celebrate the tenth year of the Women's Resource Center and I chose all poems celebrating women, the last section, mythical women such as Pallas Athene, Kali, the Furies, Medusa. I'll be doing this again at the National Women's Congress in Columbus in late June and I look forward to it.

Before the reading there was an informal supper at the

house where Sister Anne Morgan and five other sisters live. This was genial but a little hard on me as I was terrified of losing my voice if I talked too much. I have been having trouble with dryness high up in my throat. However, I felt again as I have in these past years that the most radical and alive teachers these days are nuns. The changes in the Catholic academic world where women are concerned have been monumental. Sister Anne ran in the Boston Marathon last year! She and her sister nuns each has a spacious room. I rested in Sister Claire's for half an hour after dinner and enjoyed the brilliant colors, the shelves of books, the delightful stuffed clown someone must have made for her, the huge desk made from a door, as mine was at Nelson—a room where it was quite clear someone lived who is intensely absorbed both in an inner and an outer life. The atmosphere in the whole house, an old mansard-roofed house with high ceilings and spacious rooms, was joyful. I am often in charming houses but rather rarely in one where the atmosphere is that of joy and thanksgiving. Later I talked about this with two graduate students who drove me back to Cambridge where I was spending the night. They felt strongly that from time immemorial nuns must have entered the religious life as a way of using their powers to the full, a way out of the patriarchy, in fact.

I got back here around noon with just twenty-four hours in which to repack and get myself together for the three-hour drive to the White Mountain School at Littleton, New Hampshire. When I planned this reading I had imagined driving through a spring scene, but it was still a dank gray and brown world, with some snow still around under the trees in Crawford Notch and the mountains bathed in blank fog. Bob and Sybil Carey who run the Horse and Hounds Inn in Franconia had kindly offered to take me in for the night, although the inn is closed. I got there before lunch and had an hour of pleasant exploring of the village, lunch in a joint, and then came back and slept for two hours. I was suddenly really tired that afternoon. And it felt like a strange limbo to be in a closed inn with an immense empty parking lot in front of it.

However I revived in the late afternoon when I went down to find a roaring fire at one end of the vast dining hall and a glass of Scotch and ice waiting for me, and the Careys' eight-year-old daughter to talk with while Bob disappeared into the kitchen and Sybil told me how she had begun to read Sarton, finding *Journal of a Solitude* and then going on from there. The fire bubbled; Bob came back with an exquisite scallop and mussel soup and, when we had finished that, a great platter of duckling *au poivre,* broccoli, and browned potatoes, and poured us each a glass of Beaujolais. By then I had become aware that it is possible to lead the life of Riley in an empty inn!

By the time we drove off to the school in the dusk I felt restored and ready to read again. It was not a theater this time but a large high-ceilinged room, curtained at one end at night (in the daytime, it is a huge window looking out on the Presidential range) and filled with rows of chairs, all still empty when we arrived half an hour early. It is at that moment that one's heart sinks. Would anyone come? I took refuge in the library and went over the poems once more, deciding at the last minute to open with "Mud Season," as appropriate to the dismal weather.

It was, after all, a full house, but partly through my own fault it was not an easy performance. The lectern was wobbly and rather too high, so they put it down on the floor below the stage, and that meant that I was standing on the brink and felt quite dizzy several times as though I might fall, a rather strange sensation. That tight throat wrecked the first poem, and I was terrified because I had to cough and then could not get back on the beam. But after that, all went well, and I was touched afterward to learn how many people had come from long distances away. It did not look as though many students were there and I wondered why. Perhaps they revolt aginst formal occasions, over-planned. Who knows?

It was wonderful to get home yesterday at noon and find that Edythe had made potato salad so we could have lunch here. Such a blessing.

Now it is Sunday, and tomorrow evening I fly off to St. Paul. I feel dull and tired this morning, stiff in my joints. But I know that I have to let myself go way down after these performances in order to come up again with renewed energy. Janice and I are going out for lunch, and soon I must put on sweaters and take Tamas down to the sea. At the moment at least, it is not raining.

Saturday, April 30th

MY CUP RUNNETH OVER I am so happy to be home again and to find the daffodils startling the eye all over the field and down the orchard path in all their brilliance. That was the sight that met me as Edythe drove around the curve at seven last evening, having met my plane from San Francisco and brought me home from a very rich twelve days on the road. When I finally got to bed and lay there with Tamas and Bramble beside me, I was listening to a symphony of Maine sounds—roars of waves in the distance, peepers keeping up a thrilling obligato that sounds like sleigh bells, and even closer to the house an intermittent humming of crickets or some other insect. After the perfect silence of Bill Brown's house at night in San Francisco, it seemed I was listening to an orchestra of spring rejoicing and renewal—not at all silent.

In the last twelve days I have slept in five different beds and am sorting out such a harvest of good memories it is hard to know where to begin. After the exotic splendors of San Francisco and Marin County, the hills vivid green after all the rain this winter, and that sense out there that it is still volcanic country, very young and precipitous and varied, Maine seems old, not exactly tame, but peaceful, the profile is so gentle by comparison. I felt passionately about California this time, quite overwhelmed by the beauty, but coming home I know that however passionately I responded I am married to New England and cannot imagine living anywhere else.

It was good to go back again to Unity Church at St. Paul where I had some years ago my first experience of these great audiences I now find wherever I go. Again the Unitarian church was filled, this time with an overflow of about one hundred who sat in another room and watched on closed-circuit television. I was nervous as I always am until Roy D. Phillips, the young minister, introduced me so charmingly that I felt delightfully well launched and could sail off happily into the poems. He said he had first heard of me as "a woman's poet," then began to read and found himself going back to certain poems, parts of which he quoted. He ended by saying, "I am happy to present May Sarton, *a man's poet.*" I was pleased!

Earlier that one day in St. Paul I managed to make a short visit to Sister Alice (whom I knew years ago as the poet Maris Stella) in Bethany, the retirement home for

"to find the daffodils startling the eye"

the nuns of the College of St. Catherine. She is having a hard time, but it was clear to me that she will die as she has lived—with a core of radiant light at the center, in spite of pain and what she called "the shakes." I had lunch with Sister Mary Virginia, who has been sending me poems, which I hope will be published soon. We were full of merriment and understanding, merriment because the last time we met I had taken pains to get an evening dress for the formal dinner at which the college presented me with their Alexandrine Medal. It was just after nuns were permitted to lay aside the habit if they so wished. There I was, uncomfortably clad in a long dress, and there was Sister Mary Virginia, who introduced me, in a white pant-suit with a cowboy shirt and pink tie!

Sunday, May 1st

WHEN so much happens every day it is hard to go back in a journal to what took place a week before. Yesterday I felt too pressured, but I did manage in the afternoon to get in some perennials, including a Japanese toad lily I hope I shall see flower. It was heaven to be outdoors, to stop now and then and look out on the garlands of daffodils in the gentle gray of an overcast sky, and to see Tamas lying in his favorite place under the big maple and hear the goldfinches twittering as I worked. It is still early spring in the garden, no leaves on the trees, the lilac leaves still in their pointed buds.

From St. Paul I flew to San Francisco where I moved

from friend to friend for a week before the reading at the
College of Marin, a real holiday for me to have a week
without writing a single word and intoxicated by the
beauty of the region. There, everything was in full bloom
—from roses, gigantic dusky orange ones at Bill's front
door, to masses of ranunculuses, lilacs, and spring flowers
as well as roses in Doris Beatty's lovely garden in Berkeley, to the amazing rows of bonsai on Dorothy Bryant's
porch, a resplendent show of what that art can produce
—they are her husband's work and delight. And at
Frances Whitney's we drank our coffee looking down on
a huge pink camellia in flower. As I think it all over,
perhaps the most glorious time was driving with Doris to
the Napa Valley to see the wild flowers near and around
the Pope Valley. Because of the rain, the fields everywhere, up and down the innumerable hills around San
Francisco, dotted with live oak, are bright green and look
from a distance like velvet. Then we were in wine country, driving past row on row of vines just bursting into leaf,
and I thought of Vouvray for I have not been among vines
since then, when Grace Dudley and I used to close the
iron gate at Le Petit Bois and walk out among the fields
after supper to hear the nightingales.

The variety and mystery of the landscapes we drove
through were amazing—sometimes a narrow, dark valley
with tall redwood or pines shutting out the light, sometimes a sudden coming out to open pasture, and there we
saw sheets of "gold fields," a small yellow and white
flower, punctuated by brilliant blue wild larkspur and
wild Canterbury bells that look almost like bluebells.
There were patches of pure white "meadow foam" and all
sorts of lupines and small blue iris. If one can get drunk
on flowers I certainly did. And I understood why Aldous
Huxley wanted to live in California "because of the wild

flowers." Every day was uncertain as to weather. We had set out under cloudy skies, but the sun came out, and we got out of the car to taste the chilled air, though an icy wind forced us back inside to eat our picnic in "our little flying sofa," as my mother used to call my car when I first learned to drive.

I feel at home now with Doris, partly because of her Old English sheep dog, Maggie, who is the epitome of what a sheep dog is in my dreams (as a child I dreamed of having one)—that huge fluffy head and very pink tongue, the immense paws, the size and exuberance—and when we came home her face waiting for us at the window. Doris is so thoughtful of others and so sensitive to needs; maybe Maggie who is all impetuosity and self-intoxication may be an alter ego. So Doris and Maggie together make a kind of whole and are a joy to be with.

After that glorious day in the country I went over to San Francisco on Monday to stay with Bill Brown and Paul Wonner in the Noe Valley, a really blessed two days of rest in their cool, beautiful Victorian house, before my reading on Wednesday. I have known Bill for forty-five years. We met when he was a student at Yale coming back from France on the last voyage of the *Normandie*. We do not see each other often, but for all those years we have written each other about our lives and so have been in close touch. His struggle, Paul's, and mine have been rather similar, although they are painters and I a writer. But we have all three been "outsiders," as far as fashion goes, have none of us known the kind of fame their friend Diebenkorn has, for example, and have kept on producing, *quand même.* I love the life they lead and find myself at home in it, for they work very hard and love order and peace around them as I do. Their house is filled with samples of their marvelous collection of Indian miniatures, and now with a few of Bill's new passion, birdstones, which are strange, small Brancusi-like abstracts carved from granite or obsidian by American Plains Indians as much as seven thousand years ago. I always learn something when I am with these two. And we had some great meals "out" and great talks. I kept thinking of one of Edith Kennedy's phrases about "a wide frame of reference." I find it with both these men because they read so much, because Bill is a musician as well as a painter, and because they travel with their eyes open, making discoveries wherever they go, like the birdstones and the Indian miniatures. I love them also because they have created such a lasting and fruitful relationship.

I really hated to leave Wednesday evening to be driven over to the College of Marin, and I was more nervous than usual because I knew they had sold out three weeks before. Would I be able to produce something good enough for such an audience? Always the half-hour before a performance is a kind of limbo where I wait, feeling sick and wondering how I shall ever get through it. But when I walked into the jam-packed hall and the whole audience rose to its feet in welcome, I felt happy and assured. It was quite unexpected and delightful to hear roars of laughter at almost everything I said between poems. I really don't know why, perhaps from the very enthusiasm of the response. At any rate it was kind laughter and it lifted me up.

Jean Lieberman was there at the reading to pick me and my luggage up and take me home with her to her house high up on a hill in Mill Valley for the last two nights of my stay in California. As we walked into her living room in the dark, a kind of vision of all I had seen was laid out below me, the *decrescendo* of dark hills glittering with lights down to the other shining dark of water and the bay. It is a magical scene, which I stood and looked at in many lights during the next twenty-four hours, with

sheets of rain and thunder and lightning, lost in a chiaro-
scuro of floating clouds, and at five in the morning dark
and hidden except for a broad band of yellow way off at
the horizon as the sun rose. It looks like the scenes behind
Renaissance portraits, those landscapes like dreams, imaginary places that could never be real, yet here in Mill
Valley are.

It was the perfect end to these rich days to be with
Jean, one of my very oldest friends since we were at the
Shady Hill School in Cambridge together. We have not
often met since then, as Jean's life took her to Europe for
years before and during World War II, and then she settled with her husband, Sali, and their children there in
Mill Valley, thousands of miles away from where I lived.
But those years at school, at Shady Hill and then the Cambridge High and Latin made instant intimacy and sharing
possible. I simply felt at home, at ease, with a friend to
whom nothing has to be explained, where the past flows
into and informs the present. Jean brought out a small
black leather notebook where she had copied out the
poems we had written in our teens, she and I and Letty
Field (who died tragically at fifteen) and Jean Tatlock
(who became a psychoanalyst, Oppenheimer's lover, and
committed suicide in her forties). I must say it was hard
to read those poems, the ghosts of our passionate adoles-
cence, when we all four felt everything with such intensity. It hurt to think of Letty deprived of her life so young,
of Jean Tatlock, her genius and her tragic death. All four
of us had written poems about and for Anne Thorp, and
for each other, too, sometimes. Much of the feeling expressed was romantic in the extreme as though we were
hurling ourselves forward into life we knew, then, next to
nothing about. I was stunned to see how deeply we had
been affected by Anne Thorp, and it made me renew my
resolve to finish the novel about her this year, to round out

with a celebration worthy of its subject what began more than sixty years ago in admiration and love. Like the landscape we watched in all the changing lights as we talked, Anne Thorp had provided an intimation of what passionate love would become, at first observed from a distance with a child's intense eyes, and later on to become real, no longer the magic dream, but the illuminating reality as we each went on, grew up, and entered our own destinies. But Anne and her influence had made us into poets, had given us the charge at the very start.

We did not talk only of the past, Jean and I. Last winter Sali, her husband, died after weeks of excruciating illness in the hospital. We talked about what this sudden widowhood has meant, of my hope that Jean will be able to write poems—she is a very good poet who retired only a few years ago from a demanding editing job, so there had not been time until now.

What a beautiful way it was to end my seventieth year, to round it out with this coming back to deep roots in childhood and to see how little I have changed when it comes to the essential things, how clearly marked the trajectory of my life was by the time I was fifteen.

Monday, May 2nd

THE LAST DAY of this seventieth year. I still have one thing on my mind about the trip. In the woman's bookstore in Oakland, I happened on a book, which I read that week, that was as momentous an event as anything else, *The Diary of a Good Neighbor* by Jane Somers. It is the story of Janna, a self-sufficient, self-enclosed career woman in London who gets entangled, in spite of herself, with an old, dirty, fierce woman whom she meets by accident in a shop. The novel is the story of the gradual humanization of Janna through Maudie Fowler, the old witch, whom she gradually takes on as her responsibility, grows to love, and helps to die. This is not a perfect work of art but it is nevertheless revelatory and will haunt me much as Maudie Fowler haunted Janna. I feel grateful for the chance that brought it into my hands.

As I think over this year I wish I had a long empty time in which to think it over instead of a few minutes before I take Tamas out into the wet green world! In spite of the pressures of what is ahead—to clear my desk, sow the annuals, plant perennials, get back to the novel—I feel happy and at peace. My life at the moment is a little like a game of solitaire that is coming out. Things fall into place. The long hard work is bearing fruit, and even though I make resolves to see fewer people this summer than last, I know I shall be inundated as usual, be unable to say "no," but it does not matter, for I am coming into a period of inner calm. There will be months of seeing people and months of public appearances, but as surely as the dawn, there will be months of solitude and time to work. Who could ask for more? As Robert Frost says:

I could give all to Time except—except
What I myself have held. But why declare
The things forbidden that while the Customs slept
I have crossed to Safety with? For I am There,
And what I would not part with I have kept.

CREDIT: ROD KESSLER